TRADE, TRANSFERS AND DEVELOPMENT

Trade, Transfers and Development

Problems and Prospects for
the Twenty-first Century

Edited by

S. Mansoob Murshed
Northen Ireland Economic Research Centre

and

Kunibert Raffer
University of Vienna

Edward Elgar

Published by
Edward Elgar Publishing Limited
Gower House
Croft Road
Aldershot
Hants GU11 3HR
England

Edward Elgar Publishing Company
Old Post Road
Brookfield
Vermont 05036
USA

British Library Cataloguing in Publication Data

Trade, Transfers and Development: Problems
and Prospects for the Twenty-First
Century
    I. Murshed, S. Mansoob   II. Raffer,
    Kunibert
    338.91

Library of Congress Cataloging-in-Publication Data

Trade, transfers, and development: problems and prospects for the
    twenty-first century/S. Mansoob Murshed and Kunibert Raffer, eds.
        p.   cm.
        1. Developing countries—Economic conditions.   2. Developing
    countries—Economic policy.   3. Economic development.   I. Murshed,
    Syed Mansoob.   II. Raffer, Kunibert, 1951–   .
    HC59.7.T73837 1994
    338.9'009172'4—dc20   93–22658
                                                                     CIP

ISBN 1 85278 796 1

Printed in Great Britain at the University Press, Cambridge

Contents

Figures

Tables

Notes on contributors

Graham Bird is Professor of Economics at the University of Surrey.

John-ren Chen is Professor of Economics at the University of Innsbruck, Austria.

Saadet Deger is a senior researcher at the Stockholm International Peace Research Institute (SIPRI); previously she was at Birkbeck College, University of London.

David Greenaway is Dean and Professor of Economics at the University of Nottingham, previously he was at the University of Buckingham.

Stephany Griffith-Jones is at the Institute of Development Studies (IDS) at the University of Sussex.

Raphael Kaplinsky is a Fellow at the Institute of Development Studies (IDS) at the University of Sussex. Currently he is engaged in research and advisory work in Central America, South Africa, the United Kingdom and Zimbabwe.

Toshihiko Kinoshita is Treasurer and Controller of the Export–Import Bank of Japan and Director of the Japan Society for International Development; he was special adviser to the Governor (Planning) of the Bank and Director General of the Bank's Loan Department 1.

Oliver Morrissey is a lecturer in Economics at the University of Nottingham.

S. Mansoob Murshed is at the Northern Ireland Economic Research Centre; previously he was at the universities of Surrey and Birmingham.

Sheila Page is a Research Fellow at the Overseas Development Institute, London.

Kunibert Raffer is Associate Professor at the Department of Economics, University of Vienna and Honorary Research Fellow at the Department of Commerce, University of Birmingham; in 1989 he was Visiting Fellow at the IDS, Sussex.

Somnath Sen is Reader in Economics at the University of Birmingham, he has been a consultant to SIPRI, UNICEF and the IBRD.

H.W. Singer is Emeritus Professor at the University of Sussex and Professorial Fellow at the IDS; he was a director at the UN Secretariat.

Paul Stevens is BP Professor of Petroleum Policy and Economics at the University of Dundee.

Herbert Stocker is a lecturer in economics at the University of Innsbruck, Austria.

Paul Streeten is a consultant on the *Human Development Report* to the UNDP, an Honorary Fellow of Balliol College, Oxford, and of the Institute of Development Studies at the University of Sussex.

Howard White is at the Institute of Social Studies at The Hague, Netherlands.

L. Alan Winters is Professor of Economics at the University of Birmingham and co-director of the International Trade Programme, Centre for Economic Policy Research (CEPR), London.

Abbreviations

ADB	Asian Development Bank
APEC	Asia–Pacific Economic Cooperation
BIS	Bank for International Settlements
CGE	central government expenditure
CIS	Commonwealth of Independent States
CPE	Centrally Planned Economy
DAC	Development Assistance Committee
EBRD	European Bank for Reconstruction and Development
ECOSOC	Economic and Social Council (UN)
E(E)C	European (Economic) Community/-ies
EFF	Extended Fund Facility (of the IMF)
FDI	foreign direct investment
FY	fiscal year
GATT	General Agreement on Tariffs and Trade
GDP	gross domestic product
GHG	greenhouse gas
GNP	gross national product
GSP	Gross Social Product
HDI	Human Development Index
IAC	industrially advanced country
IBRD	International Bank for Reconstruction and Development
IDA	International Development Agency
IDB	Inter-American Development Bank
IFI	international financial institutions
ILO	International Labour Organization
IMF	International Monetary Fund
IOCR	Incremented Output Capital Ratio
ITEPS	internationally traded emission permit systems
ITO	International Trade Organization
JIT	just-in-time production
KfW	Kreditanstalt für Wiederaufbau
LDC	less developed country
MFA	Multi-Fibre Arrangement
MITI	Ministry of International Trade and Industry
NAFTA	North American Free Trade Area
NGO	non-governmental organization

NIC	Newly Industrializing Country
NIS	new independent state
ODA	Official Development Assistance
OECD	Organization of Economic Cooperation and Development
OECF	Overseas Economic Cooperation Fund
OPEC	Organization of Petroleum Exporting Countries
QR	quantitative restriction
SAL	structural adjustment (loan)
SDR	special drawing right
SECAL	sectoral adjustment loan
SPC	statistical process control
TNC	transnational corporation
TOT	terms of trade
TQC	total quality control
UNCED	United Nations Conference on Environment and Development
UNCTAD	United Nations Conference on Trade and Development
UNDP	United Nations Development Programme
UNICEF	United Nations International Children's Emergency Fund
UNITAR	United Nations Institute for Training and Research

Introduction

S. Mansoob Murshed and Kunibert Raffer

As the twentieth century draws to a close and as the new millennium approaches the developmental gap between the richer and poorer nations of the world grows ever wider. Ironically this is set against the backdrop of the communications revolution which is meant to draw the world closer together. The decade of the 1980s has not been a promising phase in development experience, notwithstanding localized exceptions in East and Southeast Asia. On the basis of these recent events and the generally diminished expectations of our age the future prospects for development in the less affluent parts of the globe look very bleak. Indeed it is widely believed that growth and development will occur rapidly in some countries but hardly, if at all, in others – a view elegantly put in Lucas (1991). Baldly stated it means that some poor countries will never catch up with the standards of living and the quality of life enjoyed in the richer parts of the world. This is in sharp contrast to the commonly held opinions of the early development economists in the immediate post-war period. By and large they viewed progress in the field of development as almost inevitable, in analogy to the success of the Marshall Plan in Europe.

What factors contributed to the intellectual climacteric? As usual events, stylized facts – to use a phrase coined by the late Lord Kaldor – outpaced conventional wisdom. The early 1970s were characterized by commodity price booms, principally the sharp rises in oil prices. The perceived power of the Organization of Petroleum Exporting Countries (OPEC) grew and other commodity exporters felt that they too could exercise increased leverage in their economic dealings with the developed countries. These latter hopes encouraged the call for a New International Economic Order. The aims were to achieve better terms for the developing world in trade, aid and other fields. Above all it was felt that, for the first time, developing countries could provide an active and meaningful input into determining the global economic framework so crucial to their future. The 1970s were characterized by high liquidity in global financial markets, in part as the result of OPEC surpluses. The consequence was 'cheap money'; loans were pressed onto many developing countries by international banks, an activity which was lauded by international financial institutions (IFIs) and Northern government as successful 'recycling of OPEC surpluses'.

1

By the end of 1980 conservative governments had been elected in the UK and the USA. These governments were strongly committed to lowering inflation and thus pursued tight monetary policies. These raised interest rates. Furthermore the Reagan Administration embarked upon a major armament programme, financed not by taxation but by borrowing. The burgeoning fiscal deficits which followed further raised international interest rates. Both of these factors converted debt in the Third World into a crisis. Fears that default by debtors would seriously undermine international financial markets prompted more involuntary lending, which eventually aggravated the problem of debt. Draconian measures were imposed on debtor nations under the guise of 'structural adjustment'. These are said to have led eventually to improvements in the macroeconomic performance of some countries, but, if so, at a tremendous cost in terms of deteriorating provision of basic needs and reduced capital formation. The poor and the vulnerable suffered greatly, as evidenced by worsening indicators of infant mortality, schooling and health care, and political turmoil increased. In the aggregate there were net negative transfers to debtor nations. For the first time since political independence, the poor appeared to be subsidizing the rich. Colonial 'drain' theories (Naoroji, 1901) gained new relevance in a post-colonial world.

If the burden of debt servicing caused financial haemorrhage contributing to, if not causing, the 'lost decade' in Latin America and Sub-Saharan Africa, protectionist tendencies towards the exports of developing nations also proved to be a major handicap for the advancement of the Third World. On the one hand, developed nations, either directly or through IFIs, cajoled or forced developing countries to pursue policies aimed at export-led growth. These pressures were partially motivated by the desire to secure smooth debt servicing out of export revenues. But on the other hand, given the loss of Western competitiveness in many labour-intensive manufactures, developed countries yielded to domestic protectionist lobbies and put severe restrictions on the exports of many goods from the Third World. Protectionism, coupled with the intolerable burden of debt, served to render a severe blow to development and growth prospects of most nations in the Third World.

Two other recent developments deserve mention. One is the over-consumptionalist tendencies in some Western nations, especially in the USA and the UK. These are reflected in the balance of payments deficits of these countries and imply that in some of the richest countries expenditure exceeds income. Even the surpluses of former West Germany have been dissipated in the reunification process. The other feature worth noting is the end of the Cold War and the new relations of the former Eastern bloc with the West. The various degrees of disarray that these economies find themselves in will require major restructuring, putting immense pressure on global capital supply. All in all the great demands on international financial resources caused by the savings crisis in the West and the needs of the East will leave precious little for the South in terms of aid, loans and foreign direct investment. In spite of protestations to the contrary made by Western donors, some aid is likely to be diverted from the South to the East, as all faces in the West, particularly in Europe, are firmly turned in that direction.

All of the trends mentioned above point to a gloomy picture for most developing countries. Indeed it has been argued that developing nations have become effectively decoupled from meaningful participation in the international economic scene (Murshed, 1992). The increasing dependence of the South, particularly because of accumulated debts, has brought about strong tendencies towards a new form of neo-colonialism putting the South under the control of multilateral institutions dominated by the North. The model of centre–periphery relations recommended by Friedrich List, better known for his opposition to the 'English philosophy' of free trade as harmful to Germany's development some 150 years ago, seems to emerge. He advocated joint exploitation of the South as 'promising much richer and more certain fruits than the mutual enmity of war and trade regulations' (List, 1920, p. 211). Therefore this new form of dominance has rightly been called neo-Listian (Raffer, 1987). At present the problem of the global environment remains the only area where the South has some room for manoeuvre in its relations with the North.

The two issues of trade and transfers are all the more pressing as isolated development, just like socialism in one country, is no longer attempted or viable. In summary the new conditions prevalent in the world economy make it imperative to analyse the issues of trade and transfers between developed and developing nations. This volume will concern itself with these matters as well as assessing future prospects and opportunities faced by developing (and East European) countries within the global economy.

In Chapter 1, Hans Singer analyses present prospects for development against the background of the evolutions since the Second World War. He argues that the Bretton Woods system broke down because it was incomplete as trade was not accommodated sufficiently within the global framework. Although the 'Golden Age' of 1950 to 1970 with promising growth rates will not return and prospects are not very good in general, Singer sees windows of opportunity, expecting that the next ten to 20 years may be better for developing countries than the previous ten.

Paul Streeten surveys the evolution of development thinking evolving from the strong, and seemingly one-sided, emphasis on growth prevalent during the first post-war period, to human development; or – one might be tempted to say – from Harrod-Domar and Arthur Lewis via basic needs to the United Nations Development Programme (UNDP)'s *Human Development Report*. The hypothesis that human development, once it has reached a certain stage, leads people to call for freedom is the ray of hope presented by Streeten.

Mansoob Murshed argues in Chapter 3 that transfers to the South are necessary to induce its cooperation on the environment, justifying them on grounds of both efficiency – environmental actions have to be incentive-compatible – and equity because of the North's greater historical responsibility for environmental degradation. He expresses fears that the environment could be used as an excuse to withhold aid, trade opportunities and debt relief.

Raphael Kaplinsky assigns a critically important role in competitive production to organizational technologies. The growing openness of Southern economies forces them to confront this issue. Analysing the role of transnational corporations (TNCs) as these technologies begin to diffuse to the South, he also sees policy options for host countries to promote local firms in this field. Relatively low barriers to entry in organizational change make such policies attractive.

Next John-ren Chen and Herbert Stocker analyse the often cited case of the four Asian newly-industrializing countries (NICs) and the special conditions behind their success. Showing that a common pattern is difficult to detect and that the 'dragon' experience, while a convincing demonstration that 'miracles' are possible, can hardly be transferred to other countries. Generally applicable lessons cannot necessarily be derived from superperformers.

In Chapter 6, Paul Stevens discusses prospects for OPEC economies in the light of volatile and uncertain oil revenues and reduced market shares. These have put strains on public finances there owing to the pattern of high consumption and investment expenditure. Differences between actual and anticipated growth are likely to widen, putting political stability at risk. The inherent instability of cartels is set to continue and future OPEC membership could be confined to Arab nations.

The role of aid in promoting economic growth is discussed by Howard White (Chapter 7). He examines the question of whether or not aid crowds out domestic investment. After a careful study of the literature he concludes, on balance, that aid does promote investment, even if its impact on growth remains ambiguous.

Toshihiko Kinoshita analyses Japan's financial flows and puts current criticisms of Japan's ODA (Official Development Assistance) into perspective. Although Japan is expected, and committed, to continue as one of the main sources of finance, the expected global shortage of capital renders further steep increases unlikely. The author also points out that insights gained from Japan's development might be useful for other countries if their specific situation is duly taken into account.

Stephany Griffith-Jones argues that in Latin America progress towards resumed development after debt has been made, though not rapidly enough: prudent domestic policies have contributed, but additional debt (service) reduction remains a major issue, particularly for Sub-Saharan countries. She advocates the application of debt conversion techniques developed mainly in Latin America for commercial debt to bilateral official debt.

In Chapter 10, Kunibert Raffer discusses the problems of efficiency and financial accountability of IFIs. At present borrowers have to bear the risk of IFI errors, paying for damages by IFI staff, while IFIs even gain financially. This mechanism, reminiscent of former Communist economies, is irreconcilably at odds with the market mechanism, encouraging systemic failures and inefficiencies. Like anyone else, IFIs must therefore be made accountable for what they do.

The question as to the need for the International Monetary Fund (IMF) is tackled by Graham Bird. In many of its roles the IMF has been replaced by other institutions (such as the G-7 regarding macroeconomic coordination, even commercial banks in lending). He points out that criticisms of its activities in relation to the debt crisis and structural adjustment cannot be discounted. Nevertheless he advocates reform rather than outright abolition of the IMF.

Sheila Page then addresses concerns of developing countries regarding trade policy within the Uruguay Round and the cementation of regional trade blocs. The greatest harm to the South will come from a breakdown of multilateralism in trade policy, replaced by discriminatory bilateralism. Trade creation is likely to arise more from rent seeking than from competitive forces in the future, which makes prospects for export-led growth look less promising.

The likely consequences of the agreements between the EC and some transitional economies in Eastern Europe are analysed by Alan Winters in Chapter 13. In his opinion the present agreements to promote trade and factor movements do not go far enough, and he finds EC policies excessively restrictive, not to say self-serving, in the areas of trade, investment and migration. In the light of the pronouncements made by EC countries encouraging reform in ex-Centrally Planned Economies (CPEs), such attitudes appear ironic.

David Greenaway and Oliver Morrissey examine whether the theoretical gains of trade liberalization can actually be reaped. Liberalization policies are principally geared to removing biases in import prices, although in practice they accompany devaluation to promote exports. Reforms are usually undertaken when an economy is in difficulty, as part of an overall policy package. The authors advocate macroeconomic stabilization as a prerequisite for successful trade policy reform, stressing the importance of credibility and sequencing.

In the final chapter, Saadet Deger and Somnath Sen analyse the interrelation between security and economic crisis within the North–South framework. They argue that international economic relations must be made more equitable and efficient to attain economic security for people in the South (which means the provision of basic needs). Otherwise the North will have to face great instabilities eventually threatening its own security.

References

List, Friedrich (1920), *Das nationale System der politischen Ökonomie*, 3rd edn, Jena: G. Fischer (originally published in 1841).

Lucas, R.E. Jr. (1991), 'Making a Miracle', paper presented to the Econometric Society's European meeting, Cambridge.

Murshed, S. Mansoob (1992), *Economic Aspects of North–South Interaction, Analytical Macroeconomic Issues*, London: Academic Press.

Naoroji, D. (1901), *Poverty and Un-British Rule in India*, London: Swan Sonnenschein.

Raffer, Kunibert (1987), 'Tendencies Towards a "Neo Listian" World Economy', *Journal für Entwicklungspolitik*, 3(3).

1 Prospects for development

H.W. Singer

I A difficult starting-point

History is a seamless web. The prospects for the future of development cannot be disentangled from what happened in the past. There is a well-known story of the Irishman who asked for the best way of getting to Dublin and was told: 'If you want to go to Dublin I would not start from here if I were you.' The same, unfortunately, must be said of the prospects for development. The present is a bad starting-point for many developing countries outside East Asia. The overall picture for them during the last decade or more has been one of stagnation or decline. The debt crisis has been contained but not resolved. There is no sign of the kind of effective macroeconomic coordination, either within Europe or within the Group of 5 or 7, which could restore growth and full employment in the industrial countries and re-establish them in the role of locomotive for the Third World which they fulfilled in the 'Golden Age' of the 1950s and 1960s. Primary commodity prices continue to decline, terms of trade continue to deteriorate, the future of multilateral trade liberalization still hangs in the balance at the time of writing (October 1992) and, in spite of increasing doubts about their validity and effects, neo-liberal doctrines continue to hold sway in determining policies of stabilization and structural adjustment in developing countries.

In the light of all this, it could be said that over a large part of the Third World the immediate task ahead is not one of development but of rehabilitation and damage limitation. Indeed over much of Africa, ravished by famines and civil wars, the problem is one of survival. Nor, as we know, is the problem of civil war and threatening famine limited to Third World countries outside Europe.

II The UN/Bretton Woods system of 1944–5

To understand why we have to start from such a difficult starting-point, we have to go back to the question of why the new international economic order established in 1944/5, centred on the United Nations and the Bretton Woods institutions, collapsed in 1971/3.[1] Although the US economic deficits in 1971 and the assertion of OPEC power in 1973 were the more immediate and obvious reasons for this collapse, there were deeper underlying reasons in the deficiencies of the UN/Bretton Woods system set up in 1944/5.

Compared with the Keynesian vision, the new order established after the war was both distorted and incomplete. It was distorted in so far as the original intention of pressure on balance of payments surplus countries rather than deficit countries, or at least symmetrical pressure on both surplus and deficit countries, proved to be unworkable. Today the pressure is on the poor countries, on the deficit countries and in particular on the indebted countries. For the industrial countries, the surplus countries and the non-indebted countries there is nothing but the mildest, ineffective admonition. Global macroeconomic coordination was assumed to be in the UN General Assembly and Economic and Social Council (ECOSOC) but the hostility to the UN as a result of the Cold War and the McCarthy period soon prevented any such global policy coordination in the UN, while neither the USA under the pax americana of 1945–71, nor the Group of 5 or 7 today, nor the IMF or World Bank, have been able to take its place.

The debt crisis could not be foreseen in 1944/5. At the end of the war, Latin America and the Indian sub-continent had plenty of foreign assets and reserves while the financial affairs of Africa were a matter for their European colonial 'mother countries'. This new factor has placed the debtor developing countries – and that means the great bulk of them – in a condition of dependency and inferiority which prevents them from playing any real part in global economic affairs and which enables the Bretton Woods institutions to impose a new neo-liberal ideology under the 'Washington Consensus'.

This new relationship represents another distortion of the original post-war system. Under this system, the developing countries would have played an important, even dominant, part in global economic management in the UN General Assembly and ECOSOC, with their 'one-country-one-vote' voting system. Instead decisions are made either in the Group of 5 or 7, with no concern for developing countries other than perhaps a ritual sentence in the final communiqué, or in the IMF and World Bank with their 'one-dollar-one-vote' voting system which makes the developing countries virtually powerless. So it is worth recalling that in the original Bretton Woods system – especially in the original vision of Keynes (Singer, 1990) – the covering of balance of payments deficits by the IMF was supposed to be virtually automatic (see Dell, 1991, p. 225) while the World Bank was limited to project lending with no conditionality other than the soundness of the project.

The reasons for the World Bank getting involved in programme lending and 'conditionality' are complex, ranging from the 'fungibility' argument concerning the fallacy involved in trying to pick out the 'top priority project' for financing to the ambitions of Mr MacNamara, but the essential context was a confident belief in the World Bank, as well as the IMF, that they are in possession of a new truth which must be spread and can be imposed on unsuccessful and errant governments. The dependency imposed by the debt crisis forces the developing countries today to accept the new religion of government failure and market success, with varying degrees of conviction. By contrast, the original conception was of governments deciding policy and the international institutions acting at their command. As Arthur Lewis put it as late as 1971, 'give us the money and shut up'. Today it is the developing countries which have to shut up.

The system was not only distorted but also incomplete. The main gap was the failure to establish the International Trade Organization (ITO) which would have had commodity price stabilization as its main objective. The ITO was duly negotiated and agreed (the Havana Charter) but was not ratified by the US Congress. As a result, the post-war years have seen deteriorating terms of trade for developing countries. The deteriorating real price for oil was also responsible for the OPEC actions of 1973 and 1979 which finally delivered the death blow to the Bretton Wood System. It is a melancholy thought how different things could have been under Keynes's original proposal of a world currency based on 30 primary commodities including gold and oil, with the IMF acting as a world central bank or 'International Clearing Union'! Another major gap has already been pointed out: the failure to establish a system of democratic global economic management through the UN General Assembly and ECOSOC. Current proposals to create an Economic Security Council and to revitalize the development role of the UN can be viewed as an attempt to recapture some of the original Bretton Woods spirit.

III A decade of rehabilitation?

Thus the first overall objective must be to restore the developing countries to their growth path of the 'Golden Age' of 1950 to 1970. This would at least prevent a continuation of the divergence of income levels between rich and poor countries which has been characteristic of the overall situation since the outbreak of the debt crisis in 1982. Even this would be a more formidable task than is often realized. Compared with where they would have been if growth rates prevailing up to 1980 had continued, the developing countries during the past decade have lost cumulative income as follows: low-income countries other than China and India 35 per cent of gross domestic product (GDP); lower-middle-income countries 39 per cent; upper-middle-income countries 23; Sub-Saharan Africa 40 per cent; Latin America and the Caribbean 45 per cent; the severely indebted countries also 45 per cent. These would be the jumps in income required to bring the Third World back to the 1965–80 growth line. In manufacturing – still the flagship of economic development – the cumulative setbacks have been even more severe: 32 per cent for the low-income countries other than India and China; 53 per cent for the lower-middle-income countries; not less than 85 per cent for Sub-Saharan Africa; 57 per cent for Latin America and the Caribbean. Only the upper-middle-income countries managed to keep this cumulative loss to a relatively modest level of 10 per cent.

To make up for such heavy cumulative losses within a single decade would require nothing less than a miracle. Translating this 'miracle' into quantitative terms, the GDP of low-income countries would have to grow by 8.5 per cent per annum; lower-middle-income countries by 9.4 per cent; upper-middle-income countries by 7.9 per cent; Sub-Saharan Africa by 8.8 per cent; and Latin America and the Caribbean as well as the severely indebted countries by 10.5 per cent. Not even the four East Asian Tigers will reach such growth rates, let alone the bulk of developing countries. In any case, in any conceivable model of the world economy such growth rates would only be consistent with growth rates in the industrial countries of 5 per cent per annum or more – and not even the most optimistic forecaster would bet on this! Moreover the regime of IMF-sponsored stabilization programmes and World Bank-sponsored structural adjustment programmes with their in-built tendency towards retrenchment and austerity today would be incompatible with such required growth rates. Given that the 'decade of rehabilitation' has started under very unfavourable auspices, the required growth rates for the rest of the 1990s would be even higher than those stated above. In these circumstances, rehabilitation and damage repair would be a matter of at least two decades, and probably more. Our picture of the prospects for development must be much more modest than an early resumption of a new 'Golden Age'.

In spite of the much-vaunted 'outward orientation' achieved during the 1980s, and the undoubted fact that world trade has increased as a share of world total of national incomes, the cumulative arrears that would have to be made up by the developing countries to get back to where they would have been without the setbacks of the 1980s would be even greater for export earnings than in the case of national incomes. Even a total multilateral liberalization of world trade tomorrow – a super-Uruguay Round – would not produce the required growth rates (except perhaps for a once-for-all jump in the year or two after a super-Uruguay).

IV   Success due to the Washington Consensus?
Admittedly such gloomy quantitative projections are in relation to a very ambitious target of a return to a vanished 'Golden Age'. It could be argued more realistically that bygones are bygones, and that a more realistic target is to accept the present unfavourable starting-point as a fact of life and abandon any target involving 'catching up'. In that case, the most optimistic scenario would be one based on the 'Washington Consensus', the neo-liberal approach of the World Bank and IMF. On this interpretation, the setbacks of

the last decade were not real setbacks, but necessary periods of stabilization and structural adjustment which will turn out to be successful in 'laying the foundations for subsequent sound and sustainable growth' (to quote a favourite IMF/World Bank term). In other words, the last decade was a period of *reculer pour mieux sauter*. Perhaps so. But one has to be a strong and firm believer in the superior wisdom of the Washington Consensus, in the face of considerable evidence to the contrary, that stabilization and adjustment will in fact deliver such splendid results. The weight of the present evidence is that adjustment lending might encourage real export growth and improve the current account of the balance of payments, but that the impact on GDP growth is neutral and the effect on investment negative – this last finding being particularly serious because of its impact on future growth prospects (Greenaway and Morrissey, 1992). Furthermore the IMF and World Bank themselves would probably argue that the process of stabilization and adjustment is not yet sufficiently widespread and complete to justify expectation of striking early results during the coming decade. So an optimistic assessment of prospects as a result of the wisdom of the Washington Consensus would be highly doubtful, quite apart from the fact that the Washington Consensus itself shows some signs of internal self-doubts or even disintegration. One could venture the forecast that the pendulum will swing back at least halfway from the Washington Consensus to the old Keynesian consensus. But that in itself is not a guarantee of high growth rates in the developing countries.

There is also the opposite view, that what has happened in the past decade, far from 'laying the foundations of subsequent growth' has done exactly the opposite: that it has *destroyed* the foundations for subsequent growth. Support for this view may be derived from the fact that investment – the source of future growth – has declined even more heavily during the last decade than gross national product (GNP) or exports. For example, in the severely indebted countries, after growing by 8.4 per cent per annum in 1965–80, investment over the past decade has actually *declined* by 3.1 per cent per annum. The corresponding figures for Sub-Saharan Africa and for Latin America are no better. Now it is of course true that physical investment is not the only – and perhaps not the most important – source of economic growth, as was perhaps too readily assumed in the days of the Harrod–Domar formula. But human capital, neglected in the Harrod–Domar formula,[2] seems to have fared no better than physical investment; that, at least, is the case which UNICEF (the United Nations International Children's Emergency Fund) has made in its monumental study of *Adjustment with a Human Face* (Cornia *et al.*, 1987).

The proportion of central government expenditure spent on education has fallen from 20.5 per cent to 9.0 per cent in low-income countries; from 17.5

per cent to 13.3 per cent in lower-middle-income countries; from 15.4 per cent to 11.0 per cent in Latin America and the Caribbean; and from 15.6 per cent to 10.8 per cent in the severely indebted countries. There are similar declines in health expenditures as a proportion of government expenditure, from 5.5 per cent to 2.8 per cent in low-income countries; 5.7 per cent to 4.0 per cent in lower-middle-income countries; and from 5.9 per cent to 4.4 per cent in the severely indebted countries. Again it will take many years before such a cumulative shortfall can be made up.

All this does not look like laying the foundations for growth in terms of the human resource basis. Thus in both physical and human investment it is more a question of damage repair than new development. There remains the possibility of technological catching up. This has played a part in the past (Dowrick, 1992) and it is conceivable that the transfer of technology and knowledge can be speeded up in this age of instant telecommunication. But it is a hope rather than a certainty and in the meantime the negative forces set into motion by the decline in physical and human investment may create a Myrdalian downward cumulative process, counteracting the expectation of 'having laid the foundations of subsequent sound and sustainable growth'. To be optimistic, you have to share the belief that with the spreading of the neo-liberal gospel the quality of economic policy in developing countries has improved to such a degree as to open previously undreamed of windows of opportunity. But this is an act of faith rather than a forecast.

V   Windows of opportunity
Having disposed of unrealistic expectations, one hastens to point out that all is not gloom by any means. Even in the difficult years of the last decade there are examples of 'Tigers' among the developing countries, especially in East Asia. The example of Korea shows that there is a potential for upward mobility in the South; the line of division between North and South is by no means rigid. We can be confident that progress among the Tigers will continue even if not at the same hectic pace as sometimes in the past. In a decade or so, they may be expected to be full members of the club of industrial countries, probably sanctified by membership of the Organization of Economic Cooperation and Development (OECD). Nor will they necessarily remain alone. 'Tigerisation' may spread to other areas, including parts of China, Mexico and the present young Tigers of Malaysia, Thailand and so on. What have the old tigers and prospective new tigers in common? What can be learnt from them?

The chief lesson is that the forces of convergence so confidently proclaimed by the classics are by no means extinct. The classical view was that there will be long-term convergence or equalization of incomes among different countries, partly because of the increasing store of global technological knowledge at the disposal of currently technologically backward countries, partly because capital is assumed to flow from rich countries where capital is abundant and hence its marginal productivity is supposed to be low compared to countries where the opposite is the case, and partly because of continuing growth of world trade as a proportion of global output – spreading world trade was supposed to benefit poorer countries even more than richer countries and to lead to global factor price equalization. With the experience of the last decade or so, it would be easy to be critical of all these optimistic positions but we must be careful not to throw out the baby with the bathwater. There remains sufficient long-run force in these propositions to provide windows of opportunity.

Let us take technological catch-up. While the already mentioned study by Dowrick shows that the overall picture over the last 30 years or so was more one of divergence than convergence, it did show that technological catch-up did provide an important element of convergence which offset to a considerable degree other forces of divergence. If we can strengthen the forces of technological catch-up both by freer transfer of technology and by increased domestic capacity to develop, absorb and adapt improved technology, and at the same time weaken the forces making for divergence, the old classical optimism may still be justified. The prospect should not be too bad: the human capital of many developing countries has strongly increased with spreading literacy, education at all levels and numbers of scientists, engineers and so on. At the same time the globally available stock of technology is rapidly increasing, perhaps at an exponential rate. If the Uruguay Round succeeds with its provisions for intellectual property rights, this may also help in this direction. If we can only marry and build on these opportunities we may still be able to look forward to a prospect of gradual convergence, or at least a reasonable rate of progress in the developing countries.

Such an outcome may, however, be accompanied by increased divergence or disparities both between and within developing countries. It is the present middle-income countries which already have a better technological and human capital basis for utilizing new opportunities which will progress, leaving behind the poorer (largely African) countries. There may also be increasing disparities within countries, say between South-east China and the rest, the Punjab and Bihar, São Paulo and the Brazilian north-east. It is hoped that we will be able to develop the compensatory mechanisms, both between countries and within them, to prevent such divergences with their attendant political and social dangers.

One may also see some hopeful signs in the clear tendency towards the formation of regional blocs of free trade areas. This tendency is usually treated as an adverse rather than a favourable development. It is true that there is a danger that such regional blocs may turn protectionist ('Fortress

Europe, Fortress Western Hemisphere, Fortress East Asia and so on') and become stumbling blocks rather than stepping stones towards multilateral free trade. However it also seems to be a fact that within each of these regional blocs there is a tendency towards convergence owing to a greater willingness of the richer members of the regional bloc to provide regional funds for the benefit of the poorer members. That certainly is the experience of the European Community, it was promised by President Bush in his proposal for 'Enterprise America' combined with a Western Hemisphere Free Trade Area and the same willingness has been clearly expressed by Japan. If this favourable feature of regional blocs can be combined with successful progress towards multilateral free trade under the Uruguay Round the forces of convergence may still prevail. There remains the problem of countries not included in any of the regional blocs but for them also the benefit of multilateral trade might outweigh the absence of regional preferential treatment.

Forecasting the future is a tricky business and many forecasters have come to grief, not excluding such venerable institutions as the World Bank and IMF. But I would venture a tentative guess that the next ten or 20 years may be better for developing countries as a whole than the previous ten, even though we may not be able to restore the previous 'Golden Age'[3].

Notes

1. On 15 August 1971 President Nixon, under pressure of rising US balance of payments deficits, suspended the convertibility of the US dollar into gold at the fixed rate of US$35 per ounce which had been the anchor of the fixed exchange rate system established at Bretton Woods. November 1973 was the date when OPEC first quadrupled the price of oil, forcing the industrial countries into a perceived need for retrenchment and protective action initiating the first post-war recession and building up to the debt crisis by recycling the oil surpluses through the commercial banks.
2. This may not be entirely fair to Harrod–Domar. It is true that the rate of savings and investment was the only explicit growth factor and it did not then include human investment. However the capital–output ratio in the denominator of the formula could be interpreted to be influenced, *inter alia* by the quality of human capital and the state of technological knowledge.
3. The ideas developed in this chapter are elaborated in more detail in the forthcoming book by Singer and Roy (1993).

References

Cornia, G.A., R. Jolly and F. Stewart (eds) (1987), *Adjustment with a Human Face: Protecting the Vulnerable and Promoting Growth*, Study by UNICEF (two volumes), Oxford: Clarendon Press.

Dell, Sidney (1991), *International Development Policies, Perspectives for Industrial Countries*, Durham, London: Duke University Press.

Dowrick, S. (1992), 'Technological Catch Up and Diverging Incomes: Patterns of Economic Growth', *Economic Journal*, **102** (412).

Greenaway, D. and O. Morrissey (1992), 'Structural Adjustment and Liberalisation in Developing Countries: What Lessons Have We Learned?', paper presented at the Development Studies Association Annual Conference, Nottingham (mimeo).

Lewis, Arthur (1971), *The Evolution of Foreign Aid*, Inaugural David Owen Memorial Lecture, Cardiff: University of Wales.

Singer, H.W. (1990), 'The Vision of Keynes: The Bretton Woods Institutions', in Erik Jensen and Thomas Fisher (eds), *The United Kingdom – The United Nations*, Basingstoke: Macmillan.

Singer, H.W. and Sumit Roy (1993), *Economic Progress and Prospects in the Third World*, Aldershot: E. Elgar.

2 From growth, via basic needs, to human development: the individual in the process of development

Paul Streeten

Sometimes the changes in the fashions of thinking about development appear like a comedy of errors, a lurching from one fad to another. Economic growth, employment creation, jobs and justice, redistribution with growth, basic needs, bottom-up development, participatory development, sustainable development, market-friendly development, liberation, liberalization, human development; thus goes the carousel of slogans. A related point has been made well in a book on the World Bank: 'The besetting sin of development policy throughout its life has been vulnerability to fashion, so that when a new idea is introduced the valuable elements in the previous practice are rejected rather than assimilated' (Mosley *et al.*, 1991, p. 308). But there has been an evolution in our thinking about development. Both internal logic and new evidence have led to the revision of our views. Previous and partly discarded approaches have taught us much that is still valuable, and our current approach will surely be subject to criticisms. A brief survey of the evolution of our thinking may be helpful.

The discussion started in the 1950s, influenced by Lewis (1955) and others, who emphasized economic growth as the key to poverty eradication. Even at this early stage, sensible economists and development planners were quite clear (in spite of what is now often said in caricature of past thought) that economic growth is not an end in itself, but a performance test of development. Arthur Lewis defined the purpose of development as widening our range of choice, exactly as the UNDP's *Human Development Reports* do today.

Three justifications were given for the emphasis on growth as the principal performance test. One justification assumed that through market forces – such as the rising demand for labour, rising productivity, rising wages and lower prices of goods – economic growth would spread its benefits widely and speedily, and that these benefits are best achieved through growth. Even in the early days some sceptics said that growth is not necessarily so benign. They maintained that in certain conditions (such as increasing returns, restrictions to entry, monopoly power and unequal distribution of income and assets) growth gives to those who already have: it tends to concentrate income and wealth in the hands of the few.

This is where the second assumption came in: governments, especially democratic ones, are concerned with the fate of the poor. Therefore progressive taxation, social services and other government interventions would spread the benefits downwards. The alleviation of poverty would not be automatic (as under the first assumption) but governments would take action to correct situations in which market forces concentrated benefits in the hands of the few.

The third assumption was more hard-headed than the previous two. It said that the fate of the poor should not be a concern at the early stages of development. It was thought necessary first to build up capital, infrastructure and productive capacity in an economy to improve the lot of the poor later. For a time – and it could be quite a long period – the poor would have to tighten their belts and the rich would receive most of the benefits. But if the rewards of the rich are used to provide incentives to innovate, to save and to accumulate capital which could eventually be used to benefit the poor, the early hungry years would turn out to have been justified. Classical, neo-classical and palaeo-Marxist economists all agreed on this. Some radical egalitarian philosophers such as John Rawls (1971, p. 302) would sanction such a strategy. Inequalities, in their view, are justified if they are necessary to improve the lot of the poor.

Another powerful influence was the so-called Kuznets (1955; 1963) curve. It relates average income levels to an index of equality, suggesting that the early stages of growth are accompanied by growing inequality. Only at an income per head of about $1000 (in 1979 dollars) is further growth associated with reduced inequality. One measure of inequality is the share of the bottom 40 per cent of the population in total national income. This association has been suggested by tracing the course of the same country over time, and of different countries, with different incomes per head, at the same time. In the early stages of development, as income per head increases, inequality tends to grow. This may mean that absolute poverty for some groups also increases. But eventually the turning-point, the bottom of the U-curve, is reached, after which growing income is accompanied by greater equality and, of course, reduced poverty. The golden age is ushered in.

None of the assumptions underlying these three justifications turned out to be universally true. Except for a very few countries, with special initial conditions, such as a land reform, and special policies, such as heavy emphasis on education and health, there was no automatic tendency for income to be spread widely. Nor did governments often take corrective action to reduce poverty. Governments were themselves often formed by people who had close psychological, social, economic and political links with the beneficiaries of the process of concentrated growth, even though their motives were often mixed. And it certainly was not true that a period of enduring mass poverty was needed to accumulate savings and investment. It was found that small farmers saved at least as high a proportion of their incomes as big landowners; that they were more productive, in terms of yield per acre; and that entrepreneurial talent was widespread and not confined to large firms. Prolonged mass poverty was therefore not needed to accumulate capital and to stimulate entrepreneurship.

To judge by GNP growth, the development process since the Second World War has been a spectacular, unprecedented and unexpected success. Average annual growth of GNP per head for the low-income countries was 2.4 per cent during 1965–73, 2.1 per cent during 1973–80 and between 1980 and 1989 it was 4.1 per cent; for the middle-income countries the figures were 5.2, 2.3 and 0.5 per cent, respectively. But at the same time there was increasing diversity of growth between different developing countries and increasing dualism within many of them. Despite high growth rates of industrial production and continued general economic growth, not enough employment was created for the rapidly growing labour force. Nor were the benefits of growth always widely spread to lower-income groups.

Arthur Lewis (1954) had predicted that poor and low-productivity subsistence farmers and landless labourers would move from the countryside to the high-income, urban, modern industries. This move would increase inequality in the early stages (so long as rural inequalities were not substantially greater than urban inequalities) but, when more than a critical number of rural poor had been absorbed in modern industry, the golden age would be ushered in, when growth is married to greater equality. In this way one explanation for the statistical association of the Kuznets curve was provided.

It became evident, however, that the Lewis model, which strongly dominated not only academic thought but also political action, did not always work in reality. It did not apply for four reasons. First, rural–urban differentials were much higher than had been assumed, owing to trade union action on urban wages, minimum wage legislation, differentials inherited from colonial days and other causes. This produced an excess of migrants, at the same time impeding the rapid growth of the rural labour force. Second, the growth rate of the population and with it that of the labour force was much larger than expected: between 2 and 3 per cent per year. Third, the technology transferred from the industrial countries to the urban industrial sector of developing countries was labour-saving. Although it raised labour productivity it did not create many jobs. Fourth, in many developing countries a productivity-raising revolution in agriculture was a precondition for substantial and widespread progress in industry. This revolution did not occur.

It was not surprising, then, that attention turned away from GNP and its growth. Some even wanted to 'dethrone GNP', not for the currently fashionable reason of environmental protection, but because it neglected jobs and justice. Since 1969 the International Labour Organization (ILO) had attempted to promote jobs in the developing countries. It had organized employment missions to several countries to explore ways of creating more productive and remunerative employment. While this was an extremely useful learning exercise, it soon became evident that unemployment was not really the main problem. In *Asian Drama*, Gunnar Myrdal (1986) devoted many pages to criticizing the concepts of employment, unemployment and underemployment in the context of underdeveloped Asia. Employment and unemployment make sense only in an industrialized society where there are employment exchanges, organized and informed labour markets, and social security benefits for the unemployed, who are trained workers, willing and able to work, but temporarily without jobs. Much of this does not apply to the poorest developing countries, in which livelihoods are more important than wage employment – an instance of the transfer of an inappropriate intellectual technology from modern societies to the entirely different social, economic and cultural setting of developing countries.

Myrdal talked about 'labour utilization', which has numerous dimensions when applied to self-employed subsistence farmers, landless labourers, artisans, traders, educated young people, saffron-clad monks, beggars, caste-conscious Brahmins, or women, in societies without organized labour markets. 'Employment' as interpreted in industrial countries is not the appropriate concept. The ILO employment mission discovered or rediscovered this and they also discovered that, to afford to be unemployed, a worker has to be fairly well off. To survive, an unemployed person must have an income from another source. The root problem, it was discovered, is poverty, or low-productivity employment, not unemployment. Many of the moderately poor are not unemployed but work very hard and long hours in unremunerative, unproductive forms of activity. Among the poorest of the poor, unemployment is a common form of suffering, but its roots are quite different from those of unemployment in industrial countries.

The discovery that the problem is often unremunerative work of low productivity drew attention to the informal sector: street traders, garbage collectors and casual workers, as well as many in small-scale production, such as blacksmiths, carpenters, sandal makers, builders and lamp makers. These people often work extremely hard, are self-employed or employed by their family, and sometimes very poor. Attention was also directed to women who, in some cultures, perform hard tasks without being counted as members of the labour force because their production is not sold for cash. The problem was then redefined as that of the 'working poor.'

Labour utilization covers more dimensions than the demand for labour (the lack of which gives rise to Keynesian unemployment) and the need for cooperating factors of production such as machinery and raw materials (the lack of which gives rise to what may be called Marxian non-employment). There is a good deal of evidence that not only labour but also capital is grossly underutilized in many developing countries. This suggests other causes for underutilization than surplus labour in relation to scarce capital. More specifically, the causes of low labour utilization can be classified under three headings: consumption and level of living (including education), attitudes and institutions.

Nutrition, health and education are elements of the level of living that are important for fuller labour utilization. They have been neglected because in advanced societies they count as consumption without effect on human productivity (though possibly a negative one, as with four-martini lunches). The only exceptions admitted by literature in recent decades are some forms of education. In poor countries, however, better nutrition, health, education and training can be very productive forms of developing human resources. This is one thread that goes into the later fabric of basic needs.

The second dimension, attitudes, make a difference in the kinds of jobs people will accept. In Sri Lanka a large part of unemployment is the result of the high aspirations of the educated, who are no longer prepared to accept 'dirty' manual jobs. Caste attitudes in India also present obstacles to fuller labour utilization. In Africa those with primary education wish to leave the land and become clerks in government offices. In many societies manual or rural work is held in contempt.

The third dimension is the absence or weakness of such institutions as labour exchanges, credit facilities or a system of land ownership or tenancy providing incentives and ability to till the soil. As a result, labour is underutilized. For reasons such as these the concepts of unemployment and underemployment as understood in the North are not applicable and an approach to poverty that assumes levels of living, skills, attitudes and institutions adapted to full labour utilization has turned out to be largely a dead end. Unemployment can coexist with considerable labour shortages and capital underutilization.

Inappropriate attitudes and institutions can also frustrate some approaches to meeting basic needs. Focusing on the needs of men, women and children draws attention to the appropriate institutions (such as public services and credit facilities) to which households need access and to the attitudes (such as those towards women's welfare) that need changing to secure better distribution within the household. These issues will be more fully discussed later.

The employment concept was questioned for other reasons too. The creation of more employment opportunities, far from reducing unemployment, increases it. Those who come from the countryside to the towns in search of jobs balance the expectation of high earnings against the probability of getting a job (Harris and Todaro, 1970). As job opportunities increase, they attract more people. The influx of migrants in turn contributes to the high rate of urban drift and the growth of shanty towns. The employed urban workers, though poor by Western standards, are among the better-off when measured against the distribution of income in their own countries.

These difficulties, reinforced by the disappointments with economic growth, which had not ushered in the 'Golden Age' of egalitarian growth (as predicted by the models of Kuznets and Lewis), turned the development debate to the question of income distribution. One of the landmarks was the book, *Redistribution with Growth* (Chenery *et al.*, 1974), published for the Development Research Centre of the World Bank and the Sussex Institute of Development Studies. Among many questions about the relations between growth and redistribution,[1] it raised two sets of interest in the present context: (1) What can be done to increase the productivity of the small-scale, labour-intensive, informal sector 'discovered' by the ILO employment mission to Kenya? How can we remove discrimination against this sector and improve its access to information, credit and markets? The question is, how does redistribution affect efficiency and growth? Does helping the 'working poor' mean sacrificing productivity; is it an efficient way of promoting growth? (2) To turn the question the other way around, how does economic growth affect distribution? It was quite clearly seen that in low-income countries growth is (almost) a necessary condition for eradicating poverty, but it also seemed that economic growth sometimes reinforced and entrenched inequalities in the distribution of incomes, assets and power. Not surprisingly, when growth began with an unequal distribution of assets and power it was more difficult to redistribute incomes and to eradicate poverty.

Although it was recognized that under these conditions it would be difficult to redistribute existing assets, it was thought that the redistribution of increments of income would be politically easier (it can be seen that this approach is an elaboration of the second justification for the emphasis on growth mentioned above). A proportion of incremental income would be taxed and channelled into public services intended to raise the productivity of the poor: this is 'redistribution with growth'. But it was discovered that the results of such redistribution are very modest, at any rate for low-income countries. According to one simulation exercise, an annual transfer of 2 per cent of GNP over 25 years into public investment to build up the stock of capital available to the poor – thought to be a very 'dynamic' policy – would, after 40 years, raise the consumption of the poorest 40 per cent by only 23 per cent; that is to say their rate of consumption growth would accelerate by 0.5 per cent a year: $1 for a $200 income (Chenery *et al.*, 1974). However the model excludes, the human capital aspects of some forms of consumption and the impact on labour utilization, which are stressed by both the basic needs and the human development approach.

In spite of its title, most of *Redistribution with Growth* is concerned not with relative income shares but with the level and growth of income in low-income groups. Much of the redistribution literature measures inequality by the Gini coefficient, which runs through the whole range of incomes, from the richest to the poorest. It measures somewhat meaningless percentiles instead of socially, regionally or ethnically significant deprived groups. It does not tell who is in these decile groups, for how long, or for what reasons. Nor does it indicate the scope for mobility or the degree of equality of opportunity. Normally there is no particular interest in redistribution to the middle, which would reduce inequality but leave poverty untouched. Nor is the fate of income deciles as such of much interest, for these are not sociologically, politically or humanly interesting groups.

An empirical question is how economic growth affects the reduction of inequality and poverty, and how these reductions in turn affect efficiency and economic growth. The answers to these questions will depend on the initial distribution of assets, the policies pursued by the government, available technologies, the scope for labour-intensive exports, which enlarges the application of labour-intensive technologies, and the rate of population growth. Another empirical question is how policies to reduce inequalities and meet basic needs affect freedom and human rights.

Is it more important to reduce inequality or to meet basic needs? Is egalitarianism to be preferred to humanitarianism? In societies with very low standards of living, meeting basic needs is more important than reducing inequality, for three reasons.[2] First, equality as such is probably not an objective of great importance to most people other than utilitarian philosophers and ideologues. Second, this lack of concern is justified, because meeting basic needs is morally more important than reducing inequality. Third, reducing inequality is a highly complex, abstract objective, open to many different interpretations and operationally ambiguous.

It has been argued that, because no group ever asks to be paid *less* in the interest of social justice, people are not really concerned with equality as such (Beckerman, 1979, p. 11). Against this it could be said that in democracies better-off people *do* vote for progressive taxes, and a lack of clamour to be paid less may have something to do with the fear that the benefits might go to the fat cats rather than to the underdogs. Nevertheless most people so rarely perceive that they are overpaid that equality as such does not seem to figure prominently among their objectives. And it is fairly plain that many claims for greater social justice are only thinly disguised claims for getting more for oneself.

Removing malnutrition in children, eradicating disease, or educating girls are concrete, specific achievements meeting the basic needs of deprived groups, whereas reducing inequality is abstract. There is of course nothing wrong with an abstract moral objective, but if policies are judged by the evident reduction of human suffering, meeting basic needs scores better than reducing inequality. Internationally, also, there is more concern with ameliorating blatant deprivation than with bringing developing countries up to Western living standards. It is true that we do not have a production function for meeting adequate standards of nutrition, health and education. It is not known precisely which financial, fiscal and human resources and policies produce these desirable results. The causes are multiple and interact in a complex and still partly unknown manner. But at least it is fairly clear when the objective has been attained, and the criteria by which it is judged are also clear.

In the case of equality, however, no one knows how to achieve (and maintain) it, even how precisely to define or by what criteria to judge it. To have no clear-cut criteria for defining the optimal degree of equality does not imply ignorance as to whether inequality is too great or too small. We may be able to judge improvements in income distribution without a clear idea of the optimal distribution, as we may judge whether water in a well is higher or lower without knowing its depth. But the uncertainties surrounding differences in income and assets acceptable because of differences in age, sex, location, needs, merit and so on, and the question as to how to resolve conflicts between, for example, merit and need, make it difficult to give precise operational meaning to the objective of redistributive policies: they make 'equality' conceptually elusive. A rule is regarded as inegalitarian by Aristotle (1911, p. 107) when equals are awarded unequal shares or unequals are awarded equal shares. But what then defines 'equality'? As Robert Nozick (1974, p. 159) has written, to fill in the blank in 'to each according to his –' has been the concern of theories of distributive justice.

It might be objected that poverty necessarily contains a relative component, that it is measured against a standard set by the norms of a society and that it is therefore closely related to inequality. 'Poverty is a relative concept. Saying who is in poverty is to make a relative statement rather like saying who is short or heavy'(Abel-Smith and Townsend, 1965, p. 63).[3] Without rejecting this view, it must be asserted that an absolute core of absolute deprivation can be determined by medical and physiological criteria, without recourse to reference groups, averages or other criteria of comparison. In addition to this core of absolute poverty, it has been recognized at least since Adam Smith[4] and Karl Marx[5] that poverty contains a relative component.

Whatever doctors, nutritionists and other scientists may say about the objective conditions of deprivation, how the poor themselves perceive their deprivation is also relevant. This perception is partly a function of the reference group from which the poor take their standards of what comprises the necessities for a decent minimum level of living. Such a view need not be based on envy. The poverty norm moves up with average income because the desire to belong is an almost biological basic need and is expressed as a desire to live at a standard regarded as decent by society. This standard is different in the United States from that in Sri Lanka. But it may be questioned whether poverty should be defined in such a way that it can never be reduced, however much absolute income levels rise, if the measure of inequality remains unchanged. This would make poverty eradication rather like the attempt to catch the electric hare used to spur on greyhounds at dog races.[6] In spite of the analytical distinction between meeting basic needs and promoting greater equality, it remains, however, an empirical fact that the only societies that have been successful in meeting basic needs are those that have also reduced inequalities.[7]

After the dead end of 'employment' as interpreted in industrial countries and after the limitation and irrelevance of egalitarianism and redistribution, basic human needs were the next logical step in development thinking. The basic needs approach had at least four advantages over previous approaches to growth, employment, income redistribution and poverty eradication. First, the basic needs concept is a reminder that the objective of development is to provide all human beings with the *opportunity* for a full life. However a 'full life' is interpreted, the opportunity for achieving it presupposes meeting basic needs. In the previous decades those concerned with development have sometimes got lost in the technical intricacies of means – production, productivity, savings ratios, export ratios, capital–output ratios, tax ratios and so on – thus losing sight of the end. They came near to being guilty, to borrow a term from Marx, of 'commodity fetishism'. Being clear about the end obviously does not imply neglecting the means: on the contrary, it means efforts are directed at choosing the right means for the ultimate ends that are desired. In the past, planners have moved away from one aim of development, which is meeting basic needs, to some conglomeration of commodities and services valued at market prices, irrespective of whether they are air conditioners or bicycles, luxury houses or rural shelters, whether they benefit the rich or the poor. The basic needs approach recalled the fundamental concern of development, which is human beings and their needs.

Second, the approach went beyond abstractions such as money, income or employment. These aggregates have their place and function; they are important concepts and, though in need of revision, should not be abandoned; but they are useless if they conceal the specific, concrete objectives that people themselves seek. To consider basic needs is to move from the abstract to the concrete, from the aggregate to the specific. The evolution sketched above shows that the concepts have become decreasingly abstract and increasingly disaggregated, concrete and specific. Starting with GNP and its growth, a highly abstract and unspecified conglomerate of goods and services, irrespective of what and for whom, development thinking then turned to employment, a somewhat more specific goal. The discussion was then narrowed down to particular groups of unemployed: school leavers, recent migrants to the city, landless labourers, small-scale farmers without secure water supply, and so forth. But 'employment' was also seen to have serious limitations. Ideas were next further narrowed to identify deprived groups of individuals and families – women, children under five, the elderly, youths with specific needs, ethnic groups discriminated against, communities in distant and neglected regions.

Third, the basic needs approach appealed to members of the national and international communities and was therefore capable of mobilizing resources, unlike vaguer (though important) objectives, such as raising growth rates to 6 per cent, contributing 0.7 per cent of GNP to development assistance, redistributing for greater equality, or narrowing income gaps. People do not normally share lottery prizes or other gains in wealth with their adult brothers and sisters, but they do help when their siblings are ill, their children need education, or some other basic need has to be met. The same is true in the wider human family (Harberger, 1987). Meeting basic needs has some of the characteristics of a public good. My satisfaction from knowing that a hungry child is fed does not detract from your satisfaction. The basic needs approach therefore has the power to mobilize support for policies that more abstract notions lack.

Fourth, the basic needs approach has great organizing and integrating power intellectually, as well as politically. It provides a key to the solution of problems that are at first sight separate, but, on inspection, prove to be related. If basic needs is made the starting-point, these otherwise recalcitrant problems fall into place and become solvable (Streeten, 1976).

In one sense this was a homecoming. For when the world embarked on development 40 years ago, it was primarily with the needs of the poor in mind. Third World leaders wanted economic as well as political independence, but independence was to be used for people's self-fulfilment. The process got sidetracked, but many important discoveries about development were made: the importance of making small-scale farmers and members of the informal urban sector more productive and raising their earning power; the scope for 'efficient' redistribution, that is, redistribution that contributes to more equitable economic growth; the numerous dimensions of labour markets; and the importance of creating demand for certain types of products and the labour producing them.

As early as the 1950s pioneers like Pitambar Pant (1974)[8] in India and Lauchlin Currie, who led the first World Bank mission to a developing country (Colombia), said that development must be concerned with meeting minimum or basic human needs (though their strategies were strongly growth-oriented). Now there is a deeper understanding of the issues, of many of the inhibitions, obstacles and constraints, and also a clearer vision of the path.

The basic needs approach did not lack critics. Some criticized it for being 'absolutist' and wanting to meet the basic needs of everyone before aiming at any other objectives; others for lacking specific proposals on implementation. Ronald Dore (1978, p. 8) wrote,

> the adherents of the latest so-called 'basic needs' strategy seem ... to have a much greater zest for discussing whether or not human rights should be included in any definition of the basic needs which all developing countries should seek to secure for their citizens than for nuts-and-bolts investigation of, say, the cheapest way of ensuring that everyone has pure water to drink, or even of the factors which can successfully inhibit the use of police torture in interrogation.

Some criticized basic needs for aiming at the impossible, others for its having been well-known and pursued successfully for a long time.

As the basic needs concept entered the North–South dialogue, all sorts of misconceptions and misinterpretations grew around it (they are discussed in Streeten *et al.*, 1981, ch. 8). Opposition in developing countries grew, particularly to the use of the concept by donors, and basic needs became two five-letter words. At the same time, new concerns were incorporated in the development dialogue: the role of women, the physical environment, human rights, political freedom and governance, corruption, the waste of military expenditure, and the role of culture among them. Basic needs was regarded as too narrowly focused and it had to carry the ballast of past misinterpretations. The time had come for a wider approach that would cover all aspects of human development, in both industrial and developing countries.

In 1990 the UNDP produced its first *Human Development Report*. They have since then been published annually, complementing the World Bank's annual World Development Reports. The first report begins with the following words:

> This Report is about people – and about how development enlarges their choices. It is about more than GNP growth, more than income and wealth and more than producing commodities and accumulating capital. A person's access to income may be one of the choices, but it is not the sum total of human endeavour.

'So act as to treat humanity, whether in thine own person or in that of any other, in every case as an end, never as means only.' Thus wrote Immanuel Kant in his *Fundamental Principles of the Metaphysics of Morals*. It might serve as the motto for those concerned with human development. Like basic needs, human development puts people back at centre stage, after decades in which a maze of technical concepts, savings ratios, investment ratios, incremental capital–output ratios and similar means had obscured this fundamental vision. This is not to say that technical analysis should be abandoned. Far from it. But the ultimate purpose of the exercise, man and woman as ends, to improve the human condition, to enlarge people's choices, should never be lost sight of.

Human beings are both ends in themselves and means of production. Human development, properly interpreted, is thrice blessed: it is an end in itself; it is a means to higher productivity; and it reduces human reproductivity, by lowering the desired family size. This has been widely recognized, though it is odd that institutions like the World Bank accept without questioning Hondas, beer and television sets as final consumption goods, while nutrition, education and health services have to be justified on grounds of productivity.

Let us call those who stress the means or productivity aspect the human resource developers (or the human capital approach) and those who stress the end aspect the humanitarians. At first blush, there appears to be a unity of interest between them. Although their motives are different, both have the same cause at heart, and they should embrace each other when it comes, for example, to promoting education. This harmony of interests is reinforced by the widespread notion that 'all good things go together'. This unity of interests would exist if there were rigid links between economic production (as measured by income per head) and human development (as measured by human indicators such as life expectancy or literacy). But these two sets of indicators are not very closely related. Sri Lanka, with an income per head of $380, enjoys a life expectancy of 70 years, while Oman, with $6730 has only 54 years. South Africa's income is $2010, life expectancy only 55 years. Adult literacy is lower in Saudi Arabia than in Sri Lanka, in spite of an income per head 15 times as high. Jamaica's infant mortality rate is one-quarter that of Brazil, while its income is only one-half. Life expectancy in Costa Rica is 75 years at an income of $1600. A child born in Harlem in New York City has a lower life expectancy than one born in Bangladesh, one born in the District of Columbia than one born in Sri Lanka. A lot of these discrepancies are of course due to different income distributions. Average income per head can conceal great inequalities. But there are other reasons too. The content and access to social services, particularly in poor countries, primary education and basic health services, are also important.

Nor is there agreement on many policies between human resource developers and humanitarians. Their target groups are different, developers aiming at the potentially productive, humanitarians also concerned with the lame ducks, the unemployables. Their time horizon may be different and the content of their educational curriculum is different. Their sectoral priorities will be different, housing being least connected with raising production,[9] education most, nutrition and health in the middle. The constituencies to which they appeal for support will also be different. The human resource developers appeal to mainstream economists, bankers, including the World Bank, and technocrats; the humanitarians to churches, non-governmental organizations (NGOs), action groups and moral philosophers.

Their views on women's tasks will differ, one advocating access to the labour market, the other stressing the nurturing functions: breast feeding, preparing meals, looking after the family. Martha Nussbaum (1986) cites a story told by Plutarch. Three Spartan women were being sold as slaves. Their captors asked them what they had learned to do. The first replied, 'How to manage a household well.' The second said, 'How to be loyal.' The third said, 'How to be free.' The replies raise the question whether there is a separate women's sphere or whether freedom and autonomy are to be aimed at. But all three are slaves, anyway. And the third, Plutarch reports, commits suicide.

The approach that sees in nutrition, education and health ends in themselves rather means to higher productivity will argue for projects and programmes that enhance these ends, even when conventionally measured rates of return on these investments turned out to be zero. It amounts to standing the conventional approach on its head, or rather back on its feet again. Human development is defined as the enlargement of the range of choices. Some basic needs interpretations have run in terms of commodity bundles or specific needs satisfactions. Amartya Sen's (1985, 1987) analysis has been in terms of 'capabilities' and 'functionings', and neither satisfactions nor happiness nor commodities. Sen goes beyond the analysis of commodities in terms of their characteristics (a shirt provides warmth and decoration and if drip-dry saves ironing) which consumers value, analysing the characteristics of consumers: whether they have the capability to enjoy commodities. The same amount of food has a different significance according to whether the consumer is healthy or has parasites in her stomach, in which case the basic needs of the worms rather than the consumer's are met; or according to whether the consumer has acquired through education the knowledge of how to prepare food.

Sen also argues that human development cannot be judged only by end-states, and that the freedom to choose between different options is an important component of well-being. A given commodity bundle has a different significance to the consumer according to whether she has other options, though she does not exercise them, or whether that same bundle is the only one available. Happiness, as experienced by the individual, is not what human development can aim at or is mainly about. Not only can happiness not be delivered by the government;[10] people may be miserably poor and yet be contented. Anita Brookner (1989) in one of her novels tells of a woman who was so modest she did not even presume to be unhappy.

Human development goes beyond basic needs in that it is concerned with all human beings, not only the poor, not only poor countries, not only basic needs. Human development applies to the advanced, industrial countries as much as to middle-income and low-income countries. The indicators are of course different. Once nearly 100 per cent literacy and average life expectancy of 78 years are reached, there is not much to distinguish one industrial country from another. Years of schooling have been included in the indicator for education as a differentiating characteristic between, say, Britain and the USA, but the main indicators should be looked for elsewhere: in homelessness, drug addiction and crime rates. Divorce rates and suicide rates are more controversial. They can be regarded as indicating more options and therefore as positive achievements, particularly suicides of terminally ill elderly patients. On the other hand, they may be regarded as signs of the breakdown of a society's social fabric, a failure of upholding what some regard as the moral values of the family or the sanctity of life. A shorthand way of describing human development is a variation of Abraham Lincoln's definition of government. It is development *of* the people, *for* the people, *by* the people. Of the people implies adequate income generation through jobs, for the people implies social services for those who need help, and by the people means participation.

The move from welfare or utility, to chosen bundles of goods and services, to characteristics of these goods and services, to needs that they meet, and finally to emphasizing the enlargement of choices, has enriched our understanding. The enlargement of choices of one section should not be at the expense of the legitimate choices of another. This has two important implications: first in equity, so that one person's enlargement does not encroach on that of others; and second over time, so that our present choices do not encroach on the choices of future generations, or what has come to be known as sustainability. This concern for the future should cover not only the physical environment – raw material exhaustion without technical substitution and pollution – but also resilience to outside shocks, debt and political sustainability. A human development strategy stresses the importance of institutions for improving the human condition. Among these are not only the state, both as an agent to make markets work efficiently and to step in where they fail, and the market, but also the civil society – democratic political processes, the news media, NGOs, grassroots organizations, action groups and the public at large. It is in their interaction that the conditions for the good life should be found.

The item in the UNDP's *Report* that has caught the public's eye and caused most controversy is perhaps analytically the weakest: the Human Development Index (HDI). It is clear that the concept of human development is much wider and richer than what can be caught in *any* index or set of indicators. This is true of other indicators, such as temperature, also. But, it might be asked, why try to catch a vector in a single number? Yet such indexes are useful in focusing attention and simplifying the problem. They have a stronger impact on the mind and draw public attention more powerfully than a long list of many indicators, combined with a qualitative discussion. They are eye-catching. The strongest argument in their favour is that they show up the inadequacies of other indexes, such as GNP, and thereby contribute to an intellectual muscle therapy that helps us to avoid analytical cramps.

The Human Development Index comprises (1) income per head at real purchasing power, not at exchange rates, and with income above the poverty line counted at lower values; (2) literacy and years of schooling; and (3) life expectancy. These disparate items are brought to a common denominator by counting the distance between the best and worst performers and thereby achieving a ranking of countries. As we have seen, one of the great drawbacks of average income per head is that it is an average that can conceal great inequalities. But, it may be objected, the other components of the Human Development Index, namely life expectancy and literacy, are also averages. They can conceal vast discrepancies between men and women, boys and girls, rich and poor, urban and rural residents, different ethnic or religious groups. There are, however, several reasons why human indicators are less misleading than income per head. First, literacy and life expectancy are much less skewed in their distribution than income. There is a maximum of 100 per cent literacy. In spite of all the achievements of modern medicine, the maximum life span has not been extended. For income, on the other hand, the sky is the limit. A very few very high income earners can raise the average. Second, therefore, for the human indicators the average tells us something about the distribution. There cannot be high averages with too many people not participating.

Third, any upward move in a human indicator can be regarded as an improvement. Some might object if only the literacy of boys or the life expectancy of men is increased, but unless it can be shown that such increases worsen the fate of girls and women by, for example, increasing the ability and desire to oppress, to object would smack of envy and bitch-in-the-manger attitudes. Fourth, whereas high incomes of some can cause relative deprivation in others, this is not true for human indicators. If anything, the benefits in the health and education of anybody benefits the whole community. Fifth, international income gaps, whether relative or absolute, may be inevitably widening, but to aim at reducing international gaps in human indicators is both sensible and feasible. In fact, looking at development in human terms presents a more cheerful picture than in income terms. Since 1960 average life expectancy has increased by 16 years, adult literacy by 40 per cent, nutritional levels by over 40 per cent and child mortality rates have been halved. The international gap has closed. While average income per head in the South is 6 per cent of that in the North, life expectancy is 80 per cent, literacy 66 per cent and nutrition 85 per cent. Sixth and finally, human indicators show the troubles of overdevelopment or, better, maldevelopment, as well as of underdevelopment. Diseases of affluence can kill, just as the diseases of poverty. Income, on the other hand, does not show up the destructive aspects of wealth.

A separate index covers aspects of human freedom and human rights, clearly an important aspect of human development. Life expectancy and literacy could be quite high in a well-managed prison. Should the freedom index be integrated into the Human Development Index? There are some arguments in favour, but the balance of arguments is probably against. First, it might be said that freedom is so important that no trade-off should be possible between its loss and gains in some of the other indicators.[11] Second, political conditions are much more volatile than education and health. Once a mother knows the importance of education for her children, or of hygienic behaviour, this knowledge is not lost, even when incomes drop. So human indicators tend to be fairly stable. Political indicators, on the other hand, can change overnight with a coup. A third argument against aggregating freedom with the positive aspects of human development is that grading is more subjective and less reliable than measuring life expectancy or literacy.

Finally, one of the most interesting questions is how freedom is related to human development more narrowly interpreted, or how negative and positive rights or freedom are associated. This can be examined only if they are recorded by separate indexes, not components of the same.[12] Thus we might formulate a hypothesis that freedom, though not a necessary condition of human development, is entirely consistent with it even at quite low levels; and that human development, once it has reached a certain stage, leads to the call for freedom by the people. Here is a message of hope.

Notes

1. These questions include the following: Do conventional measures of growth involve a bias against the poor, and how can this be changed? How can strategies of redistribution be combined with strategies of growth? Is it possible to identify groups whose members

have common characteristics and to direct strategies towards those groups? What are the principal instruments of policy?

2. The following discussion is indebted to Beckerman (1979).

3. Townsend (1979, p. 915) defines poverty as 'the absence or inadequacy of those diets, amenities, standards, services, and activities which are common or customary in a society. People are deprived of the conditions of life which ordinarily define member-ship of society. If they lack or are denied resources to obtain access to these conditions of life, and so fulfil membership of society, they are in poverty.' This leads to the paradoxical conclusion that there is no poverty in societies where nearly everyone lives in conditions of deprivation which 'ordinarily define membership of society.'

4. 'By necessities I understand not only the commodities which are indispensably neces-sary for the support of life, but whatever the custom of the country renders it indecent for creditable people, even of the lower order, to be without' (Adam Smith, *The Wealth of Nations*, bk 5, ch. 2, pt 2). A.K. Sen has argued, to me convincingly, that the shame felt by these people is absolute deprivation, it is not more shame than others feel, though relative in the space of commodities.

5. 'A house may be large or small: as long as the surrounding houses are equally small it satisfies all social demands for a dwelling. But let a palace arise beside the little house, and it shrinks from a little house to a hut ... however high it [the little house] may shoot up in the course of civilization, if the neighbouring palace grows to an equal or even greater extent, the occupant of the relatively small house will feel more and more uncomfortable, dissatisfied and cramped within its four walls' (Marx and Engels, 1958, pp. 93–4).

6. A.K. Sen (1978, p. 11) concluded his discussion of relative deprivation: 'It is, however, worth noting that the approach of relative deprivation – even including all its variants – cannot really be the only basis for poverty. There is an irreducible core of *absolute* deprivation in our idea of poverty which translates reports of starvation, malnutrition and visible hardship into a diagnosis of poverty without having to ascertain first the relative picture. The approach of relative deprivation supplements rather than competes with this concern with absolute dispossession.'

7. Pre-invasion Kuwait may seem an exception to this. It achieved the eradication of absolute poverty while great inequalities remained. But this is true only for Kuwaiti citizens and excludes the many foreigners who worked there and whose incomes, though higher than those at home, were much lower than those of the Kuwaitis. In view of the removal of the resource constraint as a result of oil exports and the confinement of the benefits to Kuwaiti citizens, this may be the exception that tests the rule.

8. In a paper that was circulated in August 1962 by the Perspective Planning Division of the Planning Commission, part of which is reprinted in Srinivasan and Bardhan (1974), Pitambar Pant anticipated many features of the basic needs approach. But since he believed with Pareto in the similarity of income distributions in all societies, minimum needs had to be met by general economic growth. He postulated this growth to be much higher than the five-year-plan target, which, in turn, was higher than actual growth. Moreover he regarded the poorest 20 per cent as unreachable by economic growth.

9. The Soviet Union, however, did keep housing scarce and used its allocation to attract workers to areas where they were needed for the plan.

10. Keynes proposed the toast to the Royal Economic Society: 'to economics and econo-mists, who are the trustees, not of civilisation, but of the possibility of civilisation'.

11. This objection could be mitigated by using a geometrical rather than an arithmetic average. With a zero weight for freedom, the total index becomes zero, however high the other components.

12. It could be said that the same argument applies to the relationship between, for instance, literacy and life expectancy and that they should therefore not be lumped together.

References

Abel-Smith, Brian and Peter Townsend (1965), *The Poor and the Poorest*, London: G. Bell and Sons.

Aristotle (1911), *The Nicomachean Ethics*, London, New York: Everyman's Library.

Beckerman, Wilfred (1979), 'Presidential address to the British Association for the Advancement of Science', in W. Beckerman (ed.), *Slow Growth in Britain; Causes and Consequences*, Oxford: Clarendon Press.

Brookner, Anita (1989), *Latecomers*, New York: Pantheon.

Chenery, Hollis *et al.* (1974), *Redistribution with Growth*, London: Oxford University Press.

Dore, R.P. (1978), 'The Role of Universities in National Development', *Association of Commonwealth Universities Occasional Paper* (July).

Harberger, Arnold C. (1987), 'On the Use of Distributional Weights in Social Cost–Benefit Analysis', *Journal of Political Economy*, **86** (2) (supplement).

Harris, John R. and Michael P. Todaro (1970), 'Migration, Unemployment, and Development. A Two-Sector Analysis', *American Economic Review*, **60** (1).

Kuznets, Simon (1955), 'Economic Growth and Income Inequality', *American Economic Review*, **45** (1).

Kuznets, Simon (1963), 'Quantitative Aspects of Economic Growth of Nations, VIII: Distribution of Income by Size', *Economic Development and Cultural Change*, **11** (2).

Lewis, W.A. (1954), 'Economic Development with Unlimited Supplies of Labour,' *Manchester School of Economic and Social Studies*, **22** (2).

Lewis, W.A. (1955), *The Theory of Economic Growth*, London: Allen & Unwin.

Marx, Karl and Frederick Engels (1958), *Selected Works*, vol.1, Moscow: Foreign Languages Publishing House.

Mosley, Paul, Jane Harrigan and John Toye (1991), *Aid and Power, The World Bank and Policy-Based Lending*, vol.1, *Analysis and policy proposals*, London, New York: Routledge.

Myrdal, Gunnar (1986), *Asian Drama, An Inquiry into the Poverty of Nations*, New York: Twentieth Century Fund.

Nozick, Robert (1974), *Anarchy, State and Utopia*, New York: Basic Books.

Nussbaum, Martha (1986), 'Women's Lot', *New York Review of Books*, **33** (1), 30 January.

Pant, Pitambar (1974), 'Perspective of Development, India 1960–61 to 1975–76: Implications of Planning for a Minimum Level of Living', in Srinivasan and Bardham (1974).

Rawls, John (1971), *The Theory of Justice*, Cambridge, Mass.: Harvard University Press.

Sen, Amartya (1978), *Three Notes on the Concept of Poverty*, World Employment Programme Research Working Paper, WEP2-23/WP65, Geneva: ILO.

Sen, Amartya (1985), *Commodities and Capabilities*, Amsterdam, Oxford: North-Holland, Oxford University Press.

Sen, Amartya (1987), *The Standard of Living*, Tanner Lectures with discussion, edited by G. Hawthorn, Cambridge University Press.

Srinivasan, T.N. and Bardham, P.K. (eds) (1974), *Poverty and Income Distribution in India*, Calcutta: Statistical Publishing Society.

Streeten, Paul (1976), 'Industrialisation in a Unified Development Strategy', in Sir Alec Cairncross and Mohinder Puri (eds), *Employment, Income Distribution and Development Strategy, Essays in Honour of H.W. Singer*, Basingstoke: Macmillan; and in *World Development*, **3** (1), 1975.

Streeten, Paul *et al.* (1981), *First Things First: Meeting Basic Human Needs in Developing Countries*, New York, Oxford: Oxford University Press.

Townsend, Peter (1979), *Poverty in the United Kingdom: A Survey of Household Resources and Standards of Living*, Berkeley, Los Angeles: University of California Press.

UNDP (1990), *Human Development Report 1990*, New York, Oxford: Oxford University Press.

3 The environment and North–South interaction

S. Mansoob Murshed

Concern about the environment is at the forefront of the great issues of import at the present. Indeed it can be said that we are all 'green' today. Economic aspects of the environment are receiving a great deal of attention, at both the domestic and the international level.

The term 'environment' is commonly taken to imply nature, the atmosphere and so on. From the viewpoint of economics these should be considered to be renewable assets or resources, but until recently many of these resources were regarded as being free. The irreparable damage done to the environment by excessive or unsustainable use has only become convincingly known fairly recently. Economics has a long history of analysing the optimal use of exhaustible resources, such as minerals, with tangible values attached. Thus there is, clearly, a problem of valuing environmental resources in which there are no market transactions. We return to this point again in the next section. But where does the value of the environment spring from? First of all there are direct use values. The degradation of the environment and other environmental problems such as global warming will affect our capacity both to consume and to produce. Second, there are existence values derived from the preservation of environmental resources. Residents of some countries may derive utility from the preservation of biodiversity, say in the form of the tropical rain forest, even if they have no direct use and are located in other countries. Finally there are the so-called option values which emanate from a cautious approach to irreversible action. Even if some environmental resources have no direct uses and are not valued highly for their intrinsic worth, these may obtain in the future. Thus it could be prudent not to take irreversible action to degrade them.

Given these sources of value for the environment, where does the problem come from? The difficulties arise because of excessive use: a negative externality arises whenever acts of consumption or production exceed their socially warranted levels. The classic market-based solutions are twofold. There is the Pigovian approach which requires a benevolent agency, the government say, to tax those who act irresponsibly (the polluter) and to subsidize those who behave themselves from a socially optimal viewpoint (by adopting clean technologies). This approach is also responsible for enshrining the polluter pays principle (PPP) for the cost of cleaning up after the event. The other, more ultra-market-based, approach can be termed Coasean. This is connected with the ownership of enforceable property rights. According to this view the owner of well defined property rights, either the polluter or the polluted, will pay the other concerned party for the privilege of polluting or to desist from polluting. These actions can be effected without a governmental agency as long as there is a well established legal framework and transactions and enforcement costs are not too excessive. Finally it should be noted that, apart from market-based solutions, there is the option of direct regulation, but this does not conform well to our zeitgeist.

Perhaps the greatest stumbling-block in the way of achieving solutions to environmental problems is their global nature, involving as they do numerous countries and national governments. Many environmental problems, such as global warming, are international and the problems in achieving cooperation, leave alone solutions, are immense. This chapter will concern itself with the international aspects of environmental policy which have a bearing on North–South interaction. We begin, however, by briefly discussing the problems of development and the environment in the domestic context. The next section goes on to discuss the broad nature of the problems raised by environmental policy in the North–South sphere, including the concept of natural debt. This is followed by an analysis of the various policies suggested, including debt for nature swaps, a scheme of globally tradeable permits for greenhouse gas emission, and the links between trade (commercial) policy and the environment. The final section attempts to connect the various issues.

I   Development and the environment
In the introductory section above, mention was made of the problem of measuring the value of environmental resources. If they are regarded as mainly non-renewable resources, the value of their depletion should be deducted from national income figures in the manner in which capital stock depreciation is treated. The champions of this approach include Dasgupta (1990), Pearce and Mäler (1991) and Pearce and Freeman (1991) among others. However conventional national income accounting procedures have not yet begun to take these into account.

Once account is taken of the value of environmental resources, high levels of income achieved at the cost of environmental degradation look much less impressive. If we were to ask ourselves why such values do not enter into traditional national income accounts, it is perhaps because there are no market transactions involving environmental resources, unlike other natural resources – minerals for example. Be that as it may, Dasgupta's work does provide a framework for such national income accounting. More importantly, it enjoins us to review our measures of growth rates. Ordinary growth rates at best undervalue the depletion of the stock of environmental resources. Pearce and Mäler (1991) cite an example of the reworking of the growth rates for the Indonesian economy between 1971 and 1984. One estimate which takes into account the depreciation of the stocks of oil, timber and topsoil would reduce the annual average growth rate for that period from 7 per cent to 4 per cent, virtually halving the growth rates. Such dramatic reductions in growth rates aside, discount rates which determine the rate of present vis à vis future consumption become important in determining optimal depletion rates. Poorer nations or countries in the earlier stages of their economic development will care less about environmental degradation (which lowers the capacity to produce in the future) than richer countries (the same rich countries cared little about the environment in the earlier stages of their development).

The important point here is to view the environment as an additional category of capital – natural capital. This would be in addition to the other two widely known types of capital, human and physical. Such a procedure in addition to the problems of valuation of such a natural capital stock would involve calculations as regards its levels of depreciation, as with other types of capital. The value of the net stock of capital is arrived at after deducting depreciation; thus national accounts which estimated and deducted depreciation of natural capital would give us figures of national income considerably lower than those currently estimated.

This brings us to the much discussed view of sustainable development or growth. The idea of sustainable growth was popularized by the Brundtland report of 1987, and has as its advocates prominent economists like David Pearce. Quite crudely stated, it implies a level of economic growth or development which does not compromise the ability of future generations to enjoy similar levels of living standards (including the quality of life). Environmentally speaking it could imply either retaining intact the net stock of natural capital or some trade-off between natural and other types of capital stocks. In other words, sustainable development implies eschewing the overexploitation of the present stock of natural capital to generate high levels of income, at the expense of lower living standards (and the quality of life) for future generations. Thus there is a considerable element of intergenerational equity in this concept. According to authors such as Pearce and Mäler (1991) sustainability implies that the stock of one type of capital should only be depleted if it builds up the stock of at least one of the other two types of capital. Sustainability is violated if environmental damage is not matched by an accretion of physical or human capital. They cite the examples of degradation of the Amazonian forests not being matched by sufficient capital accumulation of the other varieties as a prime example of the violation of the rules of sustainability.

Thus the pursuit of the goals of sustainability would imply a rigorous cost–benefit analysis of the use of the environment. An example of such a study is that by Nordhaus (1991) regarding the effects of greenhouse gas (GHG) emission and the costs of containing them. His findings, based upon data for the United States, puts the net benefits of GHG control at a very modest amount. Many environmentalists, of course, would view any losses to the environment or of biodiversity as a cost outweighing any potential economic benefits. This categorical imperative is to do with 'existence' values, and the notion of a safe minimum standard has been proposed as a compromise, a level of environmental quality which development should not violate.

The above discussion points to the question as to why sustainability is violated in developing countries. The answers must be found in the desire to achieve economic growth and, above all, in poverty. These two concepts are not unrelated as far as environmental issues are concerned. The proponents of sustainability argue that the false dichotomy between economic growth or development and the environment must be removed. Growth at the expense of the environment is ultimately self-defeating. Policies to promote cleaner economic development are advocated. These include measures to check population growth as well as the adoption of better technologies and energy efficiency through carbon (energy) taxes.

While it is true that higher population growth rates in the South will put a greater pressure on resources as well as add to the consumption of fossil fuels, so intensifying global warming, the ultimate cure for high population growth rates is the eradication of poverty. Poorer families and uneducated mothers tend to have larger families, and developmental goals such as a more equitable distribution of income and education are thus environmentally friendly: the *World Development Report* (World Bank, 1992) refers to these as 'win–win' policies. This report also highlights the linkage between poverty or low income and many environmental indicators. Populations with lower incomes tend to have poorer access to safe water, sanitation and good urban air quality. Economic growth and the consequent higher income tend to solve these problems as these amenities become affordable. Cleaner technologies and energy efficiency tend to be expensive and are more affordable by richer households and societies. Above all, poorer communities, especially in rural areas, are more likely to overexploit resources such as water, reduce soil quality and fell trees in an unsustainable manner. Poverty is the root cause of this, even where an institutional mechanism is in place to prevent overuse of these resources, whether privately or commonly owned.

The eradication of poverty is the most effective manner in which these resources can be used sustainably.

Higher income is certainly no panacea: increased incomes raise total consumption, which means a rise in the emission of greenhouse gases linked to the use of cars; urban waste disposal also becomes an environmental hazard. The important point here is that certain environmental problems are linked to poverty and others to high consumption or affluence. With regard to the latter, surely it is up to the rich and the richer countries to mainly curtail consumption through economic incentives or regulation, if their avowed concern for the environment is to be credible.

II   Environmental policy in the North–South sphere: general issues

The fact that environmental problems are of an international nature cannot be overemphasized. It is, however, worthwhile distinguishing between environmental issues which are unidirectional and those which are reciprocal. Unidirectional environmental externalities arise when the polluting country is not adversely affected by pollution, but others are. The classical example is of an upstream polluting country from which pollution originates and which adversely affects one or more downstream countries. We shall not concern ourselves with this case involving a few countries, as an excellent discussion is contained in Mäler (1990). Reciprocal externalities, on the other hand, adversely affect both the originator or the source (country) of the pollution and other countries as well. Most of the issues of greatest environmental concern, such as the greenhouse effect and holes in the ozone layer, fall into this category. Reciprocal externalities could be regional as well – the European acid rain problem, for example – but they are in the main global, and from an analytical standpoint the treatment of regional and global reciprocal externalities contains many similarities. We could view the environment – the oceans, the atmosphere – as global common property (public good) and then the problem would be to prevent excessive use or misuse of the global common, which would once again require international cooperation.

Excessive use of common property leads to the familiar 'tragedy of the common'; the literature is replete with examples of this. Essentially the problem involves the 'prisoners' dilemma' situation where each party is aware that a cooperative strategy is superior to a non-cooperative one, but no mechanism exists to induce cooperation. In the example of the global environmental common property problem, the set of inducements presented to the parties concerned make them engage in (excessive) activities harmful to the environment violating the sustainability principle. There is a globally optimal level of use of environmental resources which does not violate the sustainability principle; or there exists a globally optimal level of abatement of pollutants which equates the marginal cost of abatement to the global marginal benefit from abatement. As Barrett (1990) points out for a group of countries with identical benefit and cost functions with respect to abatement, the globally optimum rule for an individual country is to equate its own marginal abatement cost to the global marginal benefit from abatement, (the global benefit from abatement is the sum of individual country benefits, as with a public good), but no global agency exists to induce or enforce this action.

In the North-South context the possibility of a subset of nations affected by reciprocal environmental externalities cooperating, as in a cartel, to act as leaders to the rest has been suggested. The outcome could resemble a Stackelberg leader–follower outcome, as Barrett (1990) elucidates. A group, say the North, could agree to cooperate to reduce their emission levels on the basis of the reaction functions of the other group, the South. The South would then in turn fix their emission levels acting as followers (fixed action by other countries) while the North behaved as Stackelberg leaders.

More generally as far as action concerning global reciprocal environmental externalities, such as the problem of global warming, is concerned, the large number of potential participants to any agreement militates against meaningful cooperative arrangements. Furthermore the huge costs of abatement also acts as a stumbling-block to cooperative behaviour. In this situation the way forward would be for a group of countries to cooperate in emission reduction, say in the North, while making side payments to some other countries, say in the South, to join such an agreement. This would be akin to a Coasean solution, and therefore potentially *efficient*. Even if one examines the Stackelberg leader–follower equilibrium described above, those countries in the leadership coalition could become better off (in terms of higher global abatement levels) by enlarging their group. But in order to induce others to join (mainly in the South) they would have to be compensated for increasing abatement and the consequently higher abatement costs in terms of forgone output and other direct costs; which would involve side payments. The important point is that side payments could secure potentially Pareto superior outcomes, inducing cooperation on the part of the South which is necessary in many areas of environmental problems. What is absolutely crucial is that cooperation or participation by the South in any global environmental scheme has to be *incentive-compatible* and this necessitates side payments.

The message implicit in the above discussion is that a globally optimum level of abatement of pollutants would equate the marginal costs of abatement amongst all pollutants. These marginal costs could be high amongst countries who have already undertaken significant levels of abatement, as in some environmentally conscious Scandinavian countries, but could also be high in countries in the South in terms of forgone output. Also the approaches outlined above deal with the *flow* concept of output involving current emission levels, but not with the *stock* of, say, greenhouse gases which have accumulated over time. The extent of global warming is related to the total stock of GHGs in the atmosphere and the *period of time* these GHGs have remained in the atmosphere. This makes the richer countries in the North the greatest contributors to the total stock of GHGs existing in the atmosphere. Clearly this is a consequence of its historically faster rates of growth and earlier industrialization. Smith (1991) estimates that the USA, for example, has emitted 70 billion tons of GHGs into the atmosphere since 1900. Valuing the clean-up cost at $20 per ton (costs incurred through reforestation) Smith puts the value of this damage at US $1.4 trillion.

The crux of the point made above is that many of the developed industrialized countries in the North have in the past emitted vast amounts of GHGs simply by virtue of their earlier industrialization and low environmental concern at these junctures. In other words they have accumulated a vast amount of natural debt. The upshot of natural debt is that countries who have large stocks of this type of debt (in the North) should pay them off. In policy terms it implies that their share of abatement of GHGs and the total cost of abatement should be reflective of their natural debt, and they should bear a higher proportion of the costs, as this would amount to the reduction of their debt. In the words of Smith (1991, p. 96):

> Since the present economic status of most countries has been achieved partly by incurring natural debts, it seems only fair to allocate responsibility for whatever needs to be done by using indices that reflect an expectation that nations should pay back the debt in the same proportion as it was borrowed.

This does not mean, however, that present growth rates of emission are highest among the nations in the North. A glance at Table 3.1 tells us that high-income countries accounted for about 46 per cent of total carbon dioxide emission in 1989, and in per capita terms released nearly three times the world average of carbon dioxide and over six times the LDC emission average. The OECD (1991) reports a slowdown in the OECD growth of carbon dioxide emission, comparing 1988 with 1971 with negative growth rates for the UK, France, Belgium, West Germany and Sweden. The rest of the world's GHG emission rose by 43 per cent in 1971–88, while the OECD average increase was 15 per cent. But the absolute rate of emissions per capita in the OECD countries (the North) remains significantly above developing countries in the South and, as Smith (1991) suggests, it will take a very long time before Southern nations catch up with the North in terms of per capita emission. For example, for 0 per cent annual average growth rates of emission for Switzerland and 5 per cent annual growth rates for Bangladesh, it will take 80 years for Bangladesh (with over ten times the population) to catch up with Switzerland. Be that as it may, the North has incurred a huge stock of natural debt even if the current (flow) accumulation to that debt is being moderated. The USA alone would be accountable for about a

Table 3.1   Global carbon dioxide emissions

Country group	Total emissions (fossil fuels & cement manufacture) (m. tons of carbon) 1965	1989	Average growth rate (%) 1980–89	Carbon dioxide emissions (tons of carbon) 1989 per capita	per $mn of GDP
Low-income	203	952	5.8	0.32	926
China*a*	131	652	5.9	0.59	1 547
India*a*	46	178	7.0	0.21	670
Middle-income	373	1 061	2.3	0.96	471
Lower-middle-income	176	478	2.3	0.70	551
Upper-middle-income	198	583	2.3	1.38	421
Low & middle-income	576	2 013	3.8	0.50	614
Sub-Saharan Africa	12	61	4.9	0.13	376
East Asia, Pacific	157	837	5.7	0.54	934
South Asia	47	201	7.0	0.18	567
Europe	191	391	1.0	2.00	809
Middle East & North Africa	37	189	4.3	0.76	516
Latin America & Caribbean	97	258	1.2	0.61	278
Other economies	535	1 089	2.0	—	—
High-income	1 901	2 702	0.5	3.26	186
Germany*a*	178	175	–1.2	2.82	147
Japan*a*	106	284	1.0	2.31	99
UK*a*	171	155	0.1	2.72	185
USA*a*	948	1 329	1.0	5.34	259
World	3 012	5 822	1.8	1.12	327

a   Top six emitters of carbon dioxide (West Germany only).

Source·   World Bank, 1992.

third of total global natural debt. Natural debt in the North means that countries in that region should take steps to reduce this debt by incurring a large proportion of abatement costs and by making transfers to the South to raise Southern abatement. These transfers could take the form of debt reduction or trade concessions for the South.

We now turn to a consideration of more specific policy proposals.

III   Debt for nature swaps

Debt for nature swaps, which are currently being undertaken on a small scale, amount to a write-down of the South's commercial international debt, the proceeds from which are diverted to finance reforestation and the preservation of the rain forest and rare species: in short, to preserve global natural resources. The retention of global biodiversity may have little direct use value in the North, apart from acting as a sink for greenhouse gases (GHGs), but its preservation yields utility to citizens in the North. Debt for nature swaps, the first of which took place in Bolivia in 1987, do not constitute an additional source of resources or transfers to the South.

The link between international commercial bank debt and environmental degradation is well documented: as many heavily indebted countries struggle to keep up debt servicing, so the pace of the destruction of biodiversity accelerates, as in the case of tropical deforestation (see Table 3.2). Some of the highest deforestation occurs in severely indebted countries. To the extent that there is concern for biodiversity, debt for nature swaps could be a Pareto improvement; see Bigman (1990), for example. The problems with debt for

Table 3.2   Deforestation in selected highly indebted countries

	Forest area (thousands of km²)				
	Total area 1980		*Annual deforestation (period)*		
	Total	*Closed*	*Total*	*Closed*	
Brazil	5145	3575	13.8	—	(1989–90)
Mexico	484	463	10.0	—	(1981–83)
Colombia	517	464	8.9	8.2	(1981–85)
Nigeria	148	60	4.0	3.0	(1981–85)
Ecuador	147	143	3.4	3.4	(1981–85)
Peru	706	697	2.7	2.7	(1981–85)
Philippines	95	95	1.4	1.4	(1981–88)

Source: World Bank, 1992.

nature swaps seem fourfold. First, there would be a temptation for some nations in the North to 'free ride' and let other nations engage in debt for nature swaps. Related to this is the problem of inducing commercial bank creditors to engage in these operations, it is easier to contemplate debt for nature exchanges as far as official debt is concerned. One way of inducing this actively on the part of commercial banks is to offer tax concessions, which in turn could have adverse fiscal consequences. It should be pointed out that some commercial banks, such as the Creditanstalt Bank in Austria, have already engaged in debt for charity swaps. Debt for nature swaps are being mainly undertaken by non-governmental organizations (NGOs). Second, there is the problem of monitoring activities in indebted Southern countries in such a way that environmentally friendly policies are actually pursued. This might require increased conditionality for existing aid and debt for nature swaps, which will increase resentment in the South. Third, there is a great danger that resources devoted to debt for nature swaps might 'crowd out' other aid and transfers from North to South. As things stand, these swaps make no new resources available but divert funds used to service debt to environmental uses. However, to the extent that existing international indebtedness contributes to net negative transfers from North to South, their diversion to environmental purposes is no bad thing from a Southern point of view. Fourth, as with commercial bank debt reduction where the private sector in the North has engaged in little 'voluntary' (although Pareto improving) debt reduction, debt for nature swaps may not go far enough in bringing about the right volume of Pareto optimal environmental control in the South. By themselves debt for nature swaps are a limited means of solving environmental problems as they are mainly geared to the preservation of biodiversity.

IV   Global tradeable permit schemes in GHG emission

An alternative or additional policy proposal to deal with global environmental problems which is currently gaining favour with an international (and North–South) dimension is the idea of internationally traded emission permit systems (ITEPS), see Grubb (1989) for a detailed proposal of such a scheme. This scheme has similarities to a carbon tax, only it would fix quantities and not directly affect prices (as a quota does when compared to a tariff). There would be a global maximum set on the total emission of greenhouse gases arrived at after international negotiations. Thereafter there would be an international initial allocation of the permits to emit GHGs. Here permits might be overissued to some nations, as in the South, to ensure their participation in the scheme. The initial allocation of permits would form the basis for revenues accruing to each country. Henceforth there would be free trade in tradeable permits and countries with high abatement costs could purchase them from countries with low abatement costs. The price of the traded permit would be market-determined but permits could be exchanged for trade concessions and debt reduction instead of cash. Ex post the total amounts paid out by a country to purchase these permits may not match the ex ante formula for revenue allocation which is based on the initial allocation of permits.

This proposal has the great merit of being flexible and allowing countries and enterprises with high abatement costs actually to buy tradeable permits and it is superior to a system of direct regulation, but when total estimates of demand for GHG emission are uncertain it is difficult to set absolute levels (upper limits) for global GHG emission. One of the great problems with such a scheme would be to induce wide participation by sovereign states, but enough participation by key countries in the South such as China, India and Brazil could be ensured by overissuing permits to them which they could sell, so obtaining revenues. There would be an additional problem of countries wishing initially to 'free ride' the system and join later at more favourable terms, but even if only a small group of countries join, benefits to the global environment will accrue and trade discrimination by scheme participants against the goods of non-members might induce participation.

A related difficulty is high transaction costs preventing international trade in tradeable permits. This would require a new international agency or an existing IFI to facilitate these transactions. The task of this agency would be also to monitor compliance with the agreement and impose fines (including withholding transfers). As Barrett (1990) has indicated, compliance can be self-enforcing: one country has an incentive to comply if non-compliance results in the same behaviour by other countries. Fines alone can only induce compliance if the marginal value of the fine equals the marginal cost of keeping up the agreed level of emission abatement. This envisaged international agency could also act as the auctioneer of tradeable permits and collect and disburse revenues.

A cause of great concern in any scheme of tradeable permits is the acquisition of market power by permit holders by actually hoarding permits. Grubb (1989) proposes that this problem can be avoided by assigning permits for a fixed term, akin to a leasehold, but even leaseholds can be hoarded for the purpose of acquiring monopoly power. Southern nations could be concerned that the North would buy up the tradeable permits. One manner of avoiding this very plausible potential inefficiency (market power) is to have schemes for issuing new permits at periodic intervals and to have other types of permit allocation mechanisms such as overlapping permits and fractional permits. Such a scheme has been proposed by Bertram (1991) with the example of overlapping fishing permits in New Zealand in mind. Permits would last for a total of L years and a fraction P/L would be retired each year. When issuing permits a mix of different length permits could be given to countries and firms within a country. At any time there would be permits of different maturity held by any country. Analytically speaking, such a scheme would have similarities to models of overlapping generations.

Perhaps the most thorny problem which any scheme of tradeable permits is likely to encounter is how to allocate the initial tranche of permits. Various proposals regarding allocation schemes exist, which can be summarized into the following categories. First, there is the so-called 'grandfathering' scheme. Under this proposal permits are assigned according to current and existing emission levels at some earlier date. This system would clearly favour developed countries as they industrialized earlier. Southern countries would object to such a scheme as it would put a constraint on their ability to industrialize (and emit GHGs), a constraint which Northern countries had not faced. The proposal would fly in the face of historical responsibility and is unlikely to be accepted by Southern countries, reducing the chances of their participation in an international scheme. Second, tradeable permit allocation could be linked to historical responsibility, related to the natural debt concept alluded to earlier. Such a scheme would favour the South by granting more permits to countries there, but is unlikely to be accepted by the North, even if such a system is more equitable than most others. Third, there is the proposal for linking the allocation of permits to GNP. This would clearly favour the richer countries in the North, especially those among them with low fossil fuel consumption per unit of GNP, such as Japan and France. Once again such a scheme would be perceived to be unfair by the South and would certainly ensure its non-participation in the scheme. Finally there are proposals to link permits to population size. Such schemes would favour developing countries, particularly the more populous nations such as China and India. In terms of equity this seems to be the most appealing proposal. As Grubb has so eloquently argued, this scheme amounts to giving *every human being an equal right to a claim on the atmosphere and the environment*. Although the merits of such a scheme are difficult to argue with on moral grounds, it is unlikely to be wholly acceptable to the wealthier North, given the perceptions about the transfers involved from North to South. One World Bank (1992) calculation places the figure at $70 billion for the North to buy emission rights from the South at $25 a ton of carbon. As Grubb (1989) has argued, a mixed scheme of permit allocation would be required, covering aspects of all of the above arguments, for the scheme to gain wide acceptability across the globe. Any scheme involving cooperation between North and South would require some transfers to the South to induce even partial cooperation. Such transfers are both efficient (on Coasean grounds) and equitable.

The model in Murshed (1992, ch. 6) analyses a macro-model of North–South interaction with an explicit scheme of tradeable permits. Such a scheme could favour both regions, especially when accompanied by transfers to the South linked to improvements in emission efficiency in that region.

V   Trade policy and the environment

The use of trade taxes, specifically tariffs, to combat emission of pollutants (unidirectional externalities) is analysed in Baumol and Oates (1988). They point out that this is clearly a second-best policy as a tariff on the goods exported by a polluting country does not directly affect production costs. For large countries with monopoly powers in international trade, they find that the tariff that maximizes welfare when pollution externalities from exporters are also considered is in excess of the optimum tariff. They point out, however, that, when a large number of importing countries are affected by pollution from a single country, if they all impose an import tax or a transnational resource charge, it will be effective in correcting the externality.

The use of trade policy to promote environmental goals is very much on the agenda. Indeed many argue that it should be enshrined in GATT (General Agreement on Tariffs and Trade) rules (GATT, 1992). Examples cited include the restriction of tuna fish exports, as dolphins are killed in catching tuna; the ban on ivory exports; restrictions on imports of wood; and restricting cassava imports from Thailand because of their effect on soil erosion there. Environmental standards must vary across countries because of the differential ability of countries to absorb environmental damage. It is justifiable to apply the same standards in connection with specific products, be they domestically produced or imported – cars for example – but it is less sensible to try and enforce vague environmental standards via trade taxes and bans. Trade taxes levied against exports of non-compliers to international environmental agreements could be justified. It is important to note that trade taxes are an indirect means of promoting environmental standards and are clearly second-best. The first best solutions lie in domestic policies.

A related issue concerns the environmental consequences of trade liberalization in developing countries. These measures were often imposed on countries in the South by multilateral agencies or IFIs as a result of the crippling macroeconomic problems faced by them in the 1980s. Export promotion was encouraged as part of the package to improve macroeconomic performance. Many successful exporters in the South export at the expense of the environment, as with timber exports. It is now the practice of the very same agencies, Northern governments and aid donors to encourage conservation of resources. There is more than a hint of hypocrisy in these pronouncements.

Finally it should be remembered that concern for the environment, real or imaginary, could become an additional weapon in the protectionist lobby's armoury. There is already an alarmingly growing protectionist tendency in the North towards Southern goods, especially in areas where the North has lost in international competitiveness. Also today's protectionism is more discriminatory, it is directed against specific countries through voluntary export restraints or even firms via anti-dumping measures. In an age of rampant regionalism, where the multilateral framework for the conduct of international trade is under grave threat, it will be sad to see the environmental card (an environmentally augmented Super 301 in the USA) used to promote discriminatory protectionist policies.

VI Conclusions
The 1980s have been dubbed the lost decade in terms of lost opportunities for development in many areas of the South. The debt crisis has meant negative net transfers to many areas of the South. Protectionist measures grow, further retarding the possibilities of export-led growth in the South. Transfers from North to South have been adversely affected by the insatiable desire of deficit countries in the North (the USA and UK, for example) for the surplus funds of the international system. The emergence of the former Soviet bloc into the international arena is bound to divert developmental assistance, soft loans and trade concessions from the South to that region, given the North's greater security considerations in the former Eastern bloc. The South, more than ever, is effectively excluded from meaningful participation in the international economic system. The environment is an exception. Notwithstanding the position taken by many Northern leaders in the Rio summit of 1992, the South cannot be ignored in the environmental sphere. This gives it some leverage, however marginal, in economic negotiations with the North.

Progress on the environment requires global cooperation, including that of the South. Such cooperation will only be forthcoming if other areas of interest to the South are adequately addressed: trade and transfers. Transfers to the South to induce cooperation are justified on both efficiency and equity grounds, the former because actions to promote environmental quality have to be made incentive-compatible. Furthermore the South too has property rights over the global environmental common and transfers to the South to promote environmental quality are justified on Coasean grounds. The equity arguments enter because of the greater historical responsibility of the North in using environmental resources in a cavalier fashion in the past – the natural debt argument. It should be noted that transfers to the South can take the form of debt forgiveness and trade concessions.

Given the backdrop of the much vaunted 'new world order', the 1992 conference in Rio de Janeiro on the environment held out much hope for many. Unfortunately these hopes, to a great extent, have been dashed. Several Northern governments, notably the USA and the UK, failed to agree to a date by which to meet the 0.7 per cent of GNP UN guideline on transfers to the South so essential to progress on the environment. The climate convention, with its many exceptions, failed to meet the expectations of many environmentalists. Above all it failed to achieve an amicable atmosphere conducive to cooperation between North and South, which is crucial to the issue of the environment. The role of the United Nations in this matter was certainly not strengthened and this will be viewed unfavourably in the South. The great fear, felt by many, is that a less than genuine concern for the environment in some Northern circles could be employed as an excuse to withhold development assistance, market access and debt relief from the South.

What of South–South cooperation on the environment? In many areas, such as water management, the prevention of soil erosion and desertification, there is scope for meaningful cooperation between nations in the South, but the scramble for access to environmental resources between neighbouring countries must not be allowed to become a source of conflict, including military conflict, for that would be the greatest tragedy of all.

References

Barrett, S. (1990), 'The Problem of Global Environmental Protection', *Oxford Review of Economic Policy*, **6**.

Baumol W.J. and W.E. Oates (1988), *The Theory of Environmental Policy*, 2nd edn, Cambridge: Cambridge University Press.

Bertram, G. (1991), 'Tradeable Emission Permits and the Control of Greenhouse Gases', *Journal of Development Studies*, forthcoming.

Bigman, D. (1990), 'A Plan to End LDC Debt and Save the Environment too', *Challenge*, July/August.

Brundtland, G. (1987), *Our Common Future. Report of the World Commission on Environment and Development*, Oxford: Oxford University Press.

Dasgupta, P. (1990), 'The Environment as a Commodity', *Oxford Review of Economic Policy*, **6**.

GATT (1992), 'Trade and the Environment', in *International Trade 1990–91*.

Grubb, M. (1989), *The Greenhouse Effect: Negotiating Targets*, London: Royal Institute for International Affairs.

Mäler, K.G. (1990), 'International Environmental Problems', *Oxford Review of Economic Policy*, **6**.

Murshed, S.M. (1992), *Economic Aspects of North–South Interaction*, London: Academic Press.

Nordhaus, W.D. (1991), 'To Slow or not to Slow. The Economics of the Greenhouse Effect', *Economic Journal*, 101.

OECD (1991), *Environmental Indicators: A Preliminary Set*, Paris: OECD.

Pearce, D. and S. Freeman (1991), 'Information Requirements for Policy Decision-makers', paper given to the International Forum on Environmental Information for the 21st Century, Montreal, May.

Pearce D. and K.G. Mäler (1991), 'Environmental Economics and the Developing World', *Ambio*, 20.
Smith, K.R. (1991), 'Allocating Responsibility for Global Warming: The Natural Debt Index', *Ambio*, 20.
World Bank (1992), *World Development Report*, Oxford: Oxford University Press.

4 The role of TNCs in the transfer of organizational technologies to LDCs*

Raphael Kaplinsky

I The challenge of the 1990s: the transfer of organizational technology

An increasing share of global manufacturing output and trade is accounted for by TNCs (a recent survey is Oman, 1991). These large firms have consequently become the dominant institutional actors affecting the global allocation of industrial resources. The new trading environment of the late 1980s and early 1990s has focused their primary attention on three major regional markets – North America, Europe and East Asia – but investments in the developing world continue to account for a substantial share of global flows of productive capital.

Although specifically export-oriented foreign direct investment (FDI) retains a significant role in production by foreign subsidiaries, most overseas production continues to be market-driven. But conditions in these overseas markets have been changing, especially in less developed countries (LDCs) where long-lived protective barriers are being significantly lowered. As in industrially advanced counties (IACs), competition in these markets is increasing. For all these reasons TNCs and locally owned firms alike – in LDCs and IACs – are being forced to confront international best practice. Here the target is moving rapidly.

Global manufacturing is undergoing a process of transformation, associated with greatly intensified patterns of competition, changes in the international location of production and divergences in national and regional rates of economic growth. Whilst there are important variations in the speed and nature of the changes occurring in different sectors and regions, the sustained growth of per capita incomes appears to be associated with the ability successfully to capture technological production rents.

Notwithstanding intense discussion on the historical significance of these changes in manufacturing competitiveness, a number of themes emerge from the various analyses. One common perception is that the basis of competitive rivalry has in large part changed because of the nature and extent of the threat posed by Japan. The 'old order', largely based upon a

*Thanks are due to Hans Singer and Kunibert Raffer for comments on an earlier draft.

world dominated by North American and European producers, was one in which price was the dominant form of competition and where, because wages were a major component of costs, labour was seen as a cost which had to be minimized. Within this mode of competition, technological rents accrued through the ability to reduce production costs. LDCs played an important role in global production, often through production by TNC subsidiaries taking advantage of their low wages, or by transnational firms marketing the output of low-wage and low-cost LDC enterprises. By contrast, in the 'new order', in which Japanese and East Asian firms are rising to dominance, competition tends to be based upon product characteristics, and technological rents accrue as much from product innovation as from process innovation. Within this, labour tends to be seen as much as an innovatory resource whose potential has to be maximized as a factor whose cost should be minimized.

It is in response to these changing market conditions and the rising intensity of competition that new rules of best practice are being forged, especially in manufacturing. There are five key areas of economic activity where the rules are being rewritten and where individual firms, sectors and economies need to encompass change:

1. in the technology of design, production and coordination;
2. in the adoption of new embodied production technologies (especially electronics-based automation technologies);
3. in the way the production process is organized and managed;
4. in relations between firms (including both vertical linkages between suppliers and assemblers and horizontal linkages between firms producing similar products); and
5. in the interlinkage between entrepreneurship and state, most clearly manifested in the industrial strategies of Japan and Korea (with regard to the central state) and to the Emilia Romagna region of Italy (with regard to the regional state).

The second and third of these factors – intra-enterprise and inter-enterprise organizational change – are of especially acute significance. International experience suggests that they require implementation before the potential of flexible automation can be realized and as a necessary component of product-enhancing corporate restructuring.

These developments in best practice have important institutional implications, including those for firm size and transnational production and ownership. The determinants of optimum location are altering, partly because of changes in the economics of location and partly because of changes in global market access, sometimes referred to as the 'politics of location' (Kaplinsky,

1991). At the same time the search for technological rents increases indirect costs of production as research and development and marketing become more intense, and these are factors which have often been promoting large-scale and transnational ownership. International experience suggests, however, that these changes do not necessarily translate into an enhanced role for TNCs, and in some countries small locally owned firms continue to thrive and would appear to have a vibrant future; moreover inter-firm collaboration (often between TNCs) may prove to be a viable alternative to a further global concentration of ownership.

These developments in the competitive environment also have wide-ranging implications for the industrial prospects of LDCs. So far, most analysts and policy makers have focused on the consequences of this changing technological environment for the international competitiveness of a relatively small group of more advanced, outward-oriented LDCs and have primarily concentrated on the implications of electronics-based automation technologies (Edquist and Jacobsson, 1988). The evidence now emerging suggests that new forms of production organization, inter-firm relations and firm–state relations may have an impact on a much wider range of countries. In particular trade policy reforms currently being introduced in most LDCs (as well as in the former communist economies) make it more difficult for productive enterprises in these countries to operate in isolation from changing patterns of global best practice. This is important both in terms of obtaining access to global markets (where, as noted, product characteristics are of growing importance) and in withstanding external competition in domestic markets. An additional factor promoting consideration of the relevance of new forms of best practice for LDCs is that many of these changes are neither capital- nor foreign-exchange intensive and consequently they might be highly appropriate for LDC operating environments.

There is much uncertainty surrounding these issues, both with regard to the general relevance of the new modes of technology, production organization and inter-firm linkages to LDCs and in relation to the policy changes necessary to allow them to avoid the pitfalls of inaction and to grasp new opportunities which are opening up. Many of these uncertainties affect the behaviour of TNCs – as producers, as purchasers and in the international transfer of technology. With technological change now primarily occurring in the domain of organization, how much will this reinforce or undermine their role in LDC industrial development? Since much of this new technological capability currently resides in TNCs, this throws into renewed focus their role in the transfer of technology. As seen earlier this takes place in a new competitive environment. Moreover in previous decades technology was primarily embodied in nature, production in LDCs was largely for domestic markets occurring behind protective barriers and cheap unskilled labour presented itself as a viable resource in the pursuit of sustained income growth.

The focus in this chapter is on the role TNCs play as carriers of new organizational technologies as they begin to diffuse to LDCs a process which mirrors the transition from mass production to flexible specialization in the IACs (often also referred to as the transition to post-Fordism, systemofacture and 'the new competition'). Owing to space constraints little empirical material will be presented but readers are referred to source texts for a presentation of these data. The section which follows briefly outlines the major characteristics of the technology transfer process and identifies different institutional 'carriers' of technology, including TNCs. Section III reviews empirical material of technology transfer to LDCs to identify the particular firm-specific characteristics of the technology transfer process; other determinants of technology transfer – that is, country- and sector-specific factors – will not be considered because of constraints of space (but see UNCTC, forthcoming). The chapter concludes with a brief treatment of the policy issues raised by this discussion of the role of TNCs in the transfer of organizational technology to LDCs.

II   The nature of and mechanisms for transferring organizational technology

The new organizational technologies evolved principally in Japan. In some cases (such as in the development of total quality control, TQC, and the introduction of statistical process control, SPC) this built upon ideas propagated by American production engineering theorists; in other cases (such as group technology) the theory emanated from the Soviet Union and in other cases again (such as just-in-time production, JIT) these developments were unique to Japan (albeit informed by principles observed by Toyota's founder in American supermarkets). The superiority of these organizational techniques means that intensive efforts are under way by corporations throughout the world designed to absorb and implement these new organizational techniques, in other words to engage in a process of technology transfer. In reviewing this recent experience in the transfer of organizational technology – both to IACs and to LDCs – and in considering the policy implications which follow, it is instructive first to consider briefly the accumulated body of policy analysis on the transfer of technology.

Three particular aspects of past experience with technology transfer will be considered, since they throw light on the range of policies applicable to the diffusion of organizational change in LDCs and the role of TNCs in this process. These are the role of technology transfer in the wider context of policies utilized to promote technological development, the range of mechanisms available for the transfer of technology and the role played by different types of technology supplying and technology-purchasing institutions.

The role of technology transfer in the wider development of technological capabilities
Ultimately the pursuit of higher living standards depends upon access to one or more types of economic rent. In previous centuries these rents were primarily based upon access to scarce natural commodities, but increasingly they are seen to derive from the appropriation of technologies (including those embodied in human skills). Thus it is necessary to identify briefly the major components in the development of technological capabilities. Six separate but related elements can be identified (Bell, 1982; Fransman, 1986; Kaplinsky, 1990).

The first is the ability to choose technology and the second concerns the effectiveness of different methods of transferring technology from suppliers of technology. The third element arises from the ability to utilize purchased technologies to their designed potential and this is complemented by a fourth element, that of 'stretching' purchased technology beyond its designed capability. This 'stretching' capability can be extended to encompass the ability to develop economically useful techniques from a body of research, the fifth element of technological capacity building. The sixth and most knowledge-intensive element of technological capability involves the capacity to undertake the research process itself.

Clearly the growth of technological capabilities does not necessarily follow this quasi-Darwinist path. Yet two important relevant aspects of international experience are clear from the comparative development of international capabilities. First, those firms/countries which begin at the research end rather than the choice end of the spectrum tend to pay heavily for their attempts to reinvent the wheel. Second, technology transfer must be seen in the context of the wider development of technological capabilities; whilst it cannot be a substitute for the development of wider capabilities its role in this wider process cannot be ignored.

Mechanisms of technology transfer
This being the case, it is helpful briefly to outline the major mechanisms available for technology transfer (UNCTAD, 1972). Five alternative (but not mutually exclusive) mechanisms can be distinguished: through the sharing of equity (ranging from wholly-owned subsidiaries to minority equity partnerships), the establishment of a licence agreement, the purchase of capital goods, the purchase of knowledge and the flow of human resources. In previous generations the two primary mechanisms of transfer utilized have been the outright purchase of capital goods and equity links but, given the

contemporary importance of organizational technologies in production, the flow of human resources (including intra-firm transfers, working abroad and through 'learning by visiting') is playing a role of growing importance.

Institutional carriers of technology

Schumpeter distinguished between three critical stages of technological change – invention, innovation and diffusion. He defined the role of entrepreneurship as that involved in the translation of inventions into innovations. From the growth perspective it is innovation rather than invention which is the key, and the function of entrepreneurship is identified as being the major factor driving technological (and hence economic) progress.

Some firms may be both inventors and innovators. When technologies are relatively simple these two processes may be fused within a single physical site, but it is generally more likely that the inventive process will have taken place somewhere distant from the site of eventual production and in some cases, when the technology is generally more complex, in different affiliates of the same enterprises as well. Production occurring across national borders in these cases involves the intra-TNC transfer of technology. In all these cases the processes of innovation and diffusion depend upon the intra-firm transfer of technology and it is here that it is possible to identify a major role played by TNCs.

A second important role is that of TNCs acting as suppliers of technology on a global scale. With respect to organizational technology this points to the growing importance of the productive services sector, sometimes referred to as the 'business services sector'(for a pioneering discussion, see USOTA, 1987). This comprises firms whose function is to collect and market specialized knowledge of relevance to those firms manufacturing goods or retailing services. This includes various sets of knowledge in corporate strategic formulation, design (and design intelligence), marketing, purchasing and production engineering and human resource development, organizational techniques discussed in detail below. Many of these firms are now specialists in these areas and are considered in national accounts to be part of the services sector, although they are often essential elements of manufacturing. Other suppliers of productive services are traditional service-sector firms, such as large transnational accountancy practices, which have diversified into production engineering specialities. In some countries (such as the UK and Germany) the government has played an important role in the expansion of the productive services sector, both by facilitating the growth in the supply of these services and by offering financial incentives to firms wishing to utilize their services.

III   Emerging experience in the transfer of organizational technology to LDCs

Overview conclusions from empirical studies

There is little case study evidence of the transfer of organizational technology to LDCs (but see Fleury and Humphrey, 1992; Kaplinsky 1991, forthcoming; Kaplinsky and Posthuma, 1992; Posthuma, 1991; Meyer-Stamer *et al.*, 1991; UNCTC, forthcoming) and much of that which is available does not provide an overview of the net benefits accruing from organizational innovation. This has three sets of implications for the conclusions which can be drawn from these studies. First, most case studies address particular subprocesses rather than the complete cycle of production, thus providing only a partial view of the impact of these changes on the overall performance of the plant, the corporate division or the firm. More damagingly, detailed studies often fail to specify the proportion of activities covered by the process of reorganization. Second, most case study material is confined to a presentation of the rewards to organizational innovation and pays scant attention to the costs. A particular shortfall is the difficulty of estimating many of the costs of reorganization, especially those which are intangible (such as lost attention of management) or those which involve a loss of output while reorganization takes place. Third, even when case studies do attempt to impute the costs of reorganization, few consider the impact of organizational change in production on corporate competitive performance, for example on profitability and market share or on the more difficult to measure 'corporate positioning' which results.

Notwithstanding these methodological difficulties, case studies allow us to draw the following five overall conclusions:

1. Organizational change, when fully implemented, represents a major enhancement of competitive positioning, contributes to significant reductions in production costs and also protects (and perhaps enhances) profitability.
2. Although organizational change has important systemic characteristics (which are in part a source of the obstacles to successful diffusion), significant gains are to be realized from a process of partial implementation. Some initial steps (such as the introduction of statistical process control, quality-at-source procedures and cellular layouts) are relatively easily introduced. Others (such as inter-enterprise just-in-time production and the endogenization of continuous improvement) appear to be much more difficult to attain.
3. There is no single path for successful implementation; each plant, firm and country has its own specific problems and must necessarily adopt a

unique approach to the implementation of what is essentially a social process.

4. The benefits of organizational change can be reaped in a wide variety of countries, including IACs, semi-industrialized economies and LDCs, large and small countries and economies with varying degrees of industrial development and skill profile.

5. The major constraint to the adoption of organizational technologies appears to lie in managerial attitudes. Relatively poor education amongst the labour force and the consequences of macroeconomic disequilibria appear to have a less damaging impact on the diffusion of these technologies in LDCs.

In considering the factors determining the process of diffusion of organizational change and the corporate and national policy implications which flow from this, it must be borne in mind that these organizational innovations do not represent a once-and-for-all change. The real change in production practice is the endogenization of change itself, that is ensuring a process of continuous improvement. Thus, moving from functional process-oriented to product-focused cellular production may provide significant returns and may help to close the gap with global 'best-practice'. But without ensuring a process of continual change, the competitive gap will merely reopen in the future.

Three primary sets of factors have influenced the effectiveness of this process of technology transfer: sector-specific, country-specific and firm-specific. Because of space constraints only the third factor will be considered below (UNCTC, forthcoming, discusses the other two factors).

Firm-specific factors affecting the diffusion of organizational reform in LDCs
Organizational change in production is subsumed within a wider arena of corporate-wide and economy-wide changes. As with other elements of social change, it is important to bear in mind that there is no single route to change and each firm, region and country will necessarily have to adopt its own path. For example, in facing the new competitive challenges outlined earlier, it is possible to distinguish two major alternatives with respect to firm size (lucidly discussed in Best, 1990). The first, involving flexible specialization within large-scale firms, is evident from the experience of Japan and Northern Germany. Very large corporations such as Mitsubishi, Toyota and Siemens achieve flexible production through internal networking, in which different affiliates or tightly linked sub-contractors work in close cooperation. The second major alternative is found in the Emilia Romagna region of Italy (the so-called 'Third Italy'), southern Germany and Jutland in Den-

mark. This involves close cooperation between small-scale firms and the sharing of indirect costs such as marketing, design and raw material procurement. The Italian *consorzii* have been especially successful in this, particularly in the 'traditional' industries such as garments, shoes, furniture, food-processing and ceramics which are supposed to be the comparative advantage of developing economies.

All of the case study material on organizational change concludes that, in each of the countries in which reform is being implemented, some firms do innovate and other firms do not. This is true even when firms operate in the same sector. Thus firm-specific attributes are almost certainly the dominant factor explaining the global diffusion of organizational reform and it is within this context that it is possible to specify the particular role played by TNCs in the transfer of organizational technology to LDCs. This being the case, it is necessary to try and understand why some firms innovate these new organizational technologies whilst other firms do not. Five possible explanations exist for this variation in firm performance – the influence of corporate trajectories (including the influence of plant histories), the ownership characteristics of entrepreneurial behaviour, the country of origin of entrepreneurship, the size of firms, and the global activities of producer services firms.

Corporate trajectories and organizational reform   Individual firms have their own histories and thus an important element of organizational change is its *sui generis* nature. This is especially true for early innovators, since followers respond to market pressures in introducing organizational changes. For example, Hewlett Packard was born out of the academic world and maintains a corporate culture which is knowledge-intensive and also promotes learning; every Friday most plants stop for a few hours and the workers are given a rundown of corporate and plant operations and are asked for their comments. Thus two-way flows of information and a culture of learning are deeply imbedded in corporate operations and the introduction of the new organizational principles in Hewlett Packard are easily understood. By contrast, until recently the Ford Motor Corporation (which had pioneered the techniques of mass production in the early twentieth century) was structured along the principles of top-down information flows and the extended division of labour. Organizational reform in this corporate culture is considerably more difficult to achieve.

Of course corporate cultures can – and do – change. In the 1980s Ford proved to be the most progressive Western car firm in adopting organizational change and its Hermasillo assembly plant in Mexico is an especially good example of its implementation (Shaiken, 1990). These differences between firms are found in all operating environments, including Japan. For example, in the car industry Nissan has long been committed to automation, whereas Toyota's distinctive focus has always lain in innovative work organization. This is clearly reflected in the particular niches which these two very large manufacturers fill in the Japanese and other markets and closely related to their development and adoption of organizational technologies (Cusumano, 1985; Hoffman and Kaplinsky, 1988).

Sometimes these corporate differences reflect the personalities of key individuals. In these cases the chief executive officer (or some other highly-placed 'change agent') plays the key role in defining a new corporate culture promoting organizational change. Individual plants, too, possess their own distinctive cultures and vary in striking ways with affiliate plants, often manufacturing the identical range of products in the same country. Much is made of the differential potential for organizational change between brownfield (plants which have been in operation for many years) and greenfield (brand new plants) sites. It is believed by many firms that greenfield sites are essential if the firm is not to be bogged down by old, inflexible work practices and attitudes. In many cases this transition to greenfield sites is fused with the desire to move to areas of low unionization.

To the extent that this brownfield/greenfield argument has merit, new entrants to production are more likely successfully to initiate and sustain organizational reform than older firms which may be weighed down by the accumulation of decades of mass production practice. Yet evidence does not wholly bear out the assertion that these obstacles are crippling to innovation. Nor is it clear that greenfield operations in countries with a tradition of mass production practices would not be detrimentally affected by the same attitudinal factors. Moreover there is also evidence that in many cases the anticipated gains from greenfield production have proved difficult to appropriate.

What is not evident from the case study material is why some firms and plants stumble upon the benefits of organizational change and become pioneers. The case of followers is easier to explain since they are responding to competitive pressures. There is almost certainly a great degree of serendipity in this process, reflecting historical accident and unanticipated encounters. However such innovations are not only a matter of chance, and the role of education and training cannot be ignored.

Ownership determinants of organizational reform   There are three major ownership-specific factors which might determine the diffusion of organizational change. The first of these concerns those firms which operate on a multi-plant and/or multidivisional basis. In these cases there might be internalization economies in that the transaction costs of acquiring knowledge of organizational reform are lower for intra-firm operations than when the knowledge is acquired in the market. The experience of Lucas is apposite here (Kaplinsky, forthcoming). It has created a special-purpose affiliate – Lucas Engineering and Systems – to diffuse the lessons of organizational reform (and other similar developments) through the global operations of the firm. Although the Engineering and Systems Division has been approached by extra-corporate customers wanting to buy its services, the affiliate has declined to market these services, partly because its hands are full with the task of its own corporate restructuring and partly because of a reluctance to spread the benefits of organizational reform to potential competitors.

Whilst these economies of internalization (and hence the intra-firm transfer of technology globally) may be evident, they are clearly not overwhelming. In Cyprus a small single-plant clothing firm (with 90 employees) proved to be a pioneering innovator, even in a country where some enterprises in the same sector were linked by corporate affiliations to enterprises in other countries which had made the transition to Rapid Response production (Kaplinsky, 1991a). Moreover global production is littered with TNCs in which some affiliates have adopted organizational reform and yet their experience has not filtered through to other affiliates, even though they sometimes operate in the same sector and in the same country. This includes Japanese electronics firms operating in Mexico which have not adopted the new organizational technologies adopted by their parents and utilized in other affiliates of global operations (Shaiken and Browne, 1991).

The second ownership-specific attribute affecting the diffusion and global transfer of organizational change arises out of the transnational operations of the firm. TNCs are exposed to a wide body of comparative international experience. Often they have affiliates producing the same (or similar) products, operating in a number of IACs and LDCs. Many of the better-managed corporations also have 'benchmark measures', enabling them to assess the comparative progress of their widespread subsidiaries. This gives them access to new developments since, when well managed, their foreign subsidiaries act as ears and eyes to new developments. The problem for many TNCs here is that their internal efforts to homogenize technology and behaviour often close their sensory perceptions to developments in foreign markets. Thus the attempt to impose a global corporate culture on a Japanese subsidiary may not allow the firm to absorb adequately the lessons to be learnt from Japanese organizational methods. Here many TNCs, some of whom have long demanded sole ownership of foreign subsidiaries, are learning the benefits to be achieved from joint ventures. This is especially the case when operating in the distinctive environment of Japan.

The third ownership-specific characteristic affecting the diffusion of organizational technology arises from the transfer of people between affiliates, a mechanism of technology transfer which is particularly appropriate to disembodied technological changes. Most TNCs have a policy of regularly transferring managers through corporate affiliates, partly in order to promote a common corporate culture, but this also has the potential benefit of facilitating the transfer of organizational technology.

In the face of these ownership-specific factors – the economies of internalization, the benefits accruing from transnational operations and the flow of people through the global operations of the firm – there are strong reasons to believe that TNCs will stand at the forefront of the global diffusion of organizational change. There are many examples which lend support to this conclusion. Unless otherwise stated, the following examples are all drawn from UNCTC (forthcoming). The Xerox and Motorola Corporations have been amongst the first large US TNCs to introduce a comprehensive programme of organizational change, specifically applying the principles of total quality control to production. In large part this follows from lessons they learnt from Japan – Xerox through its joint venture with Fuji–Xerox and Motorola as a supplier and customer of Japanese electronics firms. These TQC procedures were initially transferred to Xerox's US operations and then subsequently through its joint venture with Rank Xerox PLC to the British operations of Rank Xerox. TQC was also diffused to other of Xerox's global affiliates, including Rank Xerox's subsidiary in India. Similarly the subsidiaries of US TNCs operating in the Dominican Republic's export processing zones were also implementing TQC and JIT principles of organization. A pharmaceutical TNC, for example, possessed a corporate-wide division providing advice and training in TQC implementation. In India the introduction of organizational change by a locally owned motorcycle firm (Escorts) followed directly from its technology licence with Yamaha of Japan. But Yamaha was averse to sustaining the transfer of its organizational technology unless Escorts entered into a longer and more comprehensive link, including purchase of equity. Yamaha was reluctant to pass on the benefits of internalizing the transaction costs in absorbing organizational reform to a potential competitor.

But case studies do not always support the assertion that TNCs are more likely to introduce organizational reform than locally owned firms. In the Brazilian automobile component sector, Posthuma (1991) found that local firms were more advanced on almost every count in introducing change than their TNC counterparts. The major exception to this arose from TNC car assemblers who insisted on the use of SPC procedures by their suppliers. In the Brazilian machinery industry Meyer-Stamer *et al.* (1991) found no difference between local and foreign firms in the adoption of computer-integrated manufacturing. In fact, of their sample of 23 firms the only five who had begun to implement JIT were locally owned. Local firms were also more advanced in their utilization of TQC techniques. Whilst in both Modi Xerox and Escorts in India organizational reform stems from their links with TNCs, Crompton Greaves (a large locally controlled firm pioneering the introduction of organizational change) was wholly responsible for initiating and pushing through organizational change. Its links to its British equity holder were of no consequence in this regard.

Moreover, even when organizational change does occur under the aegis of a TNC, not all intra-corporate flows of organizational technology necessarily go through corporate headquarters, or indeed go from the firm's IAC operations to its LDC operations. In Ford's Hermasillo plant, organizational technology was transferred from Ford's partner in Japan – Ford holds 25 per cent of the equity of Mazda – directly to the Mexican plant; the implementation of organizational technologies there is far superior to that of any other of Ford's global operations (Shaiken, 1990). In the case of Lucas, its Indian joint venture has been a very successful implementer of organizational reform, but most of its progress has resulted from its own efforts.

Country of firm origin and organizational reform   Organizational reform largely originated in Japan and resulted from the operations of Japanese-owned firms. It would be logical to conclude therefore that Japanese firms operating abroad would be an important spur to organizational innovation. This would have implications both within plants (for example in introducing intra-plant JIT) and between plants (inter-firm JIT).

There is considerable evidence to support the pioneering role of Japanese TNCs in the diffusion of organizational technology outside Japan. Studies of Japanese subsidiaries in Europe and the USA show that they have been successful in introducing organizational technologies within their internal operations (Womack *et al.*, 1990). Other studies confirm that they have also had an influence on inter-firm relations; although in many cases this has involved the transplant of Japanese components suppliers to support these assembling firms, there has also been simultaneously an upgrading of local suppliers' practices (Mair, 1991). In Escorts's operations in India the link with Yamaha proved to be crucial in the implementation of organizational reform, and in Ford's Hermasillo plant the introduction of organizational technologies was driven by Ford's Japanese joint-venture partner, Mazda. In South Africa the first round of organizational innovators were spurred by the demands made by Toyota on its suppliers and many of the second-round innovators were directly attempting to emulate Toyota's South African subsidiary (Van der Riet and Hendy, 1986). An interesting feature is that Toyota's control over the operations of its South African 'subsidiary' were not mediated through equity. Because of the sensitivity of operating in South Africa during a period of international sanctions, the assembly of Toyota in South Africa was undertaken by a wholly locally owned firm.

It is perhaps surprising therefore that not all the evidence supports the assertion that Japanese TNCs are more likely successfully to implement organizational reform than non-Japanese-owned TNCs. Shaiken and Browne (1991) provide evidence that Japanese firms operating in Mexico prefer to utilize Mexican managerial methods, and Fukuda (1986) found a propensity of Japanese firms to utilize local managerial practices, even when operating in Asia. Nevertheless, despite this countervailing evidence, it is at least as likely that Japanese-originating TNCs will implement organizational reform as TNCs originating in other parts of the world. In many cases they are more likely to do so.

Firm size as a determinant of organizational reform   It is possible that firm size is an important element in the diffusion of organizational change. This may cut both ways. For example, since these changes generally require significant alterations to attitudes and in behaviour, these may be more easily accomplished within the informal context of a small-firm environment. Moreover it is sometimes argued that the very nature of organizational reform is to descale production, at least at the product and plant levels, if not the firm level (Kaplinsky, 1990). Big firms, too, may be at an advantage in some respects, particularly with regard to affording the cost of procuring consultant advice. For example, in Zimbabwe and South Africa productive services consultants estimate that the installation of a plant requires approximately one person-month of consultant input spread over a period of nine months. At current IAC prices of over $1300 per day these externally provided consulting costs (added to the intra-plant costs of reorganization) may be too high for a small firm. Also, as seen in the preceding section there may be economies of internalization in the introduction of organizational reform, and these may well be a function of size, especially when knowledge is transferred across national borders. On the other hand, large firms often tend to have inflexible corporate cultures and to be tied tightly by job demarcations agreed with trades unions; moreover external consultants need not necessarily be required, as is clear from the Cypriot apparel firm's experience discussed earlier.

Not all successful implementers are large. The Cypriot garments firm never employed more than 100 people and turnover was only around $1.5m in 1991, yet it experienced few scale-specific problems in implementing organizational reform. A second example is that of Semco, an innovative Brazilian metalworking firm (Semler, 1989). It found that the key to the successful implementation of decentralized decision taking was to reduce the size of affiliates and plants. In one particularly graphic case this was pushed through despite initially increasing overheads.

TNC producer services firms   The growing importance of knowledge in production has in part been reflected by an increasing social division of labour in which producer services firms supply specialized knowledge such as on cellular layout, JIT, TQC, SPC and design. The supply of these knowledge inputs to user firms benefits from the same internalization economies as in the case of embodied technology and a number of these consulting firms are now beginning to operate on a global basis. For example, the international accounting firm Price Waterhouse has licensed a JIT/cellular layout package from the Kawasaki Corporation of Japan which it now markets globally. Its Zimbabwean subsidiary has been one of the first to market these services in LDCs and has become the primary force behind the diffusion of organizational change in the country. In some cases its activities have been associated with significant improvements in production efficiency in Zimbabwean enterprises, but in other cases the failure of management in implementing enterprises to change their own practices has been a major factor in limiting the gains in implementation (Kaplinsky and Posthuma, 1992).

IV   Conclusions

Organizational change in production has in recent years come to assume a critically important role in the achievement of competitive production and now increasingly represents best-practice. The growing openness of LDCs forces them to confront this new best-practice. The first empirical studies suggest that it is feasible to implement these organizational technologies in LDC environments and that this is enhancing competitiveness in both domestic and export markets. Their low-cost nature and the fact that they are neither capital- nor import-intensive suggest that these organizational technologies are an appropriate technology for LDC environments. Since these techniques were pioneered in IACs, this suggests that LDCs are required to develop effective measures to promote the transfer of technology.

TNCs play a crucial role in the development and supply of these technologies. Their own adoption (or at least that of the early innovators) appears to reflect ownership- and firm-specific characteristics as well as being affected by size and the country of the TNCs' origin. TNCs may be involved in the transfer of these technologies either through their own intra-firm networks or as suppliers of organizational know-how; the emergence of global producer services firms appears to be a development of some significance in the diffusion of organizational change to LDCs.

Host-country LDCs may not wish the diffusion of organizational change to be determined by the allocative decisions of TNCs and a number of policy options exist to promote a countervailing conduit to the transfer of organizational technology which is more independent of the TNC operations. Such policy responses include programmes to promote the awareness of organizational reform, steps to promote the development of an indigenous producer services sector, incentives to local industry to adopt organizational change and a structured programme to promote the transfer of organizational change through 'learning by visiting', both to domestic enterprises and to firms abroad. The relatively low barriers to entry in organizational change (which involves a process of tacit knowledge rather than the acquisition of costly embodied technologies or highly specialized human skills) make such a countervailing policy attractive in the pursuit of sustained income growth. Finally, although there are reasons to believe that these organizational techniques can be adopted at low cost and without significant impediments, this is not independent of the modes of transfer. Employing external consultants or having to depend upon costly means of entrée to foreign plants may significantly increase the costs of technology transfer.

References

Bell, R.M. (1982), 'Technical Change in Infant Industries: A Review of the Evidence', Brighton, Science Policy Research Unit, University of Sussex (mimeo).

Best, M. (1990), *The New Competition*, Oxford: Polity Press.

Cusumano M.A. (1985), *The Japanese Automobile Industry: Technology and Management at Nissan and Toyota*, Cambridge, Mass.: Harvard University Press.

Edquist, C. and S. Jacobsson (1988), *Flexible Automation: Global Diffusion of New Engineering Technology*, Oxford: Blackwell.

Fleury, A. and J. Humphrey (1992), 'Human Resources and the Diffusion and Adaptation of New Quality Methods in Brazilian Manufacturing', report presented to Instituto de Pesquisas Economicas Aplicadas (IPEA), Brasilia.

Fransman, M. (1986), *Technology and Economic Development*, Brighton: Wheatsheaf.

Fukuda, J. (1986), *Japanese-Style Management Transferred: The Experience of East Asia*, London: Routledge.

Hoffman, K. and R. Kaplinsky (1988), *Driving Force: The Global Restructuring of Technology, Labor and Investment in the Automobile and Components Industries*, Boulder, Col.: Westview.

Kaplinsky, R. (1990), 'Technology Transfer, Adaptation and Generation: A Framework for Evaluation' in M. Chatterji (ed.), *Technology Transfer in Developing Countries*, London: Macmillan.

Kaplinsky, R. (1991), 'From Mass Production to Flexible Specialisation: A Case-Study from a Semi-Industrialised Economy', *IDS Discussion Paper 295*, Brighton.

Kaplinsky, R. (forthcoming), 'From Mass Production to Flexible Specialisation – Micro Level Restructuring in a British Engineering Firm', *IDS Discussion Paper*, Brighton.

Kaplinsky, R. and A. Posthuma (1992), 'Organizational Change in Zimbabwe's Manufacturing Sector', report prepared for United Nations University (Intech).

Mair, A. (1991), 'Parts Sourcing at Japanese Automobile Transplants: Controversy in the United States; The Case of Honda in North America; Implications for Transplants in Europe', University of Durham (mimeo).

Meyer-Stamer, J., C. Rauth, H. Riad, S. Schmitt and T. Welk (1991),'Comprehensive Modernization on the Shop Floor: A Case Study on the Brazilian Machinery Industry', Berlin: German Development Institute.

Oman, C. (1991), 'Trends in Global FDI and Latin America', paper prepared for Inter-American Dialogue, 18–20 December.

Posthuma, A. (1991), 'Changing Production Practices and Competitive Strategies in the Brazilian Auto Components Sector', D.Phil dissertation, Brighton: University of Sussex.

Semler, R. (1989), 'Managing without Managers', *Harvard Business Review*, September–October.

Shaiken, H. (1990), *Mexico in the World Economy: High-Technology and Work Organization in Export Industry*, Center for US–Mexican Studies, Monograph Series 33, University of California, San Diego.

Shaiken, H. and H. Browne (1991), 'Japanese Work Organization in Mexico', in G. Szekely (ed.), *Managing Across Borders and Oceans*, Center for US–Mexican Studies, Monograph Series 36, University of California, San Diego.

UNCTAD (1972), *Major Issues Arising from the Transfer of Technology to Developing Countries*, UN: New York.

UNCTC (forthcoming), *Transnational Corporations and the Transfer of New Management Practices to Developing Countries*, UN: New York.

USOTA (US Office of Technology Assessment) (1987), *International Competition in Services: Banking, Building, Software, Know-how*, OTA-ITE-328, Washington DC: Government Printing Office.

Van der Riet, D. and I.M. Hendy (1986), '"Just in Time": An Analysis from the South African Perspective with Particular Reference to the Western Cape', MBA Research Paper, University of Cape Town, Graduate School of Business.

Womack, J., D. Jones and D. Roos (1990), *The Machine That Changed the World*, London: Maxwell Macmillan.

5   The experience of the 'Gang of Four'

John-ren Chen and Herbert Stocker

I   Introduction

Bhagwati once stated that economic miracles are a public good, as each economist sees in them a vindication of his pet theories (Bhagwati, 1988, p. 98). This is certainly true for the growth performance of the 'Four Little Dragons' (Hong Kong, Singapore, South Korea and Taiwan). In the 1950s and 1960s there was hardly any doubt among professional economists that the new growth poles of the world economy would lie in South America, with its abundant natural resources and its 'Western-oriented' elites. The growth prospects of Asian countries, with their fast-growing populations and scarcity of all other resources were perceived as minuscule (for example, Myrdal, 1968).

The eventual outstanding economic performance of these countries came rather surprisingly and ironically just at a time when the optimism concerning the growth prospects of developing countries was fading. In this respect the model provided by these superperformers became of utmost importance in the progress of development economics and contributed effectively to the resurgence of the so-called 'new orthodoxy'.

The controversy surrounding this success, the role of institutions, policy and so on, has kept many economists busy. Essentially the argument boils down to the crucial question: is there a golden path leading to growth and wealth and, if so, have the 'Little Dragons' shown us a way which can be readily followed by others?

II   Historical backgrounds

Hong Kong was leased by the English to serve as a trading place for its commerce with the Chinese empire and remains under British rule as a Crown Colony until 1997. It is one of the most densely populated countries in the world: nearly six million people live on about a thousand square kilometres. Chinese make up almost 98 per cent of its population, but only about 60 per cent of its population was born in Hong Kong. Hong Kong's lack of any significant resources other than its diligent population, as well as the limited size of its domestic market, gave the authorities no other choice than to open its markets to world trade. Economic and political ties with Great Britain gave it access to world markets. Its prompt success made it a model for other countries, especially Taiwan, one of the first followers in this respect. A consistent non-interventionist policy has been pursued from the beginning. In addition, its non-authoritarian style of government differentiates it from the other 'Dragons'.

Singapore has several characteristics in common with Hong Kong. It is both a Chinese-dominated city-state like Hong Kong (though not as densely populated and with only about 75 per cent Chinese) and was also under British colonial rule and later under Japanese occupation during the Second World War. It was established as a trading station in 1819 and was a free port until it became independent in 1958. Its common market with Malaysia made protectionism to foster industrialization look promising but, following its separation from Malaysia in 1965, Singapore in fact removed import restrictions step by step. Ever since then, an outward-oriented growth strategy has been emphasized for quite the same reasons as in Hong Kong.

More than 20 million people live at present on the very mountainous, 36 000 square kilometres of the island of Taiwan. Taiwan became a Chinese province in the seventeenth century and a Japanese colony in 1895. The Japanese modernized administration, introduced compulsory education and improved infrastructure. The Second World War brought with it heavy destruction, but the consequences of the takeover by Chiang Kai-shek in 1945 were even worse. He was engaged in the Chinese civil war and at the time did not hesitate to deplete Taiwanese resources for this. The result was an administrative breakdown and tremendous hyperinflation. Normalization was not achieved before 1950, after which the defeated troops retreated to Taiwan and added almost 10 per cent to the population of the already densely populated island. A land reform was put into effect which, combined with the earlier hyperinflation, contributed to a reduction in the differences in wealth. This land reform also rendered the highly esteemed investment in real estate unfeasible for most people and thus caused them to find other investment outlets. This 'asset disposition effect' probably contributed to the exceptional growth performance and is outlined in more detail by Chen (1992). Additionally a currency reform accompanied by a rigid monetary policy contributed to economic stabilization.

Shortages of foreign currency and domestic savings left the government with no choice but to restrict imports. However the political situation, exacerbated by the Korean War and the military threat from mainland China gave Taiwan access to generous US aid. Economic as well as military aid fell on fertile soil and helped to increase the speed of reconstruction considerably. When foreign aid ended in the 1960s, Taiwan became a 'most favoured trading nation', emphasizing export production. However many import restrictions are still in effect which prevent an actual free trade policy (for an overview, see Chen, 1987).

South Korea is not so densely populated as the other 'Dragons', but more so than Japan or The Netherlands. It shares ethnic homogeneity and the strong influence of Confucianism with the other 'Dragons'. Modern Korean economic history can be said to have begun in 1876 when, following a long period of seclusion, a first commercial treaty was signed with Japan. This resulted in monopolistic, rapid expansion of foreign trade by Japan. Even before the annexation in 1910, the Korean currency system was linked closely with that of Japan. The first heavy investments in infrastructure were made with Japanese capital and technicians, especially in railways (Suh, 1978). Under Japanese rule after 1910, economic policy was similar to that of Taiwan, that is subordinate to Japanese needs, but with more industrial investment than in Taiwan (Fei and Ranis, 1975, cited in Datta, 1987, p. 604). The destruction in the aftermath of the Second World War was less damaging than that of the Korean War (1950–53), but the latter resulted in the division of the peninsula and the loss of most natural resources. Two land reforms in 1947 and 1950 initiated by the American military government and similar to those in Japan, together with the destruction caused by war, left most Koreans equally poor. The communist threat made South Korea, like Taiwan, one of the major recipients of foreign aid. This enormously facilitated the reconstruction of its infrastructure. For example, from '1953 to 1954, foreign aid comprised more than 68 per cent of total imports and about 60 per cent of total investment during this period' (Kwack, 1986, p. 71). It should not be overlooked, however, that defence expenditures were considerable. After initial attempts with import substitution, a very aggressive export promotion strategy was pursued, especially under the Park regime after 1961.

III Paths of development

Growth performance
The main reason why these four countries are frequently grouped together and have been given names like 'Gang of Four', 'Four Little Tigers' or simply NICs is their common outstanding record of development. In the World Bank's (1992) latest *World Development Report*, in which 125 countries are ranked according to their GNP per capita, Singapore and Hong Kong occupy the prestigious places 105 and 106, respectively, between Spain and New Zealand. South Korea takes place 96, between Portugal and Greece. There are no published data for Taiwan provided by the World Bank, but according to Taiwanese figures it ranks closely behind Ireland.

A more accurate picture of their extraordinary performance is given by the internationally comparable data set of Summers and Heston (1991). When all countries for which at least 25 annual observations are available

(121, including all OECD countries) are ranked according to their real GDP per capita growth, the 'Little Dragons' take places two to five (Botswana: 7.4 per cent, Singapore: 6.85, Taiwan: 6.75, Korea: 6.44, Hong Kong: 6.27). According to these figures, Taiwan has outpaced 40 countries in terms of per capita income, Korea 36 and Hong Kong 14 countries between 1960 and 1985 (own calculations).

The use of national accounting figures to measure welfare has often been criticized. Nevertheless the Human Development Index (HDI) published by the UNDP (1991), which combines national income and two social indicators (adult literacy and life expectancy), reveals similar results. However, if gender differences or human freedom are factored in, the situation looks worse (UNDP, 1991). Of course all efforts to measure human well-being on such an aggregate level must remain somewhat unsatisfactory and open to theoretical as well as empirical criticism. In spite of this there is little doubt that these countries have done better in almost any respect than other developing countries in the same period.

However, before discussing a 'miracle', one should closely examine the development of these countries. Pack (1988, pp. 352f) quotes several investigations which conclude that the share of growth which cannot be explained by growth in factor inputs is much lower in these countries than that typical of industrial countries. In other words, the very rapid growth in outputs was matched to an unusual extent by extra inputs of capital and employment.

Labour input
The increase of labour input in the transition period was mainly brought about by an increasing share of employment in industry, since the average working time per year is much longer in industry than in agriculture. Furthermore a considerable amount of piecework in the Taiwanese industry is accomplished in the evenings at home. A different effect was recently investigated by Dowrick (1992). Using the data set of Summers and Heston (1991) he found that the population growth rate had fallen by more than half between 1960–65 and 1984–8 in all four countries. The change in the age structure contributed to an increase in the average worker–population ratio of between 14.3 per cent in Singapore and 7.5 per cent in Korea in the same period (Dowrick, 1992, p. 609).

Dowrick also decomposed the relative growth performance for the group of Japan, Korea, Taiwan, Singapore and Hong Kong. Per capita output in this group of countries grew by 4 percentage points per annum above the sample average. Of these, 0.8 points are explained by the fact that the workforce grew faster than the population; 0.9 points are explained by capital deepening; and –0.1 points by the catching-up effect. He concludes that nearly half of this exceptional performance can be attributed to faster-than-average growth in factor inputs relative to population. Furthermore the increasing ratio of workforce to population has been relatively more important than capital deepening in three of these five countries (ibid., p. 606). However, as in most industrial countries, the proportion of old people will eventually increase and thus worsen the age–dependence ratio. Moreover the labour reserves of the agricultural sectors in Taiwan and Korea are almost fully exploited. The slightly negative catching-up effect indicates that the 'advantages of backwardness' seem to be rather exploited too. Though these results may somewhat reduce the 'miracle', they cannot really explain the outstanding success of these countries, because they cannot explain the growing demand for labour. Additionally it could reasonably be argued that the population growth rate is not exogenous but itself dependent on the income level reached.

Generally labour markets are highly competitive and open in all four countries. Even in Hong Kong, where labour unions are hardly restricted by law, their influence has been negligible. The fast-growing incomes brought about by the extraordinary economic growth probably contributed considerably to the forbearance and satisfaction of workers.

Savings, investment and industrial organization
It has already been stated above that an increase in capital stock contributed significantly to outstanding growth performance. A high domestic savings rate or foreign capital is at least necessary, although by no means sufficient, to render observed high investment rates possible. Countries like India or some former socialist countries have clearly demonstrated that a high savings rate cannot compensate for an inefficient allocation of investment. Therefore the financial sector is of crucial importance for economic development.

The financial markets of Hong Kong and Singapore have achieved an advanced stage of liberalization and internationalization. At present, both governments must try to strengthen financial supervision and regulation to conform to international standards, rather than to liberalize financial markets further. In contrast, the financial markets in South Korea and Taiwan have a dualistic structure. The banking system of both countries was under strict control of the government up to the 1980s. In Taiwan, for example, only state-owned banks were officially allowed to supply normal bank services before 1990; foreign banks were only authorized to conduct international transactions. Both countries tried to foster their industrialization by granting favourable credit concessions. The desire to enhance scale effects and the ease of implementation led both governments to privilege large firms. This led to a severe discrimination against small- and middle-sized firms, since their demand for credit was seldom satisfied. The result was a flourishing underground financial market. Especially in Taiwan, this informal financial market is very efficient when compared to the bureaucratic, state-owned banking sector. Although outlawed, the private sector has a large market share in domestic financial transactions. Above all, the informal financial sector has been important for small enterprises, the backbone of the Taiwanese success story.

In addition to this, a special form of saving clubs, known as 'Hueas', play an important role in the financial intermediation of all four countries. Their relevance for industrialization cannot be stressed enough, although formal credit institutions have probably become increasingly important in the course of time. These saving clubs are usually organized amongst relatives and friends for a limited period. When such a club is established, the members agree on a subscription, which is paid regularly at the general meetings. At each general meeting the member able to offer the highest interest rate gets all the subscriptions of the meeting, but each member can take up this credit only once. Essentially the participation in such a club allows a member to take a credit equivalent to the amount which he would have saved during the existence of the club. Because administration costs are almost negligible, these clubs can offer quite favourable loans and almost guarantee by their definition a quite efficient allocation of investment. This type of financing is particularly widespread in the construction industry.

Differential access to credit and concessionary loans are probably the key factors explaining the increasing concentration in South Korean industrial development and the highly decentralized industrial structure of Taiwan. According to Scitovsky (1986, p. 146) the number of manufacturing firms in Taiwan increased by 150 per cent between 1966 and 1976, while the average number of employees per firm increased by only 29 per cent. By contrast, in South Korea the number of firms increased by only 10 per cent, while the average number of employees per firm increased by 176 per cent. In 1981 the gross receipts of Korea's largest conglomerate were three times as great as those of Taiwan's ten largest private firms combined! *Chaebols* (large conglomerate enterprises) were favoured at the expense of small businesses in Korea, because they exploited economies of scale and were easier for the government to control. This, however, also caused inflexibilities and market imperfections. Taiwan's markets, on the contrary, were much more competitive and flexible, but did not take full advantage of scale effects.

The very ambitious targets of the South Korean development plans made it necessary to fall back upon foreign capital. Attracting foreign capital was much easier for the large *Chaebols*, often provided with government guarantees, than for the small Taiwanese enterprises. South Korea could, therefore, rely heavily on foreign capital and was hit hard by the debt crisis in the early 1980s, whereas Taiwan became a net international investor by the mid-

1970s. In the early 1980s the Korean financial sector was reformed in conjunction with a liberalization of economic policy. This reduced the share of the corporate business sector's external financing for which allocation and cost were subject to government control from 63.9 per cent in 1970–74 to 29.8 per cent in 1980–84. This contributed effectively to improving the efficiency of credit allocation in Korea (Cho, 1988, p. 105).

Inflation and development
In the 1960s and 1970s South Korea followed a policy of enhancing economic growth through inflation (easy money policy). Like most other developing countries in those times, it tried to keep interest rates down to promote investments by 'forced savings'. Inflation forces the public to reduce its real consumption and in doing so releases resources needed for domestic investment. The average Korean inflation rate between 1965 and 80 was above 18 per cent and much higher than the inflation rates of the other 'Dragons'.

Taiwan pursued a very different strategy. With the monetary reform in 1949 a rigid monetary policy was introduced to fight hyperinflation in the post-war period, since inflation was regarded as a main reason for the loss of mainland China to the communist regime. Economic stabilization was thus given importance similar to that of growth. After the collapse of the Bretton Wood System, the 'Gang of Four' tried to peg their exchange rates to the US dollar. In 1979 the exchange rate of the new Taiwan dollar was allowed to float within a range set by the central bank. Although in 1989 more flexibility was allowed, Taiwan's exchange rate regime still does not qualify as a real floating system. Whereas South Korea depreciated its currency, the won, several times to improve the country's balance of payments (Lindner, 1992), Taiwan has realized enormous trade surpluses since the mid-1970s and has accumulated foreign exchange reserves of US$ 86.6 billion (June 1992). Between 1982 and 1991 this has induced an average annual growth rate of money (M2) of about 20 per cent, but this has not yet led to a significant inflation. The consumer price index increased only at an annual average rate of 1.9 per cent in this period and wholesale prices have even decreased. The reasons may be found in the proverbial passion for gambling among the Taiwanese. The very popular lottery and stock-jobbery have most likely absorbed substantial amounts of money. However empirical evidence is not conclusive (Friedman, 1988).

Export orientation
At the beginning of industrialization the major problem for an entrepreneur is not only organizing a constant flow of materials through the plant or factory to ensure effective capacity utilization, but also to coordinate the flow of inputs from suppliers and the flow of outputs to final users. If

markets are incomplete or even missing, this can pose severe problems. In European history this frequently led to vertical integration (Chandler, 1992, p. 81). The existence of international markets can reduce the problems of availability of inputs and the marketability of outputs considerably.

The 'Four Little Tigers' in this respect followed Japan and began to benefit quite early from the existence of reliable world markets for intermediate products. This allowed them to specialize in the stages of production according to their own comparative advantage (for a detailed analysis of this 'special trade relationship', see Chen, 1975). Hong Kong started to import cotton and textiles to produce cloth; today Taiwan imports chips and exports computers. In Singapore, for instance, 'net' domestic exports in 1982 comprised only 22.4 per cent of official domestic exports (Lloyd and Sandilands, 1986, p. 191). Kubo *et al.* (1986) estimated that the import content of exports increased in South Korea from 15.8 per cent in 1963 to 25.5 per cent in 1973 and in Taiwan from 12.9 per cent in 1961 to 21.2 per cent in 1971.

This strategy, however, requires that potential importers and exporters are aware of possible gains resulting from trade. One of the major impediments for an export-oriented strategy is that, in order to open business relations, importers and exporters must first become acquainted. This is often impeded by language as well as cultural barriers. To overcome these problems, middlemen are required to establish contacts, make necessary arrangements and often to provide financing, insurance, transport and so on. Japan's great economic growth and export expansion is frequently credited to its general trading companies (*sogo shoshas*) which, at least in the beginning, almost exclusively handled Japanese foreign trade. In the course of time they became increasingly involved in international trade with third countries, notably Taiwan and Korea. In Taiwan, Japanese firms handled about 60 per cent of textile exports (Scitovsky, 1986, p. 164) until the late 1960s, when they were gradually replaced by US and European importers who opened offices in Taipei. South Korea started to build up its own trading companies along Japanese lines and was quite successful in this respect. Similar attempts in Taiwan remained rather ineffective, although enormous amounts were invested by the government (ibid., pp. 164f).

The actual export performance of all four countries is outstanding. The average growth rates of per capita exports between 1960 and 1988 of South Korea and Taiwan were more than double per capita GDP growth rates and the export share of GDP in Hong Kong and Singapore is much higher than 100 per cent (this is a result of the high import content of exports). Export growth resulted mainly from an increasing share of manufactures, thereby making fast industrialization and structural change possible. In 1978 the four 'Little Dragons' already accounted for more than 60 per cent of total LDC manufactured exports (Riedel, 1984). Since marginal factor productivities are generally higher in the export than in the non-export sector (Feder, 1983), this structural change will raise the total factor productivity of an economy. Further arguments explaining the benefits of export-oriented strategies include importing scarce capital goods with export revenues, transfer of technology, learning and spillover effects and reduction of X-inefficiencies.

The dependence on foreign countries and the vulnerability to world recessions are strong arguments against an export-oriented strategy. Balassa (1985) however found empirical evidence that outward-oriented strategies showed better results in overcoming oil shocks. Another argument against an export-oriented strategy is that aggressive export promotion strategies might induce import restrictions from industrial countries. Empirical evidence, however, demonstrated quite obviously that these countries could elude such efforts fairly effectively. We will take up this question later when we discuss the extent to which the East Asian export model can be generalized.

The role of government
One of the most controversial questions in explaining the success of NICs is the role of governments. For quite some time these countries have been perceived by more theoretically oriented economists as being typical examples of 'laissez faire' economies, where the government only fulfils the classical duties postulated by Adam Smith, namely providing external and internal security as well as supplying public goods. This is fairly true for Hong Kong. There, even the supply of money is provided by some privately owned banks and no active strategies for industrialization are pursued by the government. Hong Kong, however, provides probably the only major example of a strict capitalistic development in this century and, even there, real estate remains state-owned.

The other three 'Dragons' have relied on development plans for the last three decades to enhance economic efficiency and stability (see Koppers, 1991). The influence of these plans has been greatest in South Korea, where an aggressive and centrally controlled economic development process was pursued, and least in Taiwan, where the plans are not obligatory and the government tends to be rather supportive than interventionist (Park, 1990). In South Korea differential access to bank credit, foreign loan guarantees and tax incentives ensured private industry's close compliance with official plans. The already-mentioned high industrial concentration was a result of these policies. A further result was the growth in importance of personal contacts between government officials and private entrepreneurs. This not only gave the expression 'Korea, Inc.' some justification, but also facilitated the implementation of the plans. Pack and Westphal (1986) argued that it is the 'visible hand' of an interventionist strategy successfully 'picking winners' which explains the success of South Korea, rather than the 'invisible hand' operating through markets. However the Korean government has not always been lucky in picking its winners. The efforts to 'acquire comparative advantages' in heavy industries in the late 1970s proved to be rather ineffective and contributed to debt problems in the early 1980s. Deregulation was brought about through a liberalization of the economic policy in order to overcome some of these problems. There is little doubt, however, that South Korea's rapid achievement of international competiveness in a number of industries can be attributed to the government's selective industrial policies (Westphal, 1990, p. 41).

Similarly the government of Singapore has used development plans to foster strategic industries and foreign investment. The Economic Planning Committee comprises high government officials and representatives from the private sector to facilitate implementation (Koppers, 1991, p. 50). However the efforts of the government of Singapore to enforce a high wage policy in the 1980s have not been too successful. It had tried to do this by promoting higher value-added industries, greater capital intensity and technological progress. The efforts to establish an international financial centre were more successful, although Hong Kong managed the same without any government intervention. In Taiwan as well many prestigious projects turned out to be flops. The investment of enormous amounts of money in building an automobile industry proved to be fruitless.

With the exception of Hong Kong, public ownership in these countries, especially in banking and capital-intensive industries, is remarkably high. In Taiwan about 68 per cent of all real estate is public- or party-owned, and 30 to 40 per cent of all investment is made in state- or party-owned enterprises (Chen, Lin *et al.*, 1991). This high share is mainly a historical relic: after the Second World War, all former Japanese property was nationalized. It is also partly a result of repeated attempts to influence economic development by founding new public-owned enterprises. There is broad consensus among economists, however, that the public sector was not the driving force in any of these countries.

Although efforts to manipulate industrial incentives were prevalent in all these countries (except Hong Kong), relative prices were probably less distorted than in most developing countries. Additionally the implementation of development plans seems to have been more skilful and effective than in most other countries. Plans were not simply imposed on the private sector; rather they were achieved through close cooperation between representatives of the private sector and government officials.

Summing up, it is difficult to withstand the impression that the development in Taiwan and Hong Kong was pushed by the commercial interest of a quite diligent and well educated population, whereas the development in

Korea and Singapore was rather pulled by competent as well as lucky governments. Of course this does not mean that Koreans and Singaporeans are less diligent or that the governments in Hong Kong and Taiwan were more dim-witted than their counterparts. Rather it means that the decisive driving forces were different.

IV Recent developments and future prospects

We have already stated in the introduction that economists have seldom been successful in predicting long-term developments. This should make us cautious too. Nonetheless some developments seem to be rather easy to forecast. At this time all 'Dragons' have become service economies. Even in South Korea, which traditionally lagged behind, the share of agriculture has now been reduced to a mere 9 per cent, whereas services account for about 46 per cent (World Bank, 1992). This imposes special problems on labour markets, since the labour reserves of the agricultural sector, which fed industrial demand in the transition period, seem to be exploited. With the labour markets already under pressure, any further expansion will probably increase wages considerably and threaten their comparative advantage in labour-intensive industries. Since all the 'Dragons' are already densely populated, they are reluctant to take in new migrant workers. Furthermore the prices of real estate have boomed during the last two decades and have nearly reached Japanese levels. This has also increased investment cost.

Both effects have caused many entrepreneurs to transfer labour-intensive production processes to neighbouring low-wage countries. This is especially the case for Taiwan, which has undertaken huge direct investments in the special economic zones of the People's Republic of China and countries like Indonesia, Vietnam or Laos. However official figures are difficult to obtain since many of these investments are still not allowed by law. This rapid flow of capital from rich to poor countries is astonishing. Neither in Europe nor in America has such a rapid flow of investment goods occurred (see Lucas, 1990). The wealth of the 'Four Little Dragons' seems to flow to the neighbouring countries much more than was the case with Western countries and may create a new and very dynamic economic space.

However the 'advantages of backwardness' (the catch-up effect) seem to be rather exploited. This will call for further innovation instead of imitation, thus necessitating huge investment in research and development as well as in marketing. This necessity was clearly foreseen and things are moving fast in this respect. Taiwan, for example, has already established numerous industrial parks and districts to promote entrepreneurial talent and attract foreign high-technology firms, such as the 210-hectare park Hsinchu near Taipei, established as early as 1979. Another serious problem is the conservation and restoration of the environment, which has also been exploited and destroyed to a remarkable degree. This poses special problems in such densely populated countries and will require huge investments as well. Criminality is also increasing fast and has become another factor adversely affecting the investment climate.

All this sounds discouraging, but if we cast a closer look at these problems we find that these are more or less the same problems that most industrial countries are facing today. Therefore we suspect that the 'miracle' will come to an end sooner or later. This is not really a cause for concern, since there is little reason to fear that any of these countries will decline to previous levels. The sword of Damocles hanging over all these countries is the possibility of world recession and increasing protectionism of industrial countries. In order to meet the fears of increasing protectionism in the EC and especially in the North American Free Trade Area (NAFTA) a new process of Asia–Pacific Economic Cooperation (APEC) was launched. The 15 very heterogeneous member states (the six ASEAN members, the USA, Canada, Japan, South Korea, Australia, New Zealand, China, Hong Kong and Taiwan) account for more than half of world GDP and almost 40 per cent of world trade. Although there still is a long way to go for this process of regional integration, it gives at least an institutional setting to resolve future trade conflicts more efficiently.

In the political arena there seems to be much more uncertainty. In Hong Kong the issue of 1997 will probably become even more sensitive, although there is little doubt that Hong Kong will remain a key door between China and the world economy, especially for its booming neighbours. In South Korea a period of political and socioeconomic transition is to be expected. The situation on the labour markets and general deregulation of the economy will probably be key issues in the years ahead. Taiwan faces problems similar to those of South Korea as well as hindrances arising from its relations with China, namely the absence of any formal relations with most other countries. This poses difficulties at interregional or international levels, for instance regarding the UN. In addition fears of possible reactions by the People's Republic of China have caused many Western businessmen to neglect the Taiwanese market. Regarding its domestic policy, the repeal of martial law has improved political freedom and the situation of native Taiwanese, although this process is far from being completed.

V   Can the East Asian model be generalized?
If we ask whether the success of these countries can be replicated by followers we first have to disentangle exogenous factors which cannot be manipulated by policy and endogenous factors thought to react to changes of control or exogenous variables. This task is anything but easy to perform in a simultaneous system of such complexity. We have already seen that popula-

tion growth or political stability might sensibly be regarded as endogenous. This way one soon arrives at true but trivial conclusions like 'success breeds success'.

While investigating the development of Japan, Taiwan and South Korea, Kuznets (1988) detected five common and important characteristics that can be influenced by policy: high investment ratios, small public sectors, competitive labour markets, export expansion and government intervention in the economy. He admits that these economic characteristics are not exclusive to Japan, Korea and Taiwan (ibid., p. 35). We have already seen that not all five characteristics are fulfilled in the 'Four Little Dragons'. Moreover other factors could be added (such as adequate infrastructure or access to foreign savings). This is a clear hint of considerable arbitrariness associated with this way of proceeding. But even if we could find a catalogue of common characteristics, there would be no guarantee for any causal relationships, since in looking for common characteristics we have to face problems very similar to those in 'data mining'. Strictly speaking, we should not interpret any common characteristic as being necessarily conducive to growth. The only thing we can be sure of is that any characteristic observed in at least one successful country is not sufficient to prevent exceptional success. In this respect the lessons to be learned from these countries are not clear-cut.

If we restrict ourselves to rather robust common features, it is difficult to detect any common pattern in the development of the 'Four Little Dragons' except, of course, the primary confidence in capitalism (that is, private property and market forces) and an outward-oriented strategy. As outlined above, capitalism does not necessarily mean 'laissez faire'. All 'Dragons' but Hong Kong have experienced extensive state interventions and regulations. Especially regarding South Korea and Singapore, it would probably be more accurate to speak of state capitalism. Nonetheless market forces remained rather effective in all four countries and relative prices were less distorted than in most other developing countries. Capitalism in this sense can 'in principle' be generalized fairly easily, but the experiences of countries trying this have not always been very promising. The recent example of former socialist countries in this respect demonstrates once again that the actual implementation of such a strategy might be essential, but we cannot expect to learn too much from our survey of the 'Gang of Four', as their strategies were actually implemented long ago under very different circumstances and in a much more favourable environment.

The second point, an outward-oriented strategy, seems to be more promising. Again it must be emphasized that this is usually very different from free trade policy. All 'Dragons' but Hong Kong tried to promote exports aggressively while restricting imports, following mercantilist doctrines rather than liberal free trade prescriptions. However it has already been pointed out by Lewis (1980) in his Nobel lecture and later by Cline (1982) that the markets of industrial countries might be too small to absorb the goods if all developing countries started to export in the manner of 'The Four Little Dragons'. This would provoke import restrictions by industrial countries and thus render this strategy impossible for most countries (for a critique, see for example Riedel, 1984; Balassa, 1988, pp. 1650ff). Their models however seem to understate the flexibility of fast-growing markets. As we mentioned above, we can observe that a cascade of increasingly developed countries has evolved, where trade in capital goods contributes to an equalization of capital–labour ratios and hence wages and capital returns. For example, so-called 'Near-NICs' (Thailand, Malaysia, Indonesia, the Philippines) and China have already taken over many labour-intensive product lines such as clothing, which were under the firm control of the 'Gang of Four' not long ago. The limits of such divisions of labour between different stages of development are probably not within sight.

Summing up, we may conclude that the story of the 'Four Little Dragons' is interesting in itself, demonstrating convincingly that 'miracles' are at least possible. The lessons to be learned for other countries seem to be limited, however. Maybe the traditional focus on superperformers when looking for lessons to be learned is itself misleading. We should remember that the extraordinary success in medicine was brought about, not by studying people becoming very old, but rather by investigating the reasons for people dying very young.

References

Balassa, Bela (1985), 'Exports, Policy Choices, and Economic Growth in Developing Countries after the 1973 Oil Shock', *Journal of Development Economics*, **18** (1).

Balassa, Bela (1988), 'Outward Orientation', in Hollis Chenery and T.N. Srinivasan (eds), *Handbook of Development Economics*, vol. 1, Amsterdam: North Holland.

Bhagwati, J.N. (1988), *Protectionism*, Cambridge Mass.: MIT Press.

Chandler, Alfred D. (1992), 'Organizational Capabilities and the Economic History of Enterprise', *Journal of Economic Perspectives*, **6** (3).

Chen, John-ren (1975), 'Abwertungs- und Aufwertungseffekte in einer Volkswirtschaft mit besonderen Aussenhandelsverflechtungen', in O. Wecker and R. Richter (eds), *Dynamische Wirtschaftsanalyse*, Mohr: Tübingen.

Chen, John-ren (1987), 'Taiwan – ein Modell für ökonomische Entwicklung?', *Journal für Entwicklungspolitik*, **3** (2).

Chen, John-ren (1992), 'The Asset Disposition Effect of Land Reform and Economic Development', working paper *Internationale Ökonomik*, no.12, University of Innsbruck.

Chen, Shih-Meng S., C.C. Lin *et al.* (1991), 'Disintegrating KMT-State Capitalism: A Closer Look at Privatizing Party-Owned Enterprises', Taipei: Taipei Society (in Chinese).

Cho, Yoon Je (1988), 'The Effect of Financial Liberalization on the Efficiency of Credit Allocation: Some Evidence from Korea', *Journal of Development Economics*, **29** (1).

Cline, W. (1982), 'Can the East Asian Model of Development Be Generalized?', *World Development*, **10** (2).

Datta, Anindaya (1987), 'Understanding East Asian Economic Development', *Economic and Political Weekly*, **XXII** (14).

Dowrick, Steve (1992), 'Technological Catch Up and Diverging Incomes: Patterns of Economic Growth 1960–88', *Economic Journal*, **102** (412).

Feder, Gershon (1983), 'On Exports and Economic Growth', *Journal of Development Economics*, **12** (1/2).

Fei, John C.H. and Gustav Ranis (1975), 'A Model of Growth and Employment in the Open Dualistic Economy: The Cases of Korea and Taiwan', *Journal of Development Studies*, **XI** (2).

Friedman, Milton (1988), 'Money and the Stock Market', *Journal of Political Economy*, **96** (2).

Koppers, Simon (1991), 'Development Planning in East and Southeast Asian Economies', in S. Koppers, S. Dingens, A. Klaas and H.-E. Wermuth (eds), *Growth Determinants in East and Southeast Asian Economies*, Berlin: Duncker & Humblot.

Kubo, Yuji, Jaime de Melo, Sherman Robinson and Moshe Syrquin (1986), 'Interdependence and Industrial Structure', in H.B. Chenery, S. Robinson and M. Syrquin (eds), *Industrialization and Growth: A Comparative Study*, Oxford: Oxford University Press.

Kuznets, Paul (1988), 'An East Asian Model of Economic Development: Japan, Taiwan, and South Korea', *Economic Development and Cultural Change*, **36** (*Supplement*), April.

Kwack, Sung Yeung (1986), 'The Economic Development of the Republic of Korea, 1965–1981', in Lawrence Lau (ed.), *Models of Development*, San Francisco: ICS Press.

Lewis, Arthur (1980), 'The Slowing Down of the Engine of Growth', *American Economic Review*, **70** (4).

Lindner, Deborah J. (1992), 'The Political Economy of the Won: U.S–Korean Bilateral Negotiations on Exchange Rates', *International Finance Discussion Papers*, Board of Governors of the Federal Reserve System, no. 434.

Lloyd, P.J. and R.J. Sandilands (1986), 'The Trade-Sector in a Very Open Re-export Economy', in Chong-Yah Lim, and P.J. Lloyd (eds), *Singapore: Resources and Growth*, Singapore: Oxford University Press.

Lucas, Robert E. (1990), 'Why Doesn't Capital Flow from Rich to Poor Countries?', *American Economic Review (Papers and Proceedings)*, **80** (2).

Myrdal, Gunnar (1968), *Asian Drama – An Inquiry into the Poverty of Nations*, London: Allen Lane.

Pack, Howard (1988), 'Industrialization and Trade', in Hollis Chenery and T.N. Srinivasan (eds), *Handbook of Development Economics*, vol. I, Amsterdam: North Holland.

Pack, Howard and Larry Westphal (1986), 'Industrial Strategy and Technological Change; Theory versus Reality', *Journal of Development Economics*, **22** (1).

Park, Yung Chul (1990), 'Development Lessons from Asia: The Role of Government in South Korea and Taiwan', *American Economic Review (Papers and Proceedings)*, **80** (2).

Riedel, James (1984), 'Trade as the Engine of Growth in Developing Countries, Revisited', *Economic Journal*, **94** (373).

Scitovsky, Tibor (1986), 'Economic Development in Taiwan and South Korea, 1965–1981', in Lawrence J. Lau (ed.), *Models of Development*, San Francisco: ICS Press.

Suh, Sang-Chul (1978), *Growth and Structural Changes in the Korean Economy 1910–1940*, Cambridge Mass.: Harvard University Press.

Summers, Robert and Alan Heston (1991), 'The PENN World Table (Mark 5): An Expanded Set of International Comparisons, 1950–1988', *Quarterly Journal of Economics*, **CVI** (2).

UNDP (1991), *Human Development Report 1991*, New York: Oxford University Press.

Westphal, Larry E. (1990), 'Industrial Policy in an Export-Propelled Economy: Lessons from South Korea's Experience', *Journal of Economic Perspectives*, **4** (3).

World Bank (1992), *World Development Report 1992*, Washington DC: Oxford University Press.

6 OPEC and oil revenues

Paul Stevens

This chapter examines the effects on OPEC members of the declining oil revenues experienced in the 1980s and considers, in the light of this experience, how they may be affected in the future. The chapter consists of four sections. Section I seeks to examine the nature and causes of the decline in oil revenues. Section II considers the possible impact of this decline on the economies of the OPEC members. Section III considers the future prospects for oil revenues for the remainder of the 1990s. Finally Section IV considers how the possible revenue path may affect the member countries and the organisation itself.

I Declining oil revenues in the 1980s

Two factors underlay the decline in oil revenues in the 1980s: declining volumes of production and a decline in the unit price of oil. Between 1981 and 1985 the price decline was gradual, but in 1986 there was a precipitous collapse – the so-called 'third oil shock'. The declining requirement for OPEC oil – the call on OPEC – stemmed from two trends, both of which can be clearly seen in Figure 6.1. First there was a decline in world demand for oil which began in 1973. Towards the end of the 1970s, there was some recovery but the price rises of 1979–81 stifled this and demand declined until 1985. The prime cause of this decline, which had reversed the trend of strong and steady growth since the early 1950s, was the price changes associated with the two oil shocks. However the prime driving force was not so much the higher price itself but the expectation of higher price.

To use less oil is a two-stage process because oil is used in an energy-using appliance. In the first stage, the appliance is used less or perhaps used differently. A sharp increase in price (irrespective of expectations) will encourage such behavioural change. However, unless deprivation is acceptable, this will have a limited impact. For this reason, the short-run own price elasticity of demand for oil has been shown to be fairly low (Hawdon, 1992). The slight decline in demand registered after 1973 in part reflects such behavioural change. However to reduce oil demand significantly requires a change in the stock of oil-using appliances either to use less oil or to use some other fuel. This has two dimensions. First, it takes time to introduce such changes: new equipment must be designed and produced and the exist-

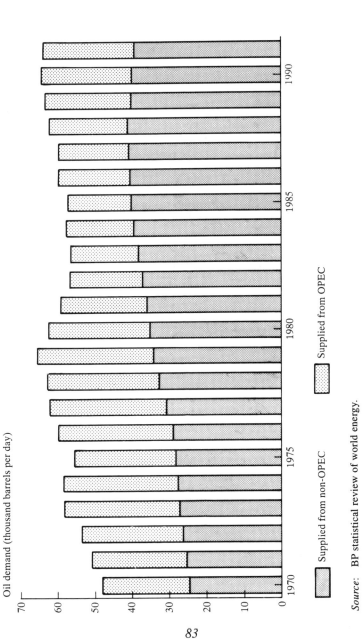

Oil demand (thousand barrels per day)

Source: BP statistical review of world energy.

Figure 6.1 World oil supply and demand, 1970–91

ing stock turned over. Thus much of the decline in demand after 1979 shown in Figure 6.1 reflects the lagged impact of the 1973 price increase. Second, the change in appliances is driven not by price but by expectations of price, since for the most part the appliance, as a piece of capital equipment, has a life span which is often long. At the start of the 1970s, a view began to develop which saw oil as a finite resource which would rapidly run out. This, with the rediscovery of the ideas of Hotelling (Hotelling, 1931; Gordon, 1967; Devarajan and Fisher, 1981), led to a widespread consensus that oil prices would go on rising for ever. It was this expectation which drove the change in appliance stock which forced down demand, thereby sowing the seeds for the destruction of the consensus.

The second reason for the reduction in the demand for OPEC oil was the steady increase in non-OPEC supply. As with demand, this also was, in part, a response to the higher prices of the 1970s. Many importers, previously facing falling real prices, in the 1970s scrambled to develop their own supplies, a process reinforced by concern over supply security. This process was encouraged by the behaviour of the major oil companies who had lost their equity oil in much of the Third World during the first half of the 1970s as a result of a series of host government takeovers. They began to seek replacements in such areas as Alaska and the North Sea. This new capacity was subject to significant lags and, as with demand, it was not until the start of the 1980s that the new supply sources began to influence the market. The consequence of the two trends outlined above was that OPEC's volume dropped steadily and steeply compared to its capacity in the 1980s. This reflected the market attitude that OPEC was the residual supplier who would act to balance the market in an effort to defend a specific price.

Price was the second factor behind OPEC's declining oil revenues. The record is outlined in Figure 6.2. The setting of oil prices is a complex and controversial subject (Mabro, 1992; Stevens, 1991) since it is a mixture of price administration in a market context. In October 1981, OPEC had set the price at $34 per barrel. However, if this price was to be maintained, OPEC had to ensure that its supply was sufficient to balance the market. Too much supply would threaten market perceptions and pressure price downwards.

During 1981, Saudi Arabia was left with the task of trying to balance the market and defend the price. As a result, Saudi Arabia's production fell from 10.0 million barrels per day (b/d) in 1981 to 6.7 million b/d in 1982 (British Petroleum, 1992). However, faced with the declining requirement for OPEC oil, this was insufficient and prices came under pressure. In an attempt to bolster Saudi Arabia's defence, in March 1982, for the first time since the mid-1960s, OPEC tried to act as a formal cartel with a production quota system.

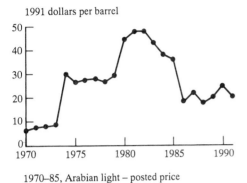

1970–85, Arabian light – posted price
1985–91, Brent – spot price

Figure 6.2   World oil price, 1970–91

As a cartel, OPEC faced two problems. First, it lacked the information on global supply and demand balances to set accurately its overall production level. OPEC compounded the problem by insisting on setting both price and production, thereby ignoring the constraint of the demand curve. The weakening of the vertically integrated structure of the international oil industry associated with the events of 1979–81 meant that such information, previously with the oil companies, had been lost. Because of the great difficulty in agreeing on the distribution of quotas between members, OPEC invariably set production levels too high for market needs. Second, there was the standard cartel problem of members cheating, thereby increasing OPEC's already inflated offering. While Saudi Arabia was willing to act as the 'swing producer', the error and the cheating could be absorbed, although the market remained increasingly sceptical. This led to an erosion of price.

However Saudi Arabia's production continued on an inexorable decline, reaching 2.4 million b/d by the Summer of 1985 (IEA, 1986). At this point, Saudi Arabia was no longer willing to suffer further and in September 1985 announced a change of policy (Mabro, 1988). This involved producing to their quota and pricing crude according to the market value of the products produced (netback pricing). In December 1985, OPEC met and declared it would seek a 'fair share' of the market. The market interpreted this as a declaration of price war and by the end of March 1986 Brent crude was trading on the spot market at $11.75 per barrel compared to $30.20 at the end of November 1985 (IEA, 1986).

The subsequent story is uncertain and much remains to be told (Yergin, 1991). It appears that the US government decided that such very low prices were against their interests as the second largest oil producer, the main creditor to a large number of (now much poorer) Third World exporters and a major investor in (now much less attractive) energy supply projects. It seems likely that pressure was applied on Saudi Arabia to change its policy yet again. This succeeded and in December 1986, with help from Iran, Saudi Arabia was able to produce an OPEC agreement for an $18 barrel which the market believed in and accepted. This belief was damaged when the Saudi–Iranian alliance was destroyed in the summer of 1987 by the killing of a large number of Iranian pilgrims at the Hajj. The underlying market weakness returned and growing market scepticism kept prices below the $18 target – at times significantly below. Cheating also worsened, notably by Kuwait and the United Arab Emirates. Their cheating reached such levels that it seems likely their actions had more to do with the politics of the Gulf than the economics of the oil market. In the summer of 1990, Saddam Hussein came up with a novel solution (not normally found in the economics literature) to the standard cartel problem of cheating – physically threatening the perpetrators. However he then proceeded to negate its undoubted effectiveness by actually invading Kuwait. The consequences of his action and its aftermath have had a very significant impact on the oil market (Stevens, 1992b). At the stroke of the UN Secretary General's pen, the excess capacity problem was solved as four million b/d was taken out of the market by sanctions. However other OPEC members, notably Saudi Arabia, were able to squeeze sufficient oil out for the market to remain comfortably supplied. During the crisis, prices rose and tended to fluctuate, but this was due to fears of the impact of hostilities rather than any market reality. On the outbreak of hostilities, prices collapsed[1] and, since the crisis, have remained several dollars below the OPEC target price of $21 per barrel agreed in July 1990. Taken together, falling volumes and falling prices meant that OPEC faced a steady decline in government revenue.

II   The impact of declining revenue

There are three methodological problems facing any assessment of the impact of the revenue patterns described above on OPEC: generalization, symmetry and complexity. The 13 members have widely divergent characteristics. Per capita income ranges from $250 to $18 430 per head; life expectancy from 51 to 71 years; adult literacy from 11 to 90 per cent; and infant mortality from 100 to 15 per thousand live births. They vary in size (both area and population), in political persuasion, in religion and in many other ways. Generalization is dangerous and misleading but constraints of space demand it. The view taken of the impact of collapsing revenues is in part dependent upon the view taken of the impact of the huge increase in revenues during the 1970s. Many argue that the large increases in oil revenues in the 1970s actually damaged the economies of the oil producers. The damage arose either because of the impact of 'Dutch disease' (Neary and Van Wijnbergen, 1986) or because of the impact on the role of the state (Stevens, 1986) or because of the impact of resource based industrialization policies triggered by the windfall (Jazayeri, 1988; Auty, 1990). Clearly, if this view is taken, the impact of a removal of the revenues would be different from that if the higher revenues were seen to have had a beneficial impact. A related issue is also the question of asymmetry. Would the impact of higher revenues experienced during the 1970s simply be reversed by the collapse or would the impact of a collapse differ from that of a rapid expansion?

The final methodological problem is the complexity of the impact. Even the most cursory analysis identifies a multi-stage process. The first stage is the direct or primary impact on economic variables from the collapse in price – export revenue falls, government tax take falls and so on. The next stage is the indirect impact. This involves the secondary impact of the primary change in domestic economic variables due to an economic transmission mechanism or a policy response. For example, lower government revenue cuts back investment projects which reduce output, employment and so on; or it forces governments to borrow, with implications for the monetary sector and so on. The second stage also involves the indirect impact stemming from any global economic impact from lower oil prices. Both oil shocks of the 1970s were associated with global economic recession although the extent of the causal link is much debated. Many anticipated that the 1986 price collapse would kick-start a global economy already showing signs of stirring. Had it happened, it might have been expected to increase oil demand by means of the income elasticity providing some offset to the revenue impact of lower unit price, although there was a growing debate over whether the OECD had effectively decoupled oil demand from economic growth (Hansen, 1990; Mackillop, 1989).

The expected economic upturn did not materialize. The global economic recovery in 1984, with GDP increasing by 4.4 per cent compared to 2.7 per cent in 1983 and 0.5 per cent in 1982, fell back to 3.3 per cent in 1985 and 3.0 per cent in 1986. The average for the rest of the decade was 3.2 per cent (IMF, 1990). Several reasons provide an explanation for the lack of stimulus to growth. The contribution of the oil price rise to the 1974–5 recession was probably overstated and the contribution to the 1980–83 recession definitely overstated. In the latter case, other factors were at work, most obviously the switch in macroeconomic policy in the early 1980s which led many to describe the slowdown as the 'policy-induced recession'. Second, for the OECD at least, oil's importance in the macroeconomic balance had diminished, reflecting the impact on oil imports of the price shock of the 1970s. In 1980, energy imports (mainly oil) into the industrial market economies were

29 per cent of merchandise exports. By 1985, the eve of the 1986 price collapse, this had fallen to 21 per cent (World Bank, 1987). Finally, in many cases, the lower price of internationally traded crude was not passed through to the final consumer and consumer governments absorbed some of the lower price by increased fiscal take on sales taxes or in setting utility prices.

The real economy

OPEC's GDP[2] inevitably fell as a result of the 1986 collapse. The poor output performance up to and including 1986 obviously reflected the fall in the value of oil output, but there were other factors which explain the continued poor performance of output compared to other Third World countries. It has been long observed that there is a type of double counting in the national accounts of oil producing countries (Al-Sadik, 1985; Stauffer, 1987). The oil is produced and sold and the revenue – logged as value added to GDP – accrues to the government. This revenue is then respent in the economy in the form of both recurrent and capital expenditure which is also logged as value added to GDP. It is on the basis of this expenditure that the private sector of the economy then responds, or not, as the case may be. In effect, in the OPEC countries a very strong and direct expenditure multiplier operates, driven by oil revenues.

This multiplier has two stages. The first is the direct impact of government capital projects which require inputs of goods and services. Initially these projects tended to rely heavily on imports. As the profitability potential became apparent, local private companies began to develop the channels, frequently through joint ventures with foreign companies by which these imports could meet the demand. This was reinforced in many cases by political structures which allowed elements of the local elites access to the decision process concerning who got what contracts. The second stage is when expectations of yet further business encourages these local groups to develop a domestic capacity to provide the inputs which then begins to creates a network of linkages.

In such a structure, a sharp decline in government spending catches the economy first by its impact on aggregate demand and second by its impact on the excess capacity installed in anticipation of ever-growing business. This was precisely the pattern experienced in 1982–6. For example, between 1982 and 1989,[3] gross capital formation – an indicator of expectations and capacity – fell as a percentage of GDP from 25.7 per cent to 18.0 per cent. By contrast, in the non-fuel exporting Third World the figures were 24.8 and 24.4, respectively. A particular problem concerned excess capacity. The first oil shock of 1973 had begun the multiplier process outlined above. In the late 1970s, the view developed that oil prices would go on rising forever and that there would be ever-increasing requirements for oil from the OPEC countries. The second oil shock gave credence to this view. The result was a scramble by the private sector to expand capacity in various sectors of the economy, with construction in particular attracting large amounts of investment. Much of this extra capacity was coming on stream just in time for the downturn in government expenditure as a consequence of the decline in oil revenue. This damaged expectations. Expectations in the Gulf States received a blow from another quarter. The oil boom had seen a dramatic expansion in the domestic banking sector, but this had occurred in a very poorly controlled institutional environment. The result in some cases was the development of dubious banking practices. The financial sector had already been hit by the collapse of the unofficial stock market in Kuwait – the Suq Al Manakh crisis (Beblawi, 1984). However, because of the deteriorating economic situation, the quantity of non-performing loans increased. The whole banking sector for the period 1982–8 at times looked on the verge of collapse, which further fuelled pessimistic expectations.

Fiscal response

During the 1970s, the OPEC governments' revenue pattern had become dominated by the contribution of oil revenues. There had been limited incentive to introduce new taxes to diversify the revenue base. Apart from the well documented problems of raising tax revenue in Third World countries (Bird and Oldman, 1975, Newbery and Stern, 1987) there were also political constraints. Many of the countries were ruled by groups who secured their political legitimacy by coercion or by the widespread provision of services and largesse. Any attempts to introduce additional taxation may well have prompted the view that there should be no taxation without representation. The existence of oil revenues had removed any fiscal links between government and the governed.

When oil revenues collapsed, therefore, the governments had very limited options. Their scope to raise alternative taxes was severely constrained, and few tried.[4] Most tried to cut expenditure. Capital projects tended to take the brunt of the cuts on the grounds that recurrent expenditure was more politically sensitive. This, however, triggered the reverse expenditure multiplier described earlier. In the event, as can be seen from Figure 6.3, most governments ran with larger budget deficits. The figure actually understates the absolute magnitude of the problem since the GDP base upon which the percentage was calculated as indicated by the previous section was falling.

The financing of such deficits varied. The Gulf States who had accumulated foreign assets began to use these to fill the gap. However, as the realization grew that the deficits might be long-standing, many turned to borrowing. Others used the money supply. The 12 major oil exporters' broad money aggregates increased on average by 15.1 per cent during 1987–9

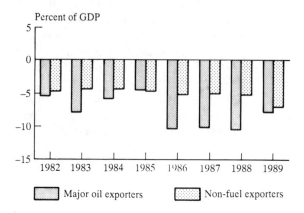

Source: IMF, *World Economic Outlook*, May 1990.

Figure 6.3 Fiscal balances, 1982–9

compared to 12.8 per cent 1982–6. Such financing was reflected in the inflation rate, which averaged 17.3 per cent during 1987–9 compared to 10.6 per cent in 1982–6.

Overall, the effect was a diminution of the governments' ability to meet the expectations of their people, expectations which had been inflated during the heady years of plenty in the 1970s. Many governments began to face political pressure and popular unrest which further locked them into problematical fiscal stances. Fiscal prudence required both lower expenditure and higher taxes. Political reality closed both options.

Balance of payments
The balance of payments picture for OPEC is presented in Figure 6.4. During the period 1982–5, when oil export volumes and prices eroded, merchandise exports fell by 29 per cent. However merchandise imports declined even more, by 35 per cent, reflecting the negative effect, described earlier, of weakening oil revenues on the economies. The result was that the trade balance, after a deterioration in 1983, recovered. Inevitably the oil price collapse in 1986 wiped out any gains and the trade balance deteriorated from $55.7 billion in 1985 to $13.9 billion in 1986, although it still registered a surplus.

The impact on invisibles was subject to many conflicting forces. Like merchandise imports, service imports fell over the period, reflecting the general economic decline. Net investment income in the period declined from $25.7 billion in 1982 to $12.4 billion in 1985. This was partly due to a

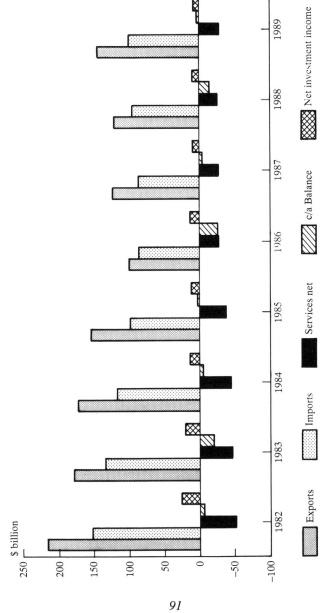

$ billion

250
200
150
100
50
0
-50
-100

Exports   Imports   Services net   c/a Balance   Net investment income

1982   1983   1984   1985   1986   1987   1988   1989

Source: IMF, *World Economic Outlook*, May 1990.

Figure 6.4   Oil exporters' current account, 1982–9

rise in interest payments from \$8.2 to \$12.7 billion despite the fact that interest rates were falling. In effect the borrowing undertaken by the exporters on the back of the second oil shock was beginning to appear as a debt-servicing problem. The net debtor fuel exporters' total external debt rose to \$274.4 by 1987 and the debt service ratio rose from 17.1 per cent (1982) to 22.7 per cent (1986). Part of the decline in net investment income can also be attributed to the liquidation of many of the assets accumulated by the net creditor oil exporters in the boom years. This liquidation was in part due to the fiscal response to the growing budget deficits outlined earlier, although hard data are difficult to obtain for the larger net creditors such as Kuwait and Saudi Arabia.

In the case of the Gulf exporters, there was also a significant reduction in workers' remittances as the economic recession in the Gulf led to a shedding of expatriate labour. The overall effect was that net services for the fuel exporters fell from a deficit of \$52.9 billion in 1982 to \$27.6 billion in 1986. This sort of level was maintained up to 1989, despite the inexorable drain coming from debt servicing.

Overall, up to 1986, the current account balance of the fuel exporters objectively was far from being a problem. The deficit of \$7.0 billion in 1982 had improved and in 1985 the balance actually registered a surplus of \$2.1 billion. The events of 1986 converted this into a \$26.7 billion deficit. Subsequently, thanks mainly to an improving trade balance, this moved back to a small surplus (\$2.9 billion) by 1989. However the real problem lay not so much with the actual numbers as with the negative impact on expectations which, for reasons outlined, were already gloomy. The declining oil revenues of the 1980s had a negative effect on output, fiscal balances and the balance of payments in OPEC. Above all, however, they had a negative impact on expectations, which forced most of the OPEC members into recession. The recession and 'conditionality' arising from debt-servicing problems led many of the OPEC members to attempt some form of economic restructuring. The ease with which such reforms can be adopted depends in part upon the prospects for oil revenue during the rest of the decade. Ample and stable revenues will help to lubricate the process.

III   Prospects for the future of OPEC revenue

The Iraqi invasion of Kuwait has had a profound effect upon the world oil market and the prospects for oil prices. In the late 1980s, a consensus was emerging in the oil industry. This was that inexorably during the 1990s, the call on OPEC, 23.4 million b/d in 1989, would grow. Estimates of the call varied from the OPEC Secretariat's figures of 30–36 million b/d by 2000 to 38–41 million b/d from a group of oil industry representatives meeting in Oxford in May 1990.

In the light of this, there was much discussion about OPEC's willingness and ability to install the necessary crude-producing capacity. It was perceived that the large excess capacity which had dogged OPEC throughout the 1980s was eroding. This was through a process of recovery in demand for OPEC oil from a trough of 17.34 million b/d in 1985 and an erosion of existing capacity through depletion and lack of maintenance. The excess capacity of 35 per cent in 1985 had fallen to 17 per cent on the eve of Saddam's invasion. The invasion and its aftermath transformed the situation. Courtesy of UN sanctions against Iraq, the tight market which some expected in the late years of the decade had arrived at the beginning of the decade. Saudi Arabia's domination of production, plus the fact that it was the only country with any excess capacity after the liberation of Kuwait, meant it could determine marginal supplies and thereby control the market. There remains the question to what extent Iran might challenge Saudi Arabia's control. Furthermore the crisis encouraged Saudi Arabia to nail its colours to the mast of low prices.

The formation of Saudi oil policy is usually a ponderous affair. The more reasons which can be found for any specific policy path, the more entrenched that policy. Three reasons dominate the low price strategy. First, there was the war itself. If it was, as many suggested, primarily intended 'to make the world safe for gas guzzlers' this meant avoiding high prices. Second, after the end of the conflict, Saudi Arabia was determined to ensure that the UN did not weaken over sanctions against Iraq. Saddam had to go and sanctions would assist his passage. While prices remained low, there was little or no pressure to allow Iraqi oil back into the market. Finally there was the drive for market share. In the short term this would assist revenues and the position of Saudi Arabia for the negotiations which would be essential when Iraq returned. However of greater importance was the longer term. The Saudi establishment still carried the scars of the two oil shocks of the 1970s. To be sure, they had generated much revenue, but the price of reduced oil demand was perceived to have been too high. Higher prices pushed oil out of the energy scene. The fear was that Saudi Arabia's huge oil reserves would simply lose any commercial value as oil continued to be backed out of the energy market. The 'market share–low price' philosophy had been present since the mid-1980s and for some technocrats much earlier. The Iraqi invasion added other imperatives which strengthened the policy.

Iraq's return would change the situation. Iraq could quickly restore its pre-war capacity providing good will from the Kurds in the North and Saudi Arabia in the South allowed the use of its 3.34 million b/d pipeline export capacity. Iraq could also quickly increase that capacity, given the number of large undeveloped fields. If Iraq came back before oil demand reflected any economic recovery, control of the market would again become difficult.

Excess capacity would dog OPEC's control efforts and a rerun of the second half of the 1980s would be probable. A lengthy exclusion might make Iraqi re-entry less traumatic. Timing is everything and there must obviously be great uncertainty involved. For Iraq to remain outside for many years is not implausible. The only clear counter to this view is something else going wrong. Currently there is very limited excess capacity in the system. Another shock affecting oil supplies could well lead to prices rising steeply. In such circumstances there would be very strong pressure to allow Iraq back in. There is a long, depressing list of potential candidates for such a trigger, most obviously from political upheavals (in Russia, Algeria, and so on).

Saudi Arabia's strategy for low prices is generating tremendous hostility in the Gulf (and indeed elsewhere). A key consequence of the Gulf War was that all in the region need even more revenue. The events created the necessity to spend to rebuild and rearm. They also greatly increased the discount rates of the rulers. Long-term perspectives are becoming a luxury in the face of short-term exigencies. Most obviously in Iran, low oil prices are playing havoc with President Rafsanjani's economic policy, upon which his survival depends. A crucial issue is how long Saudi Arabia can resist such hostility before being forced to try and push oil prices higher. Saudi Arabia is entirely dependent upon the US military umbrella. Despite profligate arms spending it would be unable to resist alone either of its larger neighbours. The general view is that US oil import dependence will ensure the maintenance of US protection. That may well be the case and would certainly be logical. However perception is more important than any logic. The current Saudi establishment will certainly remember the indecent haste with which the last Democratic incumbent of the White House ditched its primary ally in the region – the Shah. He too was supposed to act as guarantor for any anticipated oil import dependence.

In addition to regional political pressures, consumer governments are talking about raising oil prices either because oil products are an attractive source of revenue or because of environmental concerns or because the Iraqi invasion reminded consumers of their vulnerability if they are dependent upon Gulf oil. This presents a real and direct threat to the Saudi low price strategy. That the Saudis would be reluctant to increase prices because of the hard lessons learnt earlier is not in doubt. However, if prices are going to rise anyway, given the current discount rates of the Saudi establishment and the strong need for revenue, needs must when the devil drives. It would be extremely foolish for the Saudis not to pre-empt any threatened price increase.

Despite this analysis, there appears to be quite a strong consensus that prices will remain weak in 1993 and beyond. Some OPEC members may be able to offset this by increasing volume. If the consensus proves correct then

OPEC's domestic economic problems will not receive a quick dose of revenue medicine to alleviate the suffering involved in restructuring. A key uncertainty, however, will be whether in the expected environment the investment necessary for the international oil industry will be forthcoming. Much of that industry has been living upon investment decisions made prior to the first oil shock of 1973. Upstream, the lion's share of crude capacity came from fields developed in the 1950s and 1960s. Downstream, the expectations of the late 1960s of ever-lower oil prices plus ever-increasing oil demand led to a refinery building boom in the non-communist world which saw refinery capacity reach a peak of 66 million barrels per day in 1980 (British Petroleum, 1992). Tanker building imitated the refinery experience, with capacity rising from 99 million dwt in 1966 to a peak of 333 million dwt in 1977. Of the current fleet of 808 tankers over 200 000 dwt – the essential base load of the industry – in four years, 82 per cent will be over 20 years old (Shilleto, 1992). Both upstream and downstream, in the 1990s, the industry will need new capacity if even relatively pessimistic demand forecasts are accepted.

'Green' pressures are also likely to force increased spending by all of the energy industries. Oil will be no exception. The energy transformation processes must become cleaner as the result of increasingly stringent requirements on emissions. These will range from improved scrubbing techniques to significant changes in product specification, such as reformulated gasoline. Given the apparently gloomy prospects for oil prices contained in the current consensus, there is doubt that the necessary investment will be forthcoming. Given the relatively poor performance of the commercial oil companies in recent years, there are doubts that the capital markets of the world will approve of such long term investments. In related vein, will the OPEC producers be willing to invest in crude producing capacity if consumer governments are intent on using their fiscal power to reduce oil demand? The answers to these questions must be viewed as very uncertain. As the decade proceeds, the oil industry may well be characterized by feast or famine. The implication is that future oil revenues are likely to fluctuate to an even greater extent than in the past.

IV   The implications for future revenue prospects for OPEC
All the signs suggest that revenue for the remainder of the decade will be volatile and uncertain. There is a large literature on the consequences of export volatility and export dependence upon primary exports (Macbean, 1966; Glezakos, 1973; Love, 1989). Although it is far from conclusive, it seems plausible that damage is more likely to follow revenue fluctuations than benefits. An inability to provide an economic context which can meet the aspirations of the bulk of the population can only generate political

opposition and political upheaval. A casual observation of many of the OPEC members suggests such a process is already in train with the future of many of the governments and regimes coming into question. Such upheaval and uncertainty feed negative expectations, which inhibit investment, which feeds poor economic prospects, leading to further political unrest. While this is obviously undesirable for the countries themselves, it also has implications for oil consumers. The world is still dependent upon OPEC oil to fuel its economic progress. This state of affairs will not change quickly and anything which threatens the stability of oil supplies is unwelcome. Some have suggested that a way out of this potentially vicious circle lies in producer–consumer cooperation, but there are real problems with any such dialogue and little is likely to result (Stevens, 1992a). The more realistic hope lies in moves to ensure general global economic prosperity which will provide secure markets for oil and create a climate more conducive to investment in oil. This too will have its implementation problems.

As for OPEC itself, its days may well be numbered. During the 1980s, the non-Gulf members developed great resentment against the ways in which it seemed the Gulf members were manipulating the situation for their own regional political needs at the expense of the oil revenues so desperately needed. Many countries began to question the value of OPEC membership, whose only effect seemed to be to inhibit their freedom to operate in the oil market. For many years leaving OPEC has been a constant source of debate in both Nigeria and Venezuela. At the end of 1992, Ecuador will actually leave the organization. There is a logic to this. The controllers of the market have derived that power from their control over excess capacity to produce crude oil. What excess capacity may exist in the 1990s will lie largely in the Gulf States who are likely to be increasingly viewed as the residual supplier and hence the controller. As this group continues to dominate OPEC meetings, the rest may simply fade away.

Notes

1. This was due to two factors. First, the IEA announced a large-scale release of oil stocks. This had been demanded by Saudi Arabia as a *sine qua non* of starting Operation Desert Storm, since the Saudis were concerned that even a temporary very high price (widely expected during the early stages of hostilities) would create negative expectations over oil prices in the future. Second, the early reporting of the war implied that the Iraqi military threat had been easily contained and that Saudi export facilities were no longer under threat.
2. Because of the very real difficulties with data from the OPEC countries, this chapter uses, as a proxy for OPEC, data from the IMF *World Economic Outlook*. Specifically, the data refers to the category 'Twelve major oil exporters'. This group includes one non-OPEC member, Oman, and excludes two members, Ecuador and Gabon. In 1986, Oman produced 560 000 b/d of crude while Ecuador and Gabon together produced 440 000 b/d.
3. 1989 will be treated as the latest year for purpose of analysis because thereafter the figures begin to be distorted by the Iraqi invasion of Kuwait and its aftermath.

4. A classic example was seen in Saudi Arabia. The King decided to introduce taxation on expatriate workers based upon a scheme developed in the early 1970s but subsequently shelved. This was done without discussion or consultation and with no attempt to adjust the figures on exemption bands to account for inflation. The result was an unmitigated shambles, with poor Asian expatriates finding themselves liable to taxation and more affluent expatriates finding their end-of-contract payments liable to heavy taxation. Within 24 hours of the decree, very large numbers of senior expatriates resigned in all sectors. In less than one week the decree was rescinded.

References

Al-Sadik, A.T. (1985), 'National Accounting and the Income Illusion of Petroleum Exports: The Case of Arabia Gulf Cooperation Council Members', in T. Niblock and R. Lawless (eds), *Prospects for the World Oil Industry*, London: Croom Helm.

Auty R.M. (1990), *Resource-Based Industrialization: Sowing the Oil in Eight Developing Countries*, Oxford: Clarendon Press.

Beblawi, H. (1984), *The Arab Gulf Economy in a Turbulent Age*, London: Croom Helm.

Bird, R.M. and O. Oldman (1975), *Readings on Taxation in Developing Countries*, Baltimore: Johns Hopkins University Press.

British Petroleum (1992), *Statistical Review of World Energy*, London: BP.

Devarajan, J. and A.C. Fisher (1981), 'Hotelling on Exhaustible Resources', *Journal of Economic Literature*, March.

Glezakos, C. (1973), 'Export Instability and Economic Growth: A Statistical Verification', *Economic Development and Cultural Change*, **21**.

Gordon, R.L. (1967), 'A Reinterpretation of the Pure Theory of Exhaustion', *Journal of Political Economy*, June.

Hansen, U. (1990), 'The Delinking of Energy Consumption and Economic Growth', *Energy Policy*, September.

Hawdon, D. (ed.) (1992), *Energy Demand: Evidence and Expectations*, London: Surrey University Press and Academic Press.

Hotelling, H. (1931), 'The Economics of Exhaustible Resources', *Journal of Political Economy*, April.

IEA (1986), *Oil Market Report*, January/March.

IMF (1990), *World Economic Outlook*, May, Washington DC: IMF.

Jazayeri, A. (1988), *Economic Adjustment in Oil Based Economies*, Aldershot: Avebury.

Love, J. (1989), 'Export Instability in LDCs: Consequences and Causes', *Journal of Development Studies*, **25**.

Mabro, R. (ed) (1988), *The 1986 Oil Price Crisis: Economic Effects and Policy Response*, Oxford: Oxford University Press.

Mabro, R. (1992), *OPEC and the Price of Oil*, Oxford: Oxford Institute for Energy Studies.

Macbean A.I. (1966), *Export Instability and Economic Development*, London: Allen & Unwin.

Mackillop A. (1989), 'Decoupling–Recoupling and Oil Shocks', *Energy Policy*, August.

Neary J.P. and S. Van Wijnbergen (1986), *Natural Resources and the Macro Economy*, Oxford: Blackwell.

Newbery D. and N. Stern (1987), *The Theory of Taxation for Developing Countries*, Oxford: Oxford University Press.

Shilleto, K. (1992), 'Crude Oil Transportation After the Exxon Valdez', *Middle East Economic Survey*, **35** (23).

Stauffer, T. (1987), 'Income Measurement in Arab States', in H. Beblawi and G. Luciani (eds), *The Rentier State*, London: Croom Helm.

Stevens, P. (1986), 'The Impact of Oil and the Role of the State in Economic Development: A Case Study of the Arab World', *Arab Affairs*, no.1.

Stevens, P. (1991), 'Oil Prices – an Economic Framework for Analysis', in G. Bird and H. Bird (eds), *Contemporary Issues in Applied Economics*, Aldershot: Edward Elgar.

Stevens, P. (1992a), 'Economic Development and the World Energy Market', in G. Bird (ed.),

International Aspects of Economic Development, London: Surrey University Press & Academic Press.

Stevens, P. (1992b), *Oil and Politics: The Post War Gulf*, London: Royal Institute of International Affairs.

World Bank (1987), *World Development Report 1987*, Oxford: Oxford University Press.

Yergin, D. (1991), *The Prize: The Epic Quest for Oil, Money and Power*, New York: Simon & Schuster.

7 Aid, investment and growth: what prospects in the 1990s?

Howard White

A net transfer of resources of about 9 per cent of GDP on average will be required to achieve sustained growth during the 1990s. (World Bank, 1989, p. 6)

The apparent inability of development aid over more than twenty years to provide a net increment to overall growth in the Third World must give the donor community a grave cause for concern. (Mosley *et al.*, 1987, p. 636)

I Introduction

The opening quotation gives the optimistic view that more aid can lead to higher growth. If developing countries are to achieve the increase in incomes necessary to eradicate global poverty in the opening decades of the twenty-first century, then higher levels of aid are necessary (and, perhaps it may seem to some, sufficient). But, as the second quotation shows, academics can be rather more sanguine. Aid has, they argue, at best, no impact on growth and, at worst, a harmful one. Higher aid is therefore not the answer to the problem of development.

It is true that we do not have good evidence that aid is beneficial for growth. However, as argued in the next section on aid and growth, neither do we have good evidence that aid is not beneficial. If we are to properly understand the aid–growth relationship we need to look in more detail at the channels through which the link is supposed to operate. The next section does this for the case of aid's impact on investment. The fact that aid appears to lead to higher investment – which it does – does not, of course, necessarily mean that more aid results in higher growth. What also matters is the productivity of aid-financed investment. Both theory and evidence on this important issue, reviewed in the penultimate section, are scanty. Given this lack of data, we discuss some important potential sources of aid inefficiency. The conclusions that emerge from this analysis affect both research and practice.

II The aid–growth relationship

Empirical analysis of the impact of aid on growth has typically regressed real growth of income on aid inflows (perhaps aggregated with other capital inflows, or perhaps disaggregated into types of aid, such as grant or non-grant), usually with some additional regressors included (for example, change in terms of trade (TOT), domestic savings rate and various dummies; see Riddell, 1987, Michalopoulos *et al.*, 1989; White, 1992a). Such equations are misspecified, in three respects: (1) omitted variable bias; (2) single equation estimation of simultaneous relationships; and (3) parameter instability (see White, 1992a, 1992d).

First, we have only an imperfect understanding of the growth process. But it is not difficult to make a long list of variables that have at one time or another had growth regressed upon them (military expenditure, instability of export earnings, policy orientation and various social indicators, to name but a few), many of which have been found to have a 'significant' impact on growth. To the extent that aid is correlated with any of these omitted variables (as in many cases it is: for example, military expenditure) the equation is subject to a specification error that will cause the estimate of the aid coefficient to be biased.

But secondly, it is not sufficient simply to include some of the more important omitted factors. Consider, for example literacy, which is included in the model of Mosley *et al.* (1987). Its inclusion holds literacy constant whilst analysing aid's impact on growth. Yet increasing literacy may be one of the channels through which aid affects growth. This effect will not be captured by including literacy in the equation, since a single equation is being used to estimate what is, in fact, a simultaneous system.

This brings us to the third problem, which is perhaps the most serious of all. What are the channels through which aid may affect growth? During the 1960s it may have been the case that aid was used for investment in infrastructure, but since that time aid has expanded into the social sector and there has been increased use of technical assistance and aid explicitly tied to policy reforms intended (after a period of restructuring) to facilitate growth. All these things may well contribute to growth, but both the extent and the period over which it occurs will be very different in each case. It would be foolhardy to claim that a textile factory, a feeder road, a primary health clinic and a student pursuing a masters degree are all going to have the same return and, what is more, within the same time frame. Yet this is precisely what is claimed by studies that regress aid on growth. Few such studies have tried to incorporate the lags that will occur between aid-financed activities and their eventual impact on growth. But such efforts are, anyhow, futile, since the required lag structure will change as the sectoral composition of aid changes. We would therefore expect that the aid coefficient in an aid–growth regression would be unstable (in both cross-section and time series studies) – as indeed has been found on the occasions when structural stability has been tested (White, 1992b).

In summary, while studies of aid and growth do not tell us that aid has increased growth, neither do they tell us that it has not done so. There are too many problems inherent in the methodology being employed for us to put any reliance on the results of this literature one way or the other. We would be far better advised to analyse aid's impact by examining more carefully the various links in the chain running from aid to growth. What may be called the old approach to aid's macroeconomic impact – which was largely based on regression analysis – needs to be replaced by a new macroeconomics of aid, which builds on firmer theoretical foundations. In fact, there are already two distinct strands to this new macroeconomics: the fiscal response literature and 'aid as Dutch disease'. Both of these will be mentioned below, but we turn our attention now to one of the most important links in the aid–growth relationship: that between aid and investment.

III Aid and investment

The link between aid and growth in the two-gap model was seen to run through the increase in investment. Therefore some studies have regressed investment on aid: some results are summarized in Table 7.1. No studies have found a negative relationship and only one reports an insignificant result. The suggestion is that aid does indeed play a significant part in increasing investment.

But these analyses share many of the faults for which the aid–growth studies were criticized above. While omitted variable bias may not be so serious, single equation estimation of potentially simultaneous systems remains a problem. So does the possibility of misspecification on account of inappropriate pooling of data or aggregation. Levy (1988, p. 784) tests whether his data may be pooled to estimate an investment equation for Sub-Saharan Africa and finds that it cannot. One reason for this parameter instability across countries may well be differences in the relative importance of public and private investment, since the mechanisms through which aid affects these two components of investment will be very different.

In order to understand how aid does affect investment we should begin by developing a firm theoretical basis. The relationship between aid and public investment hinges upon the issue of fungibility, on the one hand, and possible feedback mechanisms (either static or dynamic) on the other. Aid's impact on private investment will be mostly indirect (though some aid is channelled to the private sector through credit schemes), these indirect effects taking the form of either crowding out or crowding in. Private investment may also be affected by a variety of feedback mechanisms. The remainder of this section of the chapter considers these issues in more detail and examines what evidence we have to date.

Table 7.1   The impact of aid on aggregate investment, from selected studies

		Aid		Other inflows	
	Sample	Current	Lagged	Current	Lagged
Areskoug (1969)	na	0.40	—	—	—
Chenery et al. (n.d.)	na	0.11	—	—	—
Massell et al. (1972)	109 observations from 11 Latin American countries, 1955–66	0.36 (1.27)	0.38 (1.39)	0.54 (6.88)	0.42 (3.03)
Chaudhuri (1978)	India time series data	3.15 (3.08)	—	—	—
Levy, V. (1987)	46 low-income countries, using two-period averages, 1968–73 & 1974–80	0.83 (3.40)	—	—	—
Levy, V. (1988)	28 SSA countries, using two-period averages, 1968–73 & 1974–82	1.19 (3.43)	—	—	—

Notes:
Results for Areskoug and Chenery et al. taken from Papanek (1972).
— denotes variable not included in regression.
Figures in parentheses are t-statistics for null hypothesis that coefficient is zero.

The impact of aid on government investment will, in the first instance, be a function of fungibility. Whilst much (though not all) aid may be nominally tied to investment projects, it does not lead to a one-for-one increase in government investment. It does not if the recipient is free to exploit fungibility: that is, it would have used its own resources for that investment project even in the absence of aid, so the aid inflow means that these resources are freed to be spent on something else (government buildings, higher civil service wages, military expenditure and so on). At best aid is, in an economic sense, *really* funding the most marginal investment project – and not that to which the funds are nominally attached – and, at worst, aid is financing developing country governments' passion for consuming 'bads' rather than 'goods'. Programme aid may also be fungible if higher aid leads to a reduction in revenue raised from taxes and borrowing.

This fungibility argument must be circumscribed in three ways. First, if aid is a large share of government revenue the room for manoeuvre on the part of the recipient is considerably less (White, 1992a). This argument has even stronger force if recipients are obliged to contribute their own funds to a project; indeed, in at least one documented case, the donor moved from full to partial cost project finance precisely to exert influence over the government's use of its own revenues. In the mid-1980s the Kenyan treasury proposed cutting the number of externally-financed development projects from 150 to only 80, partly to regain control over domestic revenues (Clark, 1986).

Second, there is considerable evidence that many governments will not spend on the projects in which donors are interested in the absence of donor finance, having a preference for prestige projects and conspicuous consumption. The evidence for this comes from (1) the high share of their own resources many countries devote to, for example, military and diplomatic expenditures (2) the (ab)use of oil revenues by oil producing developing countries, notably Nigeria; and (3) the failure to turn the massive increase in capital inflows in the years preceding the debt crisis into an improved growth performance. Third, as Cassen *et al.* (1986) point out, a donor's inputs to a project to which its name is nominally tied may improve the quality of the project as compared to what this would have been in the absence of donor involvement.

Estimates of the extent to which fungibility may divert aid away from investment have been obtained for a number of countries from the fiscal response model due to Heller (1975); such estimates are summarized in Table 7.2. The model used to produce these estimates supposes that government maximizes an objective loss function – containing government investment, taxes, borrowing and government developmental and non-developmental recurrent expenditures – subject to budget constraints, which sepa-

Table 7.2 The impact of aid on government investment, from selected studies

		Loans	Grants	Bilateral	Multilateral
Heller (1975)	Full sample, official flows	0.53	0.64	—	—
	Full sample, total flows	0.76	0.33	—	—
	Anglophone, official flows	0.41	0.09	—	—
	Anglophone, total flows	0.63	0.31	0.34	0.32
Gang and Khan (1991)	India, 1961–84	1.03	1.79	1.55	0.63
		(0.41)	(0.52)	(0.19)	(0.25)
McGillivray and Papadopoulos (1991)	Greece, 1962–80	0.62	3.64	—	—
		(0.44)	(0.74)		

Notes:
Heller's full sample comprised 11 African countries, for various years over the period 1960–70.
— denotes not calculated in study.
Figures in parentheses are standard errors.

rately include grant and loan aid. Whilst Heller's study found that grant aid in particular is not used to increase investment, the two more recent studies present a more optimistic picture. Indeed grants appear to pull other resources (notably taxes) into investment. All studies agree that loans appear to play a significant role in increasing government investment; there may be some fungibility, but it is not so great as to argue that aid is not playing a useful role in supporting government capital expenditure.

However these studies have a number of problems (see Forster, 1992; White, 1992e). First, the studies present only a partial interpretation of their results, concentrating their discussion on the apparent impact of aid through the coefficients in the budget constraints. But since the other variables in this constraint are not constant in the face of the aid inflow, these parameters do not tell us the total impact that the inflow is having on the variable of interest. In the case of the Gang and Khan (1991) study, analysis of the reduced forms suggests that aid in fact has had no impact on government investment.

Second, the fiscal response model supposes a number of target equations for the different choice variables, these targets including in some cases the lagged value of the actual variable. That is, there are implicit dynamics in the model that all the above-mentioned studies ignore. These implicit feedback effects have been incorporated in Forster's (1992) application of the model to Papua New Guinea and he finds that they can be substantial – the long-run effect of aid on government investment is about one-third higher than that obtained if the model's dynamics are ignored.

The models not only fail to analyse the feedback contained in the models themselves, they also fail to consider the possibility of feedback through the various economic variables included in the model. For example, the lag of income appears in some of the target equations, but no consideration is given to the possibility that income may increase as a result of the aid inflow.[1] Mosley *et al.* (1987) combined the Heller model with a Harrod–Domar equation, but did not recognize that the model implied a link between income and growth of income which were treated as separate independent variables. Nor did they estimate a model that bore much relationship to their theoretical exposition.

What, then, are the potential various feedback mechanisms that need to be explored? There may be, as shown in the fiscal response literature, a diversion of aid funds into non-developmental activities or to reduce taxes and borrowing. However the components of government expenditure (both consumption and investment) may well, in turn, depend on taxes (that is, government expenditure is to some extent 'supply driven'). Therefore if aid directly increases government expenditure this will (through the national accounting identity) increase income and thus taxes. The effect on taxes will feed back into a 'second round' of impacts on government expenditure patterns, including further increases in government investment. White (1992c) shows how such economic feedback effects may, in principle, more than offset any fungibility; but, in practice, the strength of these effects depends on the size of the consumption multiplier, which depends both on the propensities to import and the existence of spare capacity. If the economy is supply-constrained, the increase in domestic demand will fuel inflation, to the possible detriment of both public and private investment.[2]

Private investment may be further linked to public investment (and thus to aid) through a number of channels. First, there may be a direct complementarity between the two types of capital formation. Some projects stimulate private investment through their demand for inputs. Others have a stimulating effect via facilitating investment that would not otherwise have been profitable but becomes so with improved access or services. Second, there may be crowding out via credit rationing or the real interest rate. As shown in White and McGillivray (1992), this effect depends on aid's impact on government savings. If aid relaxes the fiscal deficit it will cheapen the cost of credit (or the quantity constraint) so that private investment may rise. Third, empirical studies find that changes in output are typically one of the

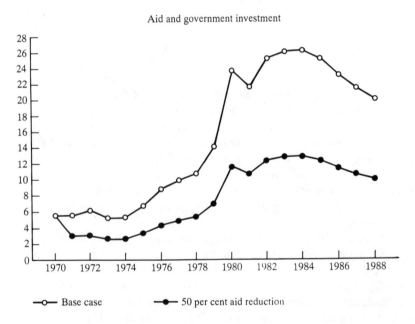

Aid and government investment

Figure 7.1   The impact of a 50 per cent reduction in aid on government investment

main determinants of private investment in developing countries (see Serven and Solimano, 1992); this is the accelerator principle. Thus aid may initiate a 'virtuous circle' with the initial aid-financed investment (and hence growth) stimulating private investment which then fuels growth. Fourth, aid may discourage investment in tradeable goods' production if, as suggested by the 'aid as Dutch disease' literature, it induces an appreciation of the real exchange rate.

From the above discussion, aid may have little effect on investment, a mixed effect (increasing public but reducing private) or strong beneficial effects on both. Which of these actually occurs can only be determined by reference to the experience of aid recipients. A model incorporating many of these effects was estimated for the case of Sri Lanka for the period 1972–88 (White, 1992d). The main findings of the Sri Lankan study were, first, that both categories of aid have a direct positive impact on government investment. Through this channel they also increase private investment, since there is strong complementarity (crowding in) between public and private investment. There is no crowding out via the real interest rate because, even though private investment *is* sensitive to this rate the latter is unaffected by the government's fiscal position. The order of magnitude of these various

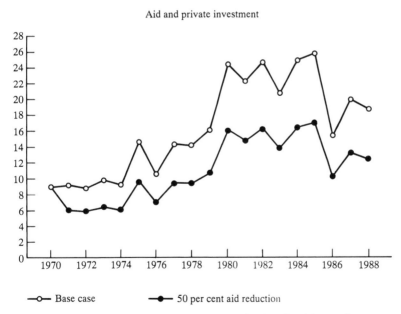

Figure 7.2   *The impact of a 50 per cent reduction in aid on private investment*

effects may be gauged from Figures 7.1 and 7.2. These graph the base case in which the exogenous variables, including the two aid flows, are given their actual values. Each figure also shows what the level of investment would have been if aid had been halved: private investment would only have been two-thirds of its actual level, and government investment less than half. The reductions in investment that result from a cut in aid are well in excess of the loss in aid.

Evidence therefore strongly supports the view that aid has played an important role in financing Sri Lanka's investment boom, thus establishing an important link between aid and growth. But it is only a link. The next step in the argument is whether or not this investment leads to higher growth.

IV   The efficiency of aid financed investment

Keith Griffin (1970) not only argued that aid (A) would displace savings, but also that more aid would lower the incremental output–capital ratio (k) since aid-financed investment was less efficient than replaced domestically financed investment. The combination of reduced domestic savings and the lower productivity of aid-financed investment led Griffin to argue that aid may actually reduce growth. He advanced the following reasons as to why such an inverse relationship between the Incremental Output Capital Ratio (IOCR) and aid might be expected:

1.   donor preference for 'monumental' projects which reflect the political motivations for aid-giving;
2.   a donor bias against funding directly productive activities in favour of infrastructure; and
3.   administrative preference for large projects.

Unfortunately Griffin presented no data in support of these arguments and his observation that 'almost no research has been done on the relationship between k and A' is nearly as true today as it was then. The evidence we have comes from Voivodas (1973), who found a negative relationship between aid and the IOCR, though not sufficiently so to render aid's impact on growth significantly negative. By contrast, Rana (1987) reported that, for a sample of Asian countries, aid was associated with *more* productive investment.

Even if there were to be more such studies, it is unlikely that they would be at all conclusive. Once again, there are problems in aggregating across countries and across sectors, and a range of other determinants of the IOCR are to be considered. Regional or country-specific analysis of sectoral IOCRs may yield useful results, but there are no such analyses.[3]

In the face of this lack of good evidence we should look in more detail at the validity of the arguments advanced for low aid efficiency. Griffin's first two arguments may have had some basis at the time he was writing, but much less so today. There are good reasons (mentioned above) to think that it is recipient governments, not donors, who favour non-developmental monument building. Second, the 1970s saw a shift of donor spending away from economic infrastructure to a range of directly productive activities. The reason Griffin gave – donors do not support public ownership of such activities – has been circumvented by the creation of mechanisms to channel funds to the private sector, a greater accommodation of donors to recipient government intervention and, most recently, a desire on the part of recipients themselves not to intervene.

The third problem that Griffin highlights – in general, a preference for quantity over quality – on the other hand, remains with us to this day (see John White, 1974). There are pressures right through the aid system for rapid disbursement. Such pressures operate from the largest agencies – some writers have explained the growth of structural adjustment lending as resulting from a need to send money into developing countries to meet debt repayment obligations – to loan officers working in rural projects (see Mosley and Dahal's (1985) account of the Small Farmers' Development Programme in Nepal). The pressure for rapid disbursement creates a number of pressures that militate against the quality of aid, such as favouring large projects over small ones and a preference for projects that are quick to implement (see Madeley, 1991).

One of the earliest documented examples of the failure of large-scale projects is the East African Groundnuts Scheme in colonial Tanganyika in which three million acres were cleared and infrastructure was constructed for the production of groundnuts. The scheme was eventually stopped with practically nothing to show for itself, very largely for reasons of a purely agricultural nature (even though only inadequate study of the area was made, there was sufficient information to tell that it was unsuitable for groundnuts because of insufficient rainfall, high clay content in the soil and the prevalence of rosette disease – see Coulson (1981) for a more detailed account). Such failures of state schemes did not prevent the Colonial Administration from compelling peasants to adopt techniques (such as terracing and tie-ridging) that were unsound given the ecological conditions. Similar problems re-emerged in the settlement schemes under the ujamaa programme in independent Tanzania, most noticeably Operation Rufiji which moved peasants out of one of the country's most prosperous farming areas on ill-founded technical grounds.

Like the Groundnuts Scheme, many more recent projects have run foul of a poor understanding of the ecological conditions and environmental consequences of project implementation. The last decade is littered with examples of such projects – such as transmigration in Indonesia and various hydropower schemes in Brazil – because more informed activitist groups have high-lighted them, but we can only suppose that such inappropriate design has always been a feature of some projects.

Environmental considerations are not the only reasons why aid, particularly in large projects, has sometimes been ineffective – there are also human ones. These human aspects revolve round the failure to consult project 'beneficiaries' (Moser, 1987) about the plans involving their future, a practice perhaps at its most brutal when the 'beneficiaries' of urban improvement learn of the project when they awake to find the bulldozers at their door (see Ayres, 1984). The importance of beneficiary participation has been stressed for some time and is, at least in principle, recognized by donors. Useful academic perspectives on the costs of non-participation come from the small, but growing, literature which may be called 'anthropological perspectives on aid ineffectiveness'.[4] Perhaps the most striking aspect of this literature is the documentation of 'beneficiary' resistance to and sabotage of development projects.

It is disturbing, but perhaps not so surprising, that 60 000 people should join a protest against the World Bank-supported Sardar Sarovar dam, when the benefits of such projects are not usually received by those that bear the cost of displacement (Adams and Solomon, 1985). At first sight, more surprising are demonstrations and strikes against projects by those meant to benefit directly from the project, as happened, for example, in the Tondo Foreshore Development Project in the Philippines. The attitude of many supposed project beneficiaries subjected to development by an outside agency is perhaps well summed up by the comments of a village chief in Lesotho on the sabotage of a village woodlot: 'Development has many enemies here' (Ferguson, 1990, p. 247).

The conclusions from the anthropological perspective concern beneficiary participation in all stages of the project cycle, though this is far from unproblematic, not least because of the complex interaction of participatory structures with the state at local and national levels. (And the currently fashionable notion of 'empowerment' is rather too vague to take us very far in the direction of policy recommendations that donor agencies can *implement*.) Research has a role to play in a more systematic analysis of successful project implementation. But participation is not the only area where academics can assist aid policy: there are macroeconomic considerations also.

In 1960 there were 88 000 miles of motorable road in Zaire, by 1985 there were only 12 000 (Davidson, 1992). Whilst this is an extreme example, the deterioration of the capital stock is a widespread phenomenon in developing countries, notably in Sub-Saharan Africa. Scarce resources are not available to prevent irreparable depreciation of assets or very low rates of capital utilization. Aid can *exacerbate* this situation by tying what resources there are to new investments. Doriye and Wuyts (1992, p. 9) demonstrate this argument empirically for the case of Tanzania. Aid involved a 'strategy [which was] extremely wasteful in resource use. This is because it was based on capacity creation without regard to the availability of resources to operate it.' It is only with the expansion of untied import-support aid under the Economic Recovery Programme in the latter half of the 1980s that any relationship has been discernible between aid and output growth.

Doriye and Wuyts further show that the Tanzanian government resorted to inflationary deficit financing to meet their local cost commitments. Ineffective aid will also be inflationary since it increases domestic demand without increasing supply. This was the case for the aid boom in Sri Lanka following the election of the new UNP government in 1977, where nearly half of project aid was channelled into the Accelerated Mahaweli Development Project alone (see B. Levy, 1987; White and Wignaraja, 1992, for a formal analysis of the way the inflationary impact of aid was translated into a real exchange rate appreciation).

Whilst this section has concentrated on some main potential sources of aid inefficiency, it should be borne in mind that the most comprehensive review of the evidence summarizes its findings thus: 'this report finds that most aid does indeed "work"' (Cassen *et al.*, 1986, p. 1). We are not seeking to reverse this conclusion but to identify outstanding issues of concern for policy and research.

V   Conclusions

Some academics have claimed that there is no relationship to be found between aid and growth, but the techniques they have used to examine this relationship have not been, and most likely cannot be, relied upon to give reliable results. The results are certainly not sufficiently sound to be used for any radical policy conclusions, such as the reduction or even abolition of development aid. From an economic perspective, we would be far wiser to study the mechanisms by which aid can affect (and damage) growth. This conclusion alone provides a research agenda that will carry us into the next century.

This chapter contributes to such a research strategy by analysing the link between aid and investment on both theoretical and empirical levels. To understand this link we must separate aid's impact on public and on private investment – the effect on both can be positive, partly because of the complementarities flowing from the former to the latter. The balance of evidence available thus far suggests that aid does indeed increase investment, but whilst this may be a necessary condition for aid to increase growth also it is by no means sufficient. Aid-financed investment must also be productive, and, although much of this investment does indeed appear to be so, some is not. Research can play an important role here in exploring the reasons for this. Two are touched on here: lack of beneficiary participation and the problem of drawing resources away from the maintenance and/or operation of the existing capital stock. Academics should not think that donors are unaware of these and other problems in aid management – in some areas they appear to be ahead of the academic community. But there are still lessons to be learnt and propagated,[5] and these are tasks that should occupy us all if the promise of the first quotation at the beginning of this chapter is to become a reality.

Notes

1. This is the same criticism that has been made of Griffin's argument that aid will displace savings (see Grinols and Bhagwati, 1976; White, 1992d).
2. The inclusion of a supply constraint in the economic feedback into the fiscal response area would create a link with the other part of the new macroeconomics of aid (namely aid as 'Dutch disease'). No paper has yet made this link explicit, but Collier and Gunning (1992) come close to so doing.
3. Norton *et al.* (1992), purporting to show that aid has enhanced agricultural productivity in Sub-Saharan Africa and Asia, do not fill this gap, for a number of reasons. The most important is that they regress the *level* of agricultural output on, *inter alia, all* ODA. Even if only aid to agriculture had been used, the aid variable may contribute to higher output by, for example, providing capital, generating new agricultural employment or opening up new land rather than increasing productivity.
4. Space precludes anything but a brief mention of this literature. Early work is to be found in the collection edited by Cernea (1985); more recent studies are Ferguson (1990) and Porter *et al.* (1991). A related development is the use of participant observation in policy and project evaluation – see Salman (1987). Official donors are not the only ones that systematically impose 'solutions' on beneficiaries – see Harrell-Bond's (1986) discussion of emergency relief in the Sudan.
5. It does seem that many of the mistakes of the past may well be about to be repeated in Eastern Europe and the Commonwealth of Independent States (CIS).

References

Adams, Patricia and Lawrence Solomon (1985), *In the Name of Progress: the Underside of Foreign Aid*, London: Earthscan.

Areskoug, Kaj (1969), *External Borrowing and its Role in Economic Development*, New York: Praeger.

Ayres, Robert (1984), *Banking on the Poor*, Cambridge, Mass.: MIT Press.

Cassen, Robert and Associates (1986), *Does Aid Work?*, Oxford: Clarendon Press.

Cernea, Michael (1985), *Putting People First: Sociological Variables in Rural Development*, New York: Oxford University Press.

Chaudhuri, P.K. (1978), *The Indian Economy: Poverty and Development*, London: Crosby Lockwood Staples.

Chenery, Hollis, H. Elkington and C. Sims (eds) (n.d.), 'A uniform analysis of development patterns', Harvard University Center for International Affairs Economic Development Report No. 148.

Clark, Colin S. (1986), 'The Aid Bargain', *Africa Report*, May–June.

Collier, Paul and Jan Willem Gunning (1992), 'Aid and exchange rate adjustment in African trade liberalisations', *Economic Journal*, **102**.

Coulson A. (1981), 'Agricultural policies in mainland Tanzania, 1946–76' in J. Heyer, P. Roberts and G. Williams (eds), *Rural Development in Tropical Africa*, London: Macmillan.

Davidson, Basil (1992), 'Africa: the Politics of Failure', *Socialist Register*.

Doriye, Joshua and Marc Wuyts (1992), 'Aid, adjustment and sustainable recovery: the case of Tanzania', SOAS Department of Economics Working Paper no. 6, London; also issued as ISS/Netherlands Interdisciplinary Demographic Institute Teaching Text, March, The Hague: Institute of Social Studies.

Ferguson, James (1990), *The Anti-Politics Machine: 'Development', Depoliticization and Bureaucratic Power in Lesotho*, Cambridge: Cambridge University Press.

Forster, Neal (1992), 'A developing country's fiscal response to foreign aid: the case of Papua New Guinea 1970–88', unpublished MA thesis, The Hague: Institute of Social Studies.

Gang, I. and H. Khan (1991), 'Foreign aid, taxes and public investment', *Journal of Development Economics*, **34**.

Griffin, Keith (1970), 'Foreign Capital, Domestic Savings and Economic Development', *Bulletin of the Oxford University Institute of Economics and Statistics*, **32** (2).

Grinols, Earl and Jagdish Bhagwati (1976), 'Foreign Capital, Savings and Dependence', *Review of Economics and Statistics*, **58**.

Harrell-Bond B.E. (1986), *Imposing Aid: Emergency Assistance to Refugees*, Oxford: Oxford University Press.

Heller, Peter S. (1975), 'A Model of Public Fiscal Behavior in Developing Countries: Aid, Investment and Taxation', *American Economic Review*, **65** (3).

Levy, Brian (1987), 'Foreign aid in the making of economic policy in Sri Lanka 1977–83', Williams College Center for Development Economics Research, Memorandum No. 106, Williamstown.

Levy, Victor (1987), 'Does Concessionary Aid Lead to Higher Investment Rates in Low-Income Countries?', *Review of Economics and Statistics*, **69**.

Levy, Victor (1988), 'Aid and Growth in Sub-Saharan Africa: the recent experience', *European Economic Review*, **32**.

Madeley, John (1991), *When Aid Is No Help: how projects fail and how they could succeed*, London: Intermediate Technology Publications.

Massell, B.F., S.R. Pearson and J.B. Fitch (1972), 'Foreign Exchange and Economic Development: an empirical study of selected Latin American countries', *Review of Economics and Statistics*, **54**.

McGillivray, Mark and Theo Papadopoulos (1991), 'Foreign capital inflows, taxation and public expenditure: a preliminary analysis of the case of Greece', Deakin University Faculty of Commerce, Working Paper No. 9108, Geelong.

Michalopoulos, Constantine, Anne O. Krueger and Vernon W. Ruttan (eds), (1989), *Aid and Development*, Baltimore: Johns Hopkins University Press.

Moser, Caroline (1987), 'Approaches to community participation in urban development programmes in Third World countries', in Michael Bamberger (ed.), *Readings in Community Participation*, vol. 2, Washington DC: EDI, World Bank.

Mosley Paul and R.P. Dahal (1985), 'Lending to the poorest: early lessons from the Small Farmers' Development Programme in Nepal', *Development Policy Review*, **3**.

Mosley, Paul, John Hudson and Sara Horrell (1987), 'Aid, the Public Sector and the Market in Less Developed Countries', *Economic Journal*, **97**.

Norton, George, Jaime Ortiz and Philip Pardey (1992), 'The impact of foreign assistance on agricultural growth', *Economic Development and Cultural Change*, **40**.

Papanek, Gustav (1972), 'The Effects of Aid and Other Resources Transfers on Savings and Growth in Less Developed Countries', *Economic Journal*, **82**.

Porter, Doug, Bryant Allen and Gaye Thompson (1991), *Development in Practice: Paved with Good Intentions*, London: Routledge.

Rana, Pradumna R. (1987), 'Foreign Capital, Exports, Savings and Growth in the Asian Region', *Savings and Development*, **1**.

Riddell R. (1987), *Foreign Aid Reconsidered*, London: James Curry.

Salman, Larry (1987), *Listen to the people: participant–observer evaluation of development projects*, New York: Oxford University Press for the World Bank.

Serven, Luis and Andres Solimano (1992), 'Private Investment and Macroeconomic Adjustment: a Survey', *World Bank Research Observer*, **7** (1).

Voivodas, Constantin S. (1973), 'Exports, Foreign Capital Inflows and Economic Growth', *Journal of International Economics*, **3**.

White, Howard (1992a), 'The Macroeconomic Impact of Development Aid: a critical survey', *Journal of Development Studies*, **28** (2).

White, Howard (1992b), 'What do we Know About Aid's Macroeconomic Impact?', *Journal of International Development*, **4** (2).

White, Howard (1992c), 'Aid and Government: a Dynamic Model of Aid, Income and Fiscal Behaviour', *Journal of International Development* (forthcoming); also published as ISS Working Paper No. 126.

White, Howard (1992d), 'Should we expect aid to increase economic growth?', ISS Working Paper, No. 127, The Hague.

White, Howard (1992e), 'Foreign aid, taxes and public investment: a further comment', (mimeo).

White, Howard and Mark McGillivray (1992), 'Aid, the Public Sector and Crowding In' ISS Working Paper, No. 126, The Hague.

White, Howard and Ganeshan Wignaraja (1992), 'Aid, Trade Liberalisation and the Real Exchange Rate: the Case of Sri Lanka', *World Development*, October; forthcoming.

White, John (1974), *The Politics of Foreign Aid*, London: Bodley Head.

World Bank (1989), *Sub-Saharan Africa: From Crisis to Sustainable Growth*, Washington DC.

8 The end of the Cold War and Japan's financial contribution to international development

Toshihiko Kinoshita

I Introduction

Although the Cold War ended amid global blessings, the general view on the future prospects of developing countries and the former Centrally Planned Economies (CPEs) does not seem so bright at the moment as uncertainties grow. It may appear somewhat strange, therefore, to see the latest IMF bullish estimates of 6.2 per cent growth in real GDP for developing countries for both 1992 and 1993, up from 3.2 per cent in 1990, and far higher than those of industrial nations for the same period, estimated at 1.7 and 2.95 per cent, respectively.

These estimates by no means guarantee that developing countries sharing 15 per cent of the world's Gross Social Product (GSP) have entered a new period of stabilized higher economic growth. With the important exception of some East and South-east Asian nations as the world's 'Growth Centre', some Asian Gulf and a few reviving Latin American countries, 40–50 highly indebted countries out of some 80 low- or lower-middle-income countries with per capita incomes below $2400 in 1989 continue to have a hard time, for instance, servicing external debt. Although it is true that recent lower international interest rates and the not-so-low import growth rates in developed nations (particularly the USA) are having a positive impact on debt payment and economic growth rates of the Third World as a whole, such a favourable situation may not continue for long.

A handful of heavily indebted Latin American countries, Brazil currently in a political mess being an exception, seem to be rebounding from the 'lost decade' of the 1980s, as a result of the 'strengthened debt strategy' (or 'Brady Plan'), improved macroeconomic management and the efforts of 'structural adjustment' in line with the IMF and the World Bank. Yet there remain many domestic and external problems. Few would predict high economic growth for South Asian and Caribbean countries (over, say, 5 per cent annually) in the coming decade. Those heavily debt-ridden, poorest developing countries like most in Sub-Saharan Africa fare even more miserably. The results of structural adjustments undertaken by them prove to be far from satisfactory and their recent terms of trade, among the worst in the post-Second World War period may long continue.

The former CPEs have recently set out to become market economies. Their economic performance, however, is worse than expected. The IMF estimates their growth rates will be −16.8 per cent in 1992 and −4.5 per cent in 1993. Furthermore the states of the former USSR are facing hyperinflation. These are the costs of basic political, economic and social reform, however. The general bearish prospects for most of these developing and newly-reforming ex-COMECON countries are attributable to the probable delay of the 'peace dividend', a prolonged economic slump in major industrialized nations, difficulties in negotiating the Uruguay Round and an increasingly inward-looking manner in many developed nations fostering protectionism and/or regionalism.

While Germany is facing the formidable costs of reunification, Japan has become the only G-7 country with a current account surplus and is now the world's top donor of Official Development Assistance (ODA), having surpassed the USA, always the top donor until recently. The Japanese have acknowledged that they must decide how to respond to growing external expectations and problems. The supply of money, technologies and ideas which has to be shared with the world will be a major issue. Various domestic pressures to the contrary must not be underestimated, however.

The author as a practitioner (within a personal capacity) gives below an overview of Japan's past 'economic cooperation' through official and private sources with special reference to ODA, examines problems to be solved and suggests the direction to be pursued. Therefore this chapter focuses on four points: Japan's financial flows to developing countries and ODA, her contribution to the alleviation of debt in developing countries, the global shortage of capital and, as a concluding remark, Japan's financial contribution.

II   Japan's financial flows to developing countries and ODA

Recent trends
Japan has recently become the biggest ODA donor. In 1991, Japan's ODA reached $11 billion, followed by the USA ($9.6 billion) and Germany ($6.7 billion). ODA is the stable mainstream of total net financial flows from Japan to developing countries (see Table 8.1). Total official and private flows fluctuate from year to year, largely influenced by yen–US dollar exchange rates. The share of private flows is around half, except in 1990, when it fell to one-third. It is mainly due to a large amount of FDI ($5–11 billion annually). ODA represents a major portion of money from official sources. 'Other Official Flows' (OOF), as opposed to ODA, fluctuate sharply. The

1988 figure of OOF was negative because of the repayment of enormous export credits and a smaller supply of new export credits. A significant amount of 'direct investment and others' should be noted in OOF currently comprising mainly untied direct loans from the Export–Import Bank of Japan (Japan EXIM) to developing countries (see Section III for details).

Table 8.1   *Japan's net flows to developing countries*

		(Net disbursements, US$ million)		
	1988	*1989*	*1990*	*1991*
I ODA	9 134	8 965	9 222	11 034
1 Bilateral	6 422	6 779	6 940	8 870
(1) Grants	2 908	3 037	3 019	3 395
(Grant assistance)	(1 483)	(1 556)	(1 374)	(1 525)
(Technical assistance)	(1 425)	(1 481)	(1 645)	(1 870)
(2) Loans	3 514	3 741	3 920	5 475
2 Multilateral	2 712	2 186	2 282	2 163
Percentage of GNP	0.32	0.31	0.31	0.32
II Other official flows (OOF)	−639	1 544	3 470	2 699
1. Export credits (over 1 year)	−1 838	−1 245	−1 028	−510
2. Direct investment and others	1 410	1 892	4 209	3 155
3. Flows to multilaterals	−211	897	290	54
Official development finance (ODF) (I+II.2+II.3)	10 333	11 754	13 721	14 243
III Private Flows	12 822	13 502	6 262	11 142
1. Export Credits (Over 1 year)	219	687	−14	602
2. Direct investment	8 190	11 290	8 144	5 003
3. Other bilateral securities & claims	2 830	1 289	−2 581	6 227
4. Flows to multilaterals	1 583	236	711	−690
IV Grants by private voluntary agencies	107	122	103	168
Total flows (I+II+III+IV)	21 423	24 133	19 057	25 043
Percentage of GNP	0.75	0.85	0.64	0.73
GNP (US$ hundred million)	28 669	28 366	29 629	33 912

Notes
Exchange rate (specified by DAC) per 1 US$: 1988: ¥128.15; 1989: ¥137.96; 1990: ¥144.80; 1991: ¥134.50.
Figures do not necessarily add up because of rounding.
Grant assistance includes administrative costs and support for NGOs.

Sources: Ministry of Foreign Affairs, *Japan's Official Development Assistance, Annual Reports*, 1990 and 1991, Tokyo. For 1991 (preliminary): Ministry of Finance, press release (5 October 1992).

It is important to note that Japan's Official Development Finance (ODF), defined by the OECD as ODA and OOF except export credits on an official basis, has increased steadily over time.

Salient features and criticism of Japan's ODA

ODA has been treated as 'the sacred area' in Japan's government budget making. In spite of budgetary constraints, therefore, the government has tried to attain the Fourth Mid-Term Target (MTT) for ODA (FY1988–92), aimed at increasing it to more than $50 billion from the actualized $25 billion of the Third MTT (1983–7). Opposition parties in the Diet have not generally denounced increases in ODA, though they have always been critical of the decision-making process involved, its use and its effect on recipients. Overall, ODA has increased very rapidly (see Table 8.2).

There are surely just and unjust criticisms both at home and abroad of Japan's ODA, whose salient features are sometimes criticized as being inferior to critics' desires. The 'lack' of a clear ODA philosophy is the first point. Mass media often use the word 'Faceless Great Donor' for Japan. It is true to some extent that the basic rationale of Japan's ODA has been obscure, although the Japanese government regards humanitarian considera-

Table 8.2   Japan's ODA performance, 1977–91

	ODA (US$ mn)	Increase (%)	ODA/GNP (%)	DAC average ODA/GNP(%)	ODA (¥ bn)	Increase (%)
1977	1 424	28.9	0.21	0.33	382	16.7
1978	2 215	55.5	0.23	0.35	466	21.9
1979	2 638	19.1	0.26	0.35	578	24.0
1980	3 304	25.3	0.31	0.37	749	29.6
1981	3 171	–4.0	0.27	0.35	699	–6.6
1982	3 023	–4.7	0.28	0.38	753	7.7
1983	3 761	24.4	0.32	0.36	893	18.6
1984	4 319	14.8	0.34	0.36	1 026	14.8
1985	3 797	–12.1	0.29	0.35	906	–11.7
1986	5 634	48.4	0.29	0.35	950	4.8
1987	7 454	32.3	0.31	0.35	1 078	13.5
1988	9 134	22.5	0.32	0.36	1 171	8.6
1989	8 965	–1.8	0.31	0.33	1 237	5.7
1990	9 222	2.9	0.31	0.35	1 335	8.0
1991	11 034	19.6	0.32	n.a.	1 473	12.2

Sources: see Table 8.1

tions and recognition of interdependence as its two basic aid rationales (Ministry of Foreign Affairs, 1991, p. 18). These represent the core of two famous reports on ODA – the Pearson Report of 1969 and the Brandt Committee's Report in 1980 (Matsuura, 1992, p. 1). Some Japanese officials used to assert, albeit informally, that no sophisticated rationale was necessary and that it was common sense that counted in their decision making. However, with Japan's ODA capacity being strengthened, rising global financial needs when a worldwide shortage of capital is expected in the coming years and, more important, the need increasingly felt by ordinary Japanese to deliver the right message to recipients and to express their willingness to share common values with the rest of the world, determination of an ODA rationale became indispensable. It is in this context that the government formulated the ODA guidelines announced in April 1991 and the so-called 'Japanese ODA Charter' in June 1990. The guidelines call for full attention to be paid to the trends of potential recipients in (1) military expenditures, development and production of weapons of mass destruction, exports and imports of arms, (2) efforts to democratize, (3) introduction of a market economy and (4) the status of human rights and personal freedom. Since the guidelines and the charter bind the government in concrete cases, their formation might well be assessed as an epoch-making achievement.

The second prevalent criticism is that ODA is too commercially motivated. As will be explained later, it is far less so now. But it is more economically oriented. The term 'commercially motivated' gives the impression that aid policy is strongly influenced by domestic commercial interests, while 'economically oriented' implies that higher priority is given to allocating aid money to support the recipient's 'economic' development. Promotion of the latter concept, such as generalizing 'untied' aid, sometimes causes conflicts with domestic commercial interests. Every donor consciously or unconsciously tends to pursue its various ideals through official aid. Some donors have encouraged recipients to become culturally similar to them, though this is not the line Japan has pursued. Thus every donor has its own style.

US official aid has been clearly strategy-oriented, with various lobbies pursuing their own goals, although concrete objectives were philosophically diversified in the early 1970s when a part of ODA was modified by the concept of Basic Human Needs (Yamazawa and Hirata, 1992, pp. 123–5). Evidently this represents an extension of domestic politics. In so far as US ODA is not necessary for commercial interest but rather is politically and socially motivated, it may well be considered less economically oriented than Japan's. While a small portion of Japanese aid was used for strategic purposes until recently, US economic aid has been largely linked with its strategic aims. However some US food aid represents domestic commercial interests. British and French ODA has been concentrated on their former colonies with a higher share of grant aid. No one can deny that it is partially commercially oriented. More than half of Britain's and France's ODA in 1989 was tied to their own goods and services. However, as the mode or explicit aim of their aid is rather different from those of Japanese ODA, one can also claim that theirs is more culture-oriented and more philanthropic.

Japan's aid programme started in the latter half of the 1950s, aimed at promoting exports with rigidly tied loans. Until the 1980s it was literally commercial and in sharp contrast to the aid of most other industrial nations. It is evident, however, that Japan's ODA is far less commercially motivated nowadays. Different approaches based on various objectives have been sought for years. Japan's untying status (the ratio of the general–untied portion of total bilateral ODA) has become one of the highest among Development Assistance Committee (DAC) member countries. Its ratio is around 80 per cent for 1989–91, according to the DAC Chairman's Reports. The figure of 81.9 per cent for 1990 ranks second only to that of New Zealand, which follows a policy of 100 per cent untiedness. For reference the ratios of the other major donors in 1989 were 34.9 (USA), 24.0 (UK), 47.8 (France), 9.1 (Italy) and 54.8 (West Germany in 1988). The ratio of Japanese firms winning the bidding for the use of soft yen loans fell sharply and steadily from 55 per cent in FY 1985 to 27 per cent in FY 1990. Considering these firms' international competitiveness it may well be said that bids on Japan's ODA loans are now quite, if not completely, open. Taking Japan's basic human needs-related economic aid granted to alleviate poverty as a further example, the share of such aid reached 22.0 per cent in 1991, while aid related to human resources development, primarily in the area of technical cooperation, accounted for 14.7 per cent. Yet some commercial considerations still exist in Japan's ODA policy; for instance, Japan favours energy resource-rich areas, but this is also related to Japan's security problem.

As previously indicated, Japan is still strongly inclined to use her ODA to foster the recipient's economic advancement. It seems that most Japanese politicians and other ODA decision makers find it easier to justify ODA to taxpayers, saying aid will encourage the recipient's economic development, thereby improving the welfare of its people and eventually the world's, rather than simply saying it is Japan's duty to give money to poor nations. Hard-hit in the Second World War the first thing Japan did was to rehabilitate her economic infrastructure and factories with US financial assistance. This post-war experience in a densely populated country, poorly endowed with natural resources, and the long path of hard toil since the Meiji Restoration in 1868, modernizing the country from a semi-developing country stage (in 1870, Japan's per capita income was only one-seventh that of the USA) are deeply imbedded in people's minds. It may unconsciously drive them to think that only those in hardship who are making earnest self-help efforts might well be given assistance (which does not preclude exceptions, however) even though they would not go as far as to say that those who do not work should not eat.

Geographical concentration on Asia is another controversial feature of Japan's bilateral aid. This might well be compared with similar geographical traits of the UK or France, concentrating their ODA (some 60 per cent) on their former colonies. Since major portions of US aid have been allocated to Israel, Egypt, Pakistan and other strategically important countries, it is more diverse geographically. Most Latin American countries have not been selected as major recipients of US ODA, mainly because of their relatively high per capita incomes. The high share of Japan's ODA going to Asia stems from the initial export-oriented aid policy of the 1950s and certain security concerns for the region's political stability. Over time the strong regional linkage with Asia began to give way to other objectives. Yet, as many of Asian per capita incomes are still low and the Japanese government wishes to continue a de facto 'good neighbour policy', Asia's share of Japan's ODA, though declining gradually, has been around 50–60 per cent. In FY 1990 it was 51.0 per cent, while the Middle East, Africa and Latin America received 20.4, 11.4 and 9.5 per cent, respectively. Highly populated Asia is by far the largest beneficiary, but the figures show that Japan's ODA now covers the entire Third World (and from now on, will include some ex-CPEs), keeping pace with the globalization of Japanese diplomacy in response to the changing international situation. Most ASEAN countries and South Asian countries have misgivings that, at their expense, a greater share of Japan's ODA will be allocated to other areas because of international politics since the end of the Cold War.

The third often criticized feature of Japan's ODA is its 'low quality'. Both the share of grants (including debt relief) and the 'grant element' of total ODA are used to measure the 'softness' of aid. As a matter of fact Japan ranks as one of the lowest among DAC nations (with her grant ratio of 52.2 per cent in 1989, for instance: MITI, 1992, p. 32). A lower grant ratio resulting in a lower overall grant element seems to reflect somewhat Japan's inclination towards an economic development orientation, as evidenced by, *inter alia*, the frequent assertion of Japanese decision makers that ODA terms should be decided in the light of the development stage of recipients and that a relatively higher share of loans might be allocated to economic infrastructure. Efforts have been made to improve the situation. The average interest rate of yen ODA loans fell to 2.54 per cent in FY 1990, from 2.70 per cent in FY 1988 and 2.69 per cent in FY 1989. The grant element consequently rose to 59.9 per cent in FY 1990, up by 1.6 per cent from the previous year. The overall grant element of Japan's ODA in 1989 jumped to

80.1 per cent from 72.5 per cent in 1988, but it still failed to meet the DAC's norm of 86 per cent. In money terms grant aid reached $3.5 billion in 1992, a 12 per cent increase over 1991.

Including some of the issues raised above, there are many factors of Japan's policy background and ODA implementation which could and should be re-examined and improved. However it is also true that Japan's ODA has begun to be better understood both by recipients and other donors, including IFIs. Currently another issue of vital importance is global environmental problems. Recognizing that it can play a leading role in this area, the Japanese government announced at the Arche Summit in 1989 that it would increase bilateral and multilateral environmental aid to ¥300 billion during the three years of FY 1989–91. Actually the target was almost achieved in the first two years (¥129.4 billion in FY1989, ¥165.4 billion in FY 1990). At the United Nations Conference on Environment and Development (UNCED) in June 1992, the government stated that it would further expand environmental aid to some ¥0.9 to 1 trillion during the five years of FY 1992–96. Aid coordination in this field would be necessary and very constructive.

III   Japan's contribution to the alleviation of debt problems

The Japanese government has striven to direct its ODF and private-sector funds to the Third World under a special programme. The details of this Japanese initiative emphasizing the alleviation of developing countries' debt pressure may not be so well known or understood, except by specific people in the governments and public sectors of recipient countries, DAC member countries and IFIs.

The 'Capital Recycling Programme', so named in 1987, actually began in the autumn of 1986 with a $10 billion component as an additional contribution to IFIs, namely the establishment of the Japan Special Fund to support technical assistance within the World Bank, a $2.6 billion contribution to the eighth replenishment of IDA, a $1.3 billion contribution to the fourth replenishment of the Asian Development Bank (ADB) and 3 billion SDRs (special drawing rights) in government loans to the IMF. It evolved into the '$30 billion package' over a three-year period beginning in May 1987 with the already mentioned $10 billion component included (see Table 8.3). It was Tokyo's initiative to supply additional funds on top of the already planned Third MTT of ODA and other financial flows, aimed at alleviating debt payment pressure and supporting economic development of Third World countries in general (Kinoshita, 1991, 1992; Islam, 1991, pp. 62–8).

The Third World 'debt crisis' emerging in 1982 became more serious in the mid-1980s. This happened when the real interest rate on the US dollar soared as a result of the Federal Reserve's contraction policy, which brought about the capital flight of dozens of billions of dollars from Mexico and

Table 8.3   Japan's Capital Recycling Programme 1987–92

	(A) US$30 billion programme 1987–1990 (3 years) (US$ billion)	(B) Enhanced portion (target amount) mid-1989–1992 (3 years)	Total 1987–1992 (5 years)
I Japan EXIM's untied loans (incl. cofinancing by commercial banks)	around 10	13.5 (8)*	23.5
II OECF's untied loans	around 5.5	7 (2)*	12.5
III Budgetary contributions, supplemental private cooperation with development banks	around 14.5	14.5	29
Total	30**	35	65 (10)*

Notes:
*Including (sums) for countries to which the *strengthened debt strategy* is applied.
**Nearly actualized in 1987–mid-1989.

other big debtors, and drastic increases in their interest payments. The world's biggest debtor, Brazil, along with Argentina, the Philippines and other major heavily-indebted developing countries, followed Mexico one after another. In 1983, 29 countries, including 13 in Latin America, had to reschedule their debts. The general optimistic idea of the 'liquidity problem' faded away as no promising signs of recovery appeared for a couple of years. The net transfer of financial resources became negative after 1984 up to 1989, for commercial banks in industrial nations, notably 'money centre banks' which used to be the biggest lenders to middle-income countries in the 1970s, began to suspend or curtail their supply of new money substantially. There arose a misgiving that an overall collapse or a moratorium by major debtors might occur without a coordinated and effective action, which would cause catastrophe in the world financial system.

The conventional prescription for countries in default, though not very frequently used between 1945 and 1982, was to reschedule debt payments subject to severe IMF conditionalities, which proved to be ineffective for many big debtors at this stage. In September 1985, James Baker, Secretary of the Treasury, announced the Baker Plan. It called for the strengthening of the role of the World Bank and the Inter-American Development Bank (IDB), for new money from commercial banks, with the IMF as an active player urging 15 (later 17) heavily indebted countries to adopt structural adjustment measures including the adoption of 'privatization' and 'export-oriented' policies, thereby attaining 'sustainable economic growth'. The concept of more growth rather than contraction to ameliorate the current situation was a transformation of the way of thinking. The Japanese government promptly agreed to the proposal. The $10 billion recycling programme announced in 1986 was just to support it, an additional $20 billion programme following in 1987.

The Japanese government recognized a necessity effectively to hasten the recycling of its funds for the rest of the world, mainly because its current account surplus began to grow rapidly, from $35 billion (2.8 per cent of GNP) in 1984 to $85.9 billion (4.3 per cent) in 1986. In 1986 the government announced that it would lead Japan towards a domestic demand-driven economy in line with the 'Mayekawa Report'. The 'emergency economic measures' promulgated in May 1987 endorsed this plan by describing a concrete programme, and the $30 billion recycling programme was also included. Tackling the global debt overhang was not an easy task, however. Quick cooperative action on this issue was expected, though it was also foreseen that it would take some time to increase physical capacity, particularly the capacity for high-level economic analysis to scrutinize mainly the balance-of-payments support (or structural adjustment (SAL) type) loans for dozens of potential borrowers in the two implementing agencies. Furthermore it was made clear that export promotion should by no means be a target of this programme.

The government intended to favour cofinancing with IFIs, to implement the programme on a completely untied basis, and additional support to IFIs in Tokyo's capital market. Implementation agencies for Categories I and II were Japan EXIM (cofinanceable on a case-by-case basis with commercial banks in Japan) and Overseas Economic Cooperation Fund (OECF). Terms and sectors financed by the respective agency were to reflect the demarcation of its ordinary financial activities. Japan EXIM gives loans to eligible sectors (for instance manufacturing and energy-related industries) of recipients whose per capita income is relatively higher (most Latin American countries are included). Interest rates are non-concessional, loans generally for 10–20 years, roughly similar to those of IFIs. The reverse applies for OECF loans bearing ODA terms. Japan EXIM had seldom supplied untied loans before 1986, when it cofinanced a Colombian project with the World Bank. By 1987, OECF had refrained from providing quickly disbursed commodity credits which might bring about moral hazards without the use of very cautious programmes. It is notable that Japan's ODF comprising untied loans of this kind from Japan EXIM and OECF would not have increased as fast as shown in Table 8.1 without this recycling programme.

A drastic and qualitative change in the international debt strategy was seen in 1989. The macroeconomic performance of highly indebted middle-income countries had not improved three years after the announcement of the Baker Plan. The strains of adjusting to the persistent foreign debt problem centred on increased politicization of the debt issue in many countries. For instance, a violent riot occurred in Venezuela in February 1989. On 10 March, N. Brady, US Secretary of the Treasury, proposed a new epoch-making debt strategy, often called the Strengthened Debt Strategy, or simply the Brady Plan. Its concept is that, if highly indebted middle-income countries conclude an agreement with the IMF, 'voluntary' (albeit under de facto official auspices) debt (service) reduction of commercial bank debts could take place. The concrete application was to be decided on a case-by-case basis, as in the Baker Plan. The Japanese government, having proposed a similar plan ('Miyazawa Plan') in 1988, offered prompt and strong support on various occasions, including the statement at the IMF interim committee meeting in April 1989 that Japan EXIM could provide up to $4.5 billion, financing parallelly with the IMF over the next several years.

By the end of June 1989, just two years after the announcement of the programme (one year ahead of target) $28.5 billion, or 94.5 per cent of total funds, had been committed. The pace of disbursement was also extremely fast compared with conventional lending, owing to the high proportion of quick disbursement lending such as policy-based lending (SAL) and local cost financing.

Consequently the Japanese government announced a major expansion of the programme at the Arche Summit in July 1989, namely, that it would scale up the total programme to $65 billion over the five years between 1987 to 1992 (see Table 8.3), more than doubling the original programme. Under the expanded recycling programme, a total of at least $10 billion will be committed by Japan EXIM ($8 billion) and OECF ($2 billion) to selected debtor nations which may be eligible for the new debt strategy. The $8 billion include (up to) $4.5 billion in IMF parallel lending.

Mexico became the first country to undergo an application of the strengthened debt strategy after the conclusion of an agreement with the IMF's Extended Fund Facility (EFF), a growth-oriented and outward-looking structural adjustment framework. It should be noted that commercial bankers agreed to choose one of three options: reduction of principal by 35 per cent, debt service reduction or suppling new money equivalent to a quarter of the old debt loanable in four years. The Paris Club agreed to reschedule $2.6 billion. IFIs decided to supply not only new money but additional money for so-called 'credit enhancement'. Japan EXIM offered $1.9 billion in new money for this operation in IMF parallel lending and cofinancing with the World Bank. Thus an overall debt reduction of $12.7 billion in present value (against the $48.1 billion debt to commercial banks) was successfully brought about and $1 billion in new money was committed. Similar operations continued with the Philippines, followed by Costa Rica, Venezuela and Uruguay. Through these operations some $20 billion in present value were reduced, worth almost one-quarter of the targeted old commercial banks loans. Together with IFIs, Japan EXIM contributed substantially to the operations for the Philippines ($300 million) and Venezuela ($600 million). This strengthened debt strategy has proved to be mostly successful. The confidence of foreign and domestic investors has increased. Money once flowing out of these countries has begun to flow back.

Besides robust financial support from Japan to heavily indebted middle-income countries, centred on Latin America, dozens of developing countries in Asia, the Middle East and Africa have been beneficiaries of the Capital Recycling Programme (see Table 8.4). This reflects the idea that money should be allocated globally in line with various objectives – for instance, to avoid moral hazard as much as possible by supporting such countries as India, Pakistan, Indonesia, Turkey, Algeria, Colombia and Hungary which are paying their debts on schedule without plunging into the need to reschedule. As of mid-1992, the total amount committed in this programme just surpassed the target of $65 billion.

It is the the the Japanese government's policy to continue contributing to the Third World and to Central and Eastern Europe in the same manner, though new target figures have not been revealed. It is unknown whether targets or some other guidepost will be announced again in the future.

IV   The global shortage of capital

Demand for and supply of international finance
Many organizations, including the IMF and the World Bank, have pointed out the global shortage of capital which will occur in the coming years. Japan's Economic Planning Agency (EPA, 1992, p. 41) estimated the global net capital shortage in 1993 to be $93 billion. However the real shortage is very difficult to assess. Assuming sustainable economic growth rates of, say, 5 per cent in the Third World, one can estimate total financial needs. Evidently requirements will not be fully met by foreign sources. EPA estimates show that the capital shortage will be $56 billion in developed countries and $37 billion in developing countries in 1993. Adding the expected financial needs of ex-CPEs, the amount needed will be far larger.

On the demand side the shortage may be attributable to many factors, such as the enormous costs of Germany's reunification, the continuing large fiscal

Table 8.4 Results of the Capital Recycling Programme 1982–92

Category	(A) Target	(B) Commitments	End of June 1992 (B)/(A)
	(US$ billion)		%
I Japan EXIM	23.5	23.7	100.9
II OECF	12.5	15.0	120.0
III Budgetary contributions and supplemental private cooperation with development banks	29.0	28.5	98.3
Total	65.0	67.2	103.4

(Breakdown of I and II (end of May 1992)

Category I (including cofinancing portion of commercial banks)*

Regionally

	cases	$ billion	%
Asia, Pacific	31	6.70	36.3
Middle East, Africa, Europe	19	3.12	17.0
Latin America	28	5.59	30.3
IMF's ESAF	1	3.04	16.4
Total	79	18.47	100.0

By ways of financing

Co-financing with

	cases	$ billion	%
World Bank	29	7.67	41.5
ADB	6	0.46	2.5
IDB	5	0.62	3.4
World Bank & ADB	3	1.13	6.1
World Bank & IDB	1	0.30	1.6
Parallel lending with IMF	3	1.60	8.7
Independent bilateral loans	32	3.65	19.8
Loan to IMF's ESAF	1	3.04	16.4
Total	80	18.47	100.0

Category II

Regionally

	cases	$ billion	%
Asia	60	7.90	52.4
Middle East, Africa	29	3.67	24.3
Latin America	29	3.36	22.3
Europe (Poland)	1	0.15	1.0
Total	119	15.09	100.0

Notes:

Some numbers may not add up due to rounding.

*Difference between $18.5 billion (end of May) and $23.7 billion (end of June): Japan EXIM's commitment of $7 billion to China (energy development loan).

deficit of the USA (an all-time high of 4.9 per cent of GDP, or $290 billion for FY1992) and the costs of democratization and economic reform in ex-CPEs, especially Russia, which is facing severe financial difficulties with external debt estimated at some $75 billion. Ex-CPEs were donors to allied developing countries until recently, but have now slashed their economic aid drastically and are asking their borrowers to repay as soon as possible.

On the supply side there are problems, such as the general reluctance of commercial banks to lend money again to Third World countries, particularly those where they had to reduce debts, and to ex-CPEs (BIS – Bank for International Settlements – regulations aggravate this trend) and the very prudent attitude of foreign investors in highly indebted countries, although some countries, such as Mexico, Venezuela and Chile have been rather successful in inducing foreign investment through good macroeconomic management and continuous structural adjustment. Consequently long-term external finance must come mainly from official sources (Ahmed and Summers, 1992, pp. 4–5).

It has become generally recognized that Germany will not be able to increase ODA substantially for the time being (if it does not in fact reduce it) because of severe fiscal constraints due to reunification; the new US government beginning early in 1993 will not be able to reduce its huge fiscal deficit substantially and some strategic portion of US ODA may be curtailed now because its importance was dramatically reduced with the end of the Cold War (Israel will remain the strategically most important country, though); and some European countries will reduce ODA to traditional African and Asian clients because of stringent fiscal situations. Sweden and Italy have already begun to slash theirs. Some countries, however, will take more action to favour new friendly countries in ex-CPEs, whom they regard as having the same historical origin.

Recommendable measures for donors and recipients

Donor side   First, the significance of the interdependence between developed and developing countries should be emphasized in order to eliminate the so-called 'aid fatigue'. Second, attempts should be made to raise the level of ODA as much and on as soft terms as possible. For that purpose donors should decrease fiscal deficits, if any and try to increase such OOF as ordinary funds of IFIs, bilateral untied and FDI-support loans, such as those of Japan EXIM and KfW of Germany, and export credits from export credit agencies (including officially supported insurance and guarantees). It should not be forgotten that most of the financial needs of ex-CPEs (except the former USSR's Central Asian states) and those developing countries with relatively high per capita incomes will, if conditions are met, be funded by export credits and other OOF, not by ODA. Official technical assistance – mainly as ODA – will be an exception, however. Third, there should be continuing special programmes (for instance New Toronto Scheme, a more concessional debt-relief plan) to support the poorest severely indebted developing countries, centring on Sub-Saharan countries mainly indebted to official sources. For a long-term strategy, the steady investment in primary education to which donors might allocate more funds will be most important. Technical collaboration should also be intensified, particularly in agriculture to secure food supply.

Recipient side First, domestic savings should be mobilized by all possible means. Local governments can play a catalytic role so that small depositors, for instance, can save at nearby financial institutions safely and easily. Needless to say, good service, security and the protection of clients' secrets are indispensable. Economic reforms are the fundamental self-help efforts by which donors' official aid is justified domestically. Second, best efforts should be made to induce FDI. Successful experiences in East and Southeast Asia could be quite a good reference for other developing countries. A continuing South–South dialogue will be quite effective in exchanging opinions on how to build up good investment climates for foreign and domestic investors.

Other actions and considerations

It is now crucial to provide as much private and official money as possible for economic growth, structural adjustment and the alleviation of debt pressures (including rescheduling) for the Third World and ex-CPEs. However it is no less important to maintain the free multilateral trading system for all. The IFI prescription of export-oriented policies for developing countries will only be effective as long as the free trade system, which steadily increases world trade, is maintained. Therefore the Uruguay Round must end successfully, *inter alia* with regard to agricultural trade.

It is true that debt reduction for selective countries has been successful and that similar operations have been and will be adapted in somewhat different ways to the poorest developing countries. However one should not forget moral hazard. These operations have forced commercial banks to slash dramatically their lending to the Third World. Also some donor governments experience 'aid fatigue' when responding to the worse than expected scenario. The basic principle that borrowed money must be repaid as originally contracted is a foundation of modern lending. Exceptions should be exceptions. The past debt crisis of middle-income countries could be regarded as a kind of 'government failure' by borrowers and 'market failure' by lenders based on logical reasons: limitless growth of the Eurodollar market in the 1970s due to huge inflows of oil dollars, evolution of financial technologies in private banking, fallibility of forecasts such as general expectations of very low or even negative future real interest rates, the selection of the wrong growth strategy and the easy-going attitude regarding external borrowing in many developing countries. There was another reason, namely the rapid deterioration of the balance of payments of non-oil producing countries when international oil prices soared twice in the 1970s. But this was not necessarily decisive. Oil exporters like Mexico became big debtors, while many Asian oil importers attained high growth without serious debt problems. Repetition of similar market and government failures should not be allowed. Structural adjustment policies urging quicker deregulation, including privatization of state enterprises, may not ensure that they will not happen again. Now that rather large-scale capital inflows are seen in some big Latin American debtors (mainly to their private sectors) both private and official debt should be administered properly. IFIs could work well in this area by setting up, for example, an early warning system for both lenders and borrowers. Should this principle be accepted worldwide, commercial lending to the Third World in a healthy way will become very popular.

Together with the recipient's authorities, private lenders and investors should devise ways to support newly-born privatized enterprises in developing and ex-COMECON countries. Sometimes these firms are financially too fragile for foreign (or even domestic) lenders or investors. IFIs, including the new European Bank for Reconstruction and Development (EBRD), and other official lenders are having a hard time coping with such fragility. Local governmental financial institutions or first-class banks are expected to intermediate financial transactions.

V   Concluding remarks: Japan's financial contribution
Japan could remain the top ODA donor in the 1990s, until the EC, not its members, supplies all European ODA or until drastic increases in the 'peace dividend' enable a rapid increase in US ODA. The approach of the 'ageing society', the bursting of the 'bubble economy' resulting in a drastic fall in tax revenues in Japan and the general lack of enthusiasm about aid to the Third World in North America and Western Europe are influencing Japanese decision makers. The number of Japanese who do not wish to increase ODA (currently about 20 per cent of the world's total) seems to be increasing. However the government and the majority of Japanese feel it their duty to play an active role as a donor. After serious discussion, the government will decide to increase its ODA level, though at a lower pace than in the 1980s. The objectives of Japan's ODA from now on will be more diversified as more attention will be paid to solving problems such as aids, immigrants,

refugees and drugs, as well as the global environment. The de facto 'good neighbour policy' of ODA will continue even so.

Meanwhile Japan has committed herself to supporting the former CPEs in various ways. For Central and Eastern European countries, further efforts are being made by Japan EXIM to realize cofinancing with the EBRD and to support possible – eagerly awaited – Japanese direct investments. Main commitments and forthcoming financial contributions already announced are as follows. For Hungary, Japan EXIM had disbursed a $200 million untied loan, cofinancing with the World Bank's SAL, before August 1991, when it committed a $150 million untied loan of the same character in August 1991. Japan EXIM committed a $200 million untied loan to Czechoslovakia in December 1991, cofinancing with the World Bank's SAL. Basic agreements were reached with Bulgaria and Romania that Japan EXIM would loan around $100 million to each country, cofinancing with the World Bank's SAL. Japan EXIM is ready to consider a total loan of $100 million to the Baltic States, cofinancing with the World Bank's Rehabilitation Loan, subject to the approval of the IMF's stand-by arrangement. EXIM's mission was sent there in October 1992. As for the former USSR, Japan's policy towards Russia is strongly determined by the 'North Islands problem', which should be solved. The government announced in December 1990 that Japan EXIM would provide $100 million in export credits for humanitarian support (the loan agreement was signed in October 1992). It announced in October 1991 a $2.5 billion package plan, comprising an additional $500 million from Japan EXIM for humanitarian assistance for food, medicine, their transportation and $2 billion measures 'to smooth the trade activities' ($1.8 billion in export insurance and $200 million in loans by Japan EXIM). In January 1992 the government decided to supply $50 million (¥6.5 billion) of grants for food and so on, and followed this with two announcements that it would contribute $20 million to the National Science Technology Centre and give technical support of $25 million towards security measures for nuclear power stations. At the Tokyo Conference on Assistance to New Independent States (NIS) of the former USSR (29–30 October 1992) the government further announced additional grants of $100 million for humanitarian support by supplying food, medicine and so on to help during the winter. Foreign Minister Watanabe said that the previous $50 million grant aid had been expended, centring on the far-eastern part of Russia, and the new $100 million will be used similarly, with due consideration to the other NIS as well. Also he expressed Japan's wishes for a quicker realization of ODA to Tajikistan, Kazakhstan, Turkmenistan, Uzbekistan and Kyrgyzstan.

Although no new targets for the Capital Recycling Programme were announced when the programme's term ended in mid-1992, it is the government's policy to continue the flow of Japanese capital in the same manner.

Keeping a higher level of OOF will be crucial because big financial needs of indebted developing countries whose per capita incomes are relatively high shall be largely funded by official long-term credits on semi-commercial terms. Japan is expected to continue as one of their main sources on top of ODA.

The Japanese private sector has been a major investor in the form of FDI. East and South-east Asian countries have been major beneficiaries since the signing of the Plaza Accord, which caused the exchange rate of the yen to soar. They in turn began to export large amounts of manufactured goods such as colour televisions and other electric domestic appliances to Japan, in addition to a high level of conventional exports of textiles and clothing, which began to transform mutual trade patterns more horizontally. There is some potential interest in Japanese business circles in investing in Latin America and ex-CPEs. However they are wary of taking big risks. It is strongly expected, therefore, that effective measures will be taken by these potential beneficiaries to create better investment climates by (1) fostering political stability, (2) investment in necessary infrastructure and basic education by local governments, (3) adopting good macroeconomic management, and (4) not discriminating against FDI in favour of domestic investment. The Japanese government can contribute in some ways to support their efforts: first, by supporting infrastructure improvements with official funds; second, by providing technical assistance to modernize their capital and financial markets and legal structures; and third, by encouraging the active use of private-sector organizations providing information about investing in those countries (Nakahira, 1992 p. 13).

Last but not least, it is important that Japan is also expected to be a source of ideas for 'nation building' or comprehensive market-oriented reform for these countries. In addition to the transfer of technologies through official technical cooperation and FDI, it is frequently asserted that some ideas or know-how based on Japan's post-Second World War experiences and possibly those of East and South-east Asian countries could provide useful lessons to countries in difficult situations. It is certain that they have grown up in a market-friendly framework of intense competition and private property but also that a greater role for the government in economic activities is considered one of the strongest driving forces for their higher economic development in the past (Sakurai, 1992, pp. 17–19). This point, however, is controversial (see, for instance, Sweeney, 1992, p. 65). Some argue that such an assertion will encourage those resisting deregulation and make the situation worse. But it is also true that the often over-hasty enforcement of IFI 'laissez-faire' economic policies has raised questions. The World Bank for one is making a comprehensive study, titled 'Asian Miracle', on the impact of the greater role of government in Japan and other Asian countries, and heated dialogues continue. The author believes that, since many countries facing economic difficulties are also facing growing global uncertainties and a general lack of mature entrepreneurship, enforcement of a simple 'one-size-fits-all' doctrine may not necessarily be beneficial to different countries in different development stages, as has been shown in the poorest countries of Africa. How to create and intensify the basis of market mechanisms in different situations should be the main target. However more academic and empirical studies on Japan, Korea, Taiwan and Singapore are required before the application of a certain model, if any, to a given country. Adopting a given strategy, everyone should ponder very carefully international perspectives, the specific problems of the country and the existence of vested interests wishing to maintain the status quo.

Bibliography

Ahmed, Masood and Lawrence Summers (1992), 'A Tenth Anniversary Report on the Debt Issue', *Finance & Development*, **29** (3).

EPA (Economic Planning Agency) (1992), *Sekai keizai hakusyo shiryo-hen -heisei 3nenban-* (White Paper on World Economy: Series of Data for 1992), Tokyo.

Islam, Shafiqul (ed.) (1991), *Yen for development: Japanese Foreign Aid and the Politics of Burden-Sharing*, New York: Council on Foreign Relations Press.

Kinoshita, Toshihiko (1991), 'Development in the International Debt Strategy and Japan's Response', *Exim Review*, **10** (2).

Kinoshita, Toshihiko (1992), 'Ruiseki saimumondai to shikin kanryuu' (Debt problem and capital recycling), in Takatoshi Ito (ed.), *Kokusai kin'yuu no genjoo* (Current Situation of International Finance), Tokyo: Yuuhikaku.

Kohama, Hirohisa (1992), *Oda no keizaigaku* (Economics of Development Co-operation), Tokyo: Nihon Hyoronsha.

Lin, Ching-yuan (1989), *Latin America vs East Asia: A Comparative Development Perspective*, Armonk, NY, London: Sharpe.

Matsuura, Koichiro (1992), 'Japan's Aid Policy', speech (draft) at the Tokyo Workshop on US–Japan Partnership in Development Co-operation, 12–13 October.

Ministry of Foreign Affairs (1991), *Japan's Official Development Assistance 1990 Annual Report*, Tokyo.

Ministry of Foreign Affairs (1992), *Wagakuni no seifu kaihatsu enjo – 1991* (Japan's Official Development Assistance 1991 Annual Report) 2 vols, Tokyo.

MITI (Ministry of International Trade and Industry) (1992), *Keizai kyooryoku no genjo to mondaiten – heisei 3-nenban* (Current Situation and Problems of Economic Co-operation for 1991), Tokyo.

Nakahira, Kosuke (1992), 'Economic and Financial Co-operation in Asia and Pacific', keynote speech, EXIM Japan's Symposium, 28–9 October, Tokyo.

Sakurai, Makoto (1992), 'Economic Development in the 1990s: The Key Issues in Development and Development Policy', speech at the Tokyo Workshop on US–Japan Partnership in Development Co-operation, 12–13 October.

Sweeney, Paul (1992), 'The World Bank Takes Another Look at Its Priorities', *Global Finance*, **6** (9).

World Bank (1991), *World Development Report 1991*, Washington DC: Oxford University Press.

Yamazawa, Ippei and Hirata Akira (eds) (1992), *Nihon, Amerika, Yoroppa no kaihatsukyooryoku seisaku* (Development Co-operation Policies of Japan, the US and Europe), Research Institute of Developing Economies, Research Series no. 422.

9 New debt reduction techniques*

Stephany Griffith-Jones

I Introduction

This chapter will briefly argue in the following section that debt reduction in severely indebted low-income (SILICs) and low–middle-income countries (SILMICs) is needed. Section III will examine the techniques of commercial debt reduction, with reference to Latin America. Debt reduction techniques employed before the Brady Plan will be discussed, focusing on debt–equity swaps (DES), especially in Chile, where commercial DES are seen to have been most successful. Then we will examine debt reduction and other techniques introduced in the context of the Brady Plan. Special reference will be made to Mexico, seen as one of the most successful cases, especially in terms of broad objectives, such as restoration of creditworthiness and potential for economic growth. Fairly brief references to Venezuela and Costa Rica will be included, before we examine extra-Brady debt reduction techniques, such as buybacks, illustrated by Bolivia.

In Section IV we will briefly discuss the application of some of these techniques to official bilateral debt reduction and especially conversion. This is particularly relevant to the countries of Sub-Saharan Africa (SSA), as such a large proportion of their external debt is owed to official bilateral creditors and interesting new initiatives are opening up in this field. Section V draws brief conclusions.

II Need for debt reduction

The total stock of developing countries' external debt grew very rapidly between 1982 and 1991, particularly so in SILICs, whose total debt outstanding and disbursed (DOD) has more than doubled, from $79 billion to $175 billion. Total interest arrears of SILICs have also increased significantly, from $1.3 billion (1982) to $12.9 billion (1991), reflecting their growing incapacity to service debts.

Two factors make debt a greater burden for SILICs than for other highly indebted regions: far more severe poverty, which implies that output and income contractions linked to excessive debt overhang are particularly damaging in terms of human welfare; and greater structural weaknesses of those

*This chapter draws on a study prepared for United Nations Institute for Training and Research UNITAR.

economies, as well as their greater difficulty in adapting to changes in the international environment. As a result of these structural weaknesses and in some cases of mistaken policies, SILIC export performance was disappointing in the 1980s, with an annual average decline of 2 per cent, leading to a further deterioration in debt service and debt–export ratios (see Table 9.1). In the late 1980s both debt service and debt–export ratios were significantly higher in SILICs than in either 1980 or 1982. There is therefore an urgent need for greater debt reduction.

Table 9.1 Export growth and debt ratios

		Ratios					
	Export growth	*Debt service*			*Debt–export*		
	(1982–9, %)	*1980*	*1982*	*1989*	*1980*	*1982*	*1989*
SILICs	–2.0	10	20	23	96	214	493
SIMICs	3.5	36	49	29	196	297	294

Source: Based on World Bank (1992).

Severely indebted middle-income countries, by contrast, especially upper-middle-income ones, experienced a decline of total DOD in 1991, mainly as a result of declining private debt since 1988, reflecting the impact of Brady deals, as well as fairly large amounts of debt conversions, mainly for equity but also for development purposes. Second, SIMIC export performance during the 1980s was far better than for SILICs. Debt service ratios have declined quite substantially, even though they are still at a fairly high level. In 1992, debt has stopped being a constraint on growth and development for many SIMICs (such as Chile and Mexico). Surprisingly, overabundance of foreign exchange inflows and reserves has become the new source of concern (see Griffith-Jones *et al.*, 1992).

An important element explaining the increase in all developing countries' debt since 1982 is the very rapid rise of bilateral DOD, particularly in SILICs, where it rose from $32 billion (1982) to $80 billion, representing over 45 per cent of total debt in 1991. This rapid rise in bilateral debt occurred despite ODA debt cancellations of over $8 billion between 1983 and 1990 for SILICs, and the successive application of Toronto, Venice, Houston and now 'enhanced Toronto terms' in Paris Club agreements for SILICs and SILMICs. It is principally due to the effect of exchange rate changes since 1985 and interest capitalization practices of the Paris Club. A further source of concern is the increase in multilateral debt, especially in SILICs. Their outstanding debt obligations to multilaterals rose from around $11 billion to almost $35 billion during 1982–91. It is not clear what can and should be done to reduce the burden of multilateral debt (servicing), given the need to safeguard the creditworthiness of these institutions that allows them to exert valuable leverage, raising private funds with public funds of a significantly smaller size. However the large burden of multilateral debt service (and the difficulty of reducing it) further increases the need for action reducing/converting both SILIC and SILMIC official bilateral and commercial debt. These trends clearly suggest the need for bilateral debt (service) reduction beyond that envisaged in the 'enhanced Toronto terms' for SILICs and beyond that already granted to SILMICs.

Export credit agencies need to accept the same realities commercial banks have recognized, engaging not just in cancellation but also in conversion to reduce bilateral debt to realistically serviceable levels. Conversion options should particularly be used, not just in cases where debt reduction has been insufficient, but also where they would imply other gains (including those in efficiency) and where undesirable effects are marginal or can be easily counteracted by debtor government policy. Regarding official bilateral debt, a number of measures for debt reduction have and are being implemented for SILICs and SILMICs, but there is evidence that for an important number of them progress is still insufficient (see World Bank (WDT); Mistry, 1992). It is disappointing that neither the British proposal (Trinidad terms) by John Major nor the Dutch proposal by Jan Pronk were adopted by the Paris Club. The Paris Club consensus of December 1991 (already applied to Benin and Nicaragua) dilutes the Trinidad terms quite considerably. Under these 'enhanced Toronto terms', creditors can opt for: (1) cancellation of 50 per cent of eligible maturities being consolidated; (2) halving interest rates on non-concessional debt; (3) stretching export credit and concessional debt repayments further; or (4) capitalising reduced interest rates in a way equivalent in net present value. The Trinidad terms would have implied a much more significant step towards solving SSA's bilateral debt problems.

Because of insufficient action for SILICs on bilateral debt reduction, on help with servicing multilateral debt and even slower progress on commercial debt reduction (see Mistry and Griffith-Jones, 1992) there is great urgency in promoting far greater debt (service) reduction to levels sufficient to restore confidence in sustainable recovery. It is important that, as in the Latin American cases described below, sufficient reduction is accompanied by macroeconomic stabilization and economic restructuring (where necessary) to maximize the benefits of future growth.

III Techniques of commercial debt reduction with special reference to Latin America

Debt conversion programmes

Debt–equity swaps Debt–equity conversions of private bank debt have been extensively used during the last several years in a number of developing countries to reduce debt, promote foreign investment, encourage privatization and further other development objectives (Table 9.2).

Table 9.2   Volume of debt conversion, 1985–90*

	1985	1986	1987	1988	1989	1990	Total
	(US$ million)						
Argentina	469			764	1 180	7 038	9451
Brazil	537	176	336	2 095	942	483	4 569
Chile	323	974	1 997	2 927	2 767	1 096	10 084
Costa Rica		7	89	44	124	17	281
Ecuador			127	261	31	42	461
Honduras			9	14	47	32	102
Jamaica			4	5	16	23	48
Mexico		413	1 680	1 056**	532	435	4 116
Nigeria				70	304	217	591
Philippines		81	451	931	630	378	2 471
Uruguay				104	53		157
Venezuela			45	49	544	716	1 354
Total	1 329	1 651	4 738	8 320	7 170	10 477	33 685

*Official conversions (face value); without large-scale cash buybacks and debt exchanges
**Estimated prepayment of private debt at a discount of US$6–8 billion since August 1987 (related to signing of FICORCA restructuring agreement) not included.

Sources: Central banks of Argentina, Brazil, Chile, the Philippines, Jamaica, Venezuela, Mexico: Ministry of Finance; IMF.

The total volume of commercial debt extinguished through official programmes, $33.6 billion according to IMF estimates, is around 15 per cent of total commercial debt of all heavily indebted countries. Though debt conversions clearly did not lead to overcoming the debt overhang of most heavily indebted countries (except Chile's) they did make a meaningful contribution to debt reduction in several of them.

Reportedly (UNCTC, 1990) Brazil was the first Latin American country to establish a small, semi-formalized debt–equity programme. Argentina and Chile followed. The Chilean programme was sustained for a very long period without interruptions, led to major debt reduction and is widely regarded as a clear success. Since Chile established the first institutionalized programme in May 1985, many highly indebted countries (mostly in Latin America) have adopted similar schemes. After a rapid expansion of debt conversions in 1987 and 1988, *some* countries slowed down or suspended conversions because of concerns such as domestic monetary implications and the possible lack of additionality of investments. In other countries (especially Chile) debt conversions grew rapidly, until their very success reduced the stock of available debt to sell. The revival of DES in countries like Argentina, Mexico and the Philippines was largely linked to privatization, partly in response to potentially adverse inflationary effects. The advantage of debt conversions for privatization is that they do not lead to the monetization of foreign debt. Both fiscal and monetary expansionary impacts are avoided by privatizing publicly owned enterprises and swapping their equity. Furthermore if privatization leads to efficiency gains in loss-making enterprises the debtor government will gain from a reduction of external debt and of subsidies. However, if the government swapped debt for equity in currently profitable enterprises, the reduction in government income could have a future negative fiscal impact, although this case is perhaps less frequent.

Another factor explaining the recent expansion of debt conversion programmes is that several recent bank debt restructuring agreements (especially in the context of the Brady Plan), contain commitments of debtor countries to engage in DES. The increased use of market-based debt reduction techniques (especially DES) has been facilitated by and has in turn contributed to a marked growth in the secondary market. According to *Latin Finance*, the total trading volume of LDC debt reached around $100 billion in 1990. NMB, the largest European traders, estimates that real figures were at least $150 billion. This contrasts sharply with 1983 or 1984, when total trading in LDC debt reached $0.5 billion. Closely related to the dramatic increase in volume, a streamlining and simplification of procedures, particularly documentation, have occurred. All post-Brady bonds are perfectly tradeable and assignable documents. Procedures and documentation have by now become so simplified that trading can be done over the counter. As deals were initially so complex and there were so many who were sceptical about the secondary market's future, its impressive recent development may also show important potentials for significant *official* debt trading, especially for swapping debt for equity or development.

Reviewing experiences and literature on commercial debt conversion seems to lead to three broad conclusions. First, the economic effects of debt conversions are very heterogeneous amongst countries and sometimes in different periods within one country. Factors which seem to contribute to more positive results include (1) a stable macroeconomic environment, with low fiscal and quasi-fiscal deficits; (2) existing or parallelly developing domestic capital markets, which can attenuate or eliminate monetary effects (as was particularly well illustrated by Chile); (3) clarity of programme objectives; and (4) carefully designed programmes controlling problems, such as excessive monetary expansion or misuse ('round-tripping') of funds.

Second, DES yield valuable positive results if the policy framework, circumstances and programme design are right. Major reductions in commercial debt contributed very importantly to reducing Chile's debt overhang, helping the country to return to international capital markets. Elsewhere debt reduction has been far less meaningful, although Mexico and Venezuela have now returned to international capital markets too, this being an important objective of their debt strategy. It could be argued that for them debt conversions played some (though not a major) role. It should be stressed that other factors besides Brady context debt conversions played an important role in Mexico, including prudent domestic macroeconomic policies and external events such as the likely creation of NAFTA.

An important bonus of debt–equity conversions has in several cases been its helping to attract foreign direct investment (FDI) and the return of domestic flight capital. The literature debates how much FDI is additional. The answer depends on counter-factual assumptions. However, especially in some countries (again Chile, to a lesser extent Mexico), there is ample evidence to suggest that conversions have contributed directly and indirectly to accelerating the pace of foreign investment. The origin of FDI has diversified. Naturally the subsidy granted to investors had an important influence. Policy makers in countries like Chile stress that favourable publicity concerning the country's economic performance, a favourable business climate and economic openness generated by Chile's early adoption of debt conversion played an important indirect role. This 'kick-starting' of FDI to countries where previously both foreign and domestic investments were depressed was a very valuable bonus in middle-income countries, which could possibly be replicated in other, relatively poor countries. There are three important caveats. First, debt conversion will be effective in helping catalyse FDI and possibly other private (portfolio) flows if they are part of a policy package making the country attractive. Second, there may be some trade-off between applying criteria selectively to enhance positive development and macroeconomic effects – such as demanding new flows to accompany debt conversion, as in Argentina, and/or restricting the sectors for which DES can be used as in the Philippines – and the magnitude of conversions and FDI. Less selectivity and fewer preconditions achieve greater volumes, though development and macro impacts may have flaws. Greater selectivity may limit volumes but their development impact may be enhanced. Finally, and most important, it is not certain whether indirect positive FDI effects will occur to the same extent in low-income as they did in middle-income countries. Debt conversion can also be used as a vehicle facilitating the return of flight capital. A special window was opened in Chile for residents, giving a smaller subsidy than to foreigners but implicitly offering tax and legal amnesty.

To the extent that additional FDI goes into tradeables (especially if they bring along know-how, additional markets and more efficient technology) foreign exchange earning/saving will be promoted. There is evidence that important shares of FDI entering through debt conversions have gone into such activities. As pointed out above, conversion programmes have increasingly boosted privatization, providing an additional source of demand for equity. In some countries (such as Chile) debt conversion reduced the debts of state-owned enterprises, making them more attractive to potential private shareholders. Debt conversions need to be properly structured to avoid excessive subsidies to foreigners.

In countries such as Chile, Brazil and Ecuador the debt crisis coincided with and largely caused financial problems for the domestic private, especially the financial, sector. Debt conversion programmes helped strengthen it, particularly by lowering excessive debt levels. This strengthening of the private sector (and especially the banks) seems to have contributed to a recovery of domestic private investment.

Regarding all these positive effects, an important caveat should be made. A high degree of transparency in such operations is important to avoid excessive hidden subsidies either to foreign investors buying shares of privatized companies or to the domestic private sector, even if no subsidies were needed, as reportedly happened in Ecuador, Brazil and also Chile. Transparency and supervision prevent open corruption, making programmes domestically more attractive, increasing the likelihood that they will remain. Continuity of debt conversion programmes, as in Chile, seems to yield better results than stop–go experiences, as in Costa Rica or Jamaica.

The third conclusion is that, although swaps have important beneficial effects for debtor economies, they also have problematic effects, which can be partly or totally counteracted by efficient programme design and implementation. Monetary and fiscal effects with inflationary potential are meaningful if swaps are large, if debt is exchanged against local currency, if this issue is not regulated carefully in time, and if no compensatory measures are taken. If the scale of conversion is small relative to the money supply the problem is not meaningful. However experiences such as Brazil's illustrate that, in a context of high inflation and high budget deficits, conversions can accentuate an already serious problem. If conversion is made against bonds placed in domestic capital markets, the monetary impact is diminished, but there may be a negative effect on increased interest rates. Conversion against instruments such as bonds is only feasible in countries having or creating fairly deep domestic capital markets.

Net effects of conversions on balances of payments could be negatively accentuated if debt was previously not serviced fully, if there were considerable 'round-tripping', if foreign investment is not 'additional' and if the outflow of profit remittances and capital is higher than interest and amortization payments saved. Finally the important subsidy normally implied could lead to inappropriate allocation of resources, unless important net efficiency gains exist. The subsidy can be regulated by central banks, either through a market (auctioning, as in Chile, under Art. 18 used by residents) and/or through administrative measures, such as fixing a lower value for the local currency swapped per unit of debt (called redenomination rate).

Debt-for-development swaps   The growth of debt–equity programmes has been accompanied by increased interest in other forms of conversions, which can be broadly called debt-for-development swaps. Debt-for-nature swaps attracted most publicity and a large share of operations, largely reflecting priorities in developed countries and active lobbying by Northern environmental NGOs. However some other pioneering debt-for-development swaps have been carried out. Six banks donated their Sudanese debt (more than $20 million) to UNICEF. These operations allow for funding of high-priority social spending (from a developing country perspective).

Most frequently international charitable organizations or developed country governments purchase commercial debt at a discount, converting it into local currency instruments either at par or at a discount less steep than in the secondary market. Banks have also donated debt to an international NGO with the condition that it be 'paid' in local currency for previously agreed conservation or social purposes. Frequently other parties, such as financial intermediaries and local NGOs, are involved. The number of parties involved and differences in their objectives imply complexity and often administrative and other costs. This may be one of the important factors explaining the fairly limited scale of commercial debt-for-development transactions. Their total identified face value reached around US$ 485 million by April 1992. Assuming that some transactions have not been identified, the total could reach US$ 500–600 million. This sum could be increased fairly significantly by increased interest in these transactions. However it is incredibly small, representing around 2 per cent of total commercial DES, which have accumulated to around $38 billion by early 1992.

Until now at least they have not made a meaningful contribution to reducing the debt overhang and cannot be expected to. They have contributed marginally and have had a number of other positive effects (and some costs). Their greatest value lies in highlighting high priority areas in social and environmental spending, shifting resources to such areas (Mistry and Griffith-Jones, 1992).

Debt (service) reduction techniques and the Brady Plan

Examining the reasons making the previously almost taboo subject of debt reduction almost universally acceptable in 1989 and a key element in the US Treasury's new strategy seems worthwhile. First, impatience with adjustment and negative net transfers had clearly spread from relatively limited circles of intellectuals in debtor nations. Parties supporting a more radical stance on debt gained many votes or power. The riots in Venezuela in February 1989 illustrated the deep resistance to declining or stagnating living standards and investment levels since 1982. Increasingly these concerns were shared by creditor governments, international organizations, banks and public opinion in industrial countries. The need to sustain fragile young democracies and the need to provide hope to people in highly indebted countries were often quoted as reasons. A strong intellectual case was made by influential economists in the industrialized world, such as Paul Krugman, John Williamson and Jeffrey Sachs, that debt relief was in the economic interest of debtors and creditors. Excessive debt burdens are a disincentive for debtors to take painful or politically unpopular measures, as potential fruits would go mostly to creditors. Second, they pointed out that attempts to extract full contractual debt service risked confrontations from which both parties would lose. Excessive debt burdens have direct negative effects on the local economy, particularly via lower investment, higher taxation and higher inflation, but also indirect ones, for example by discouraging flight capital repatriation. By forgiving part of a country's debt, creditors may increase expected payments, increasing the incentive for orderly adjustment and desirable structural reforms.

The Brady Plan included a number of innovative elements. It explicitly recognized the need for commercial debt (service) reduction. Its second important element was that IMF and World Bank funds (plus governments contributions, particularly by Japan) were made available. A final innovative aspect was its recognition of the need to loosen existing legal, regulatory, tax and accounting constraints limiting the possibility of debt (service) reduction.

Evaluation of Brady deals   Mexico, Venezuela, Costa Rica and Uruguay are amongst Latin American countries that have already signed Brady deals. Rather than evaluating each in depth, we will put more emphasis on Mexico – the first deal where results can be assessed for a longer period and which influenced and will influence other deals – with some reference also to Costa Rica, because of its special characteristics.

Academic literature and ex post evaluation increasingly emphasized the *positive indirect effects* of what is widely accepted as a satisfactory deal, on both the domestic and the foreign private sector. A multi-annual deal not only reducing debt service, but also shifting amortizations for an important number of years was seen to reduce uncertainty and to provide confidence, for example regarding perceived exchange rate sustainability. It was hoped that a satisfactory deal would significantly lower high domestic interest rates, attract additional private flows not linked to the deal from abroad and encourage private capital to return. These indirect benefits on domestic interest rates and on capital flows have been especially positive in Mexico.

Total average cash flow savings for the 1990–94 period are estimated at $4.1 billion by the Ministry of Finance (Aspe, 1990). $2.1 billion thereof are due to restructuring of amortization, $0.3 billion to new money, and could have been achieved through the previous conventional restructuring process. However savings on interest payments – around $1.6 billion (Van Wijnbergen, 1991) – are reported to have provided sufficient financing for a growth target of 4 per cent on average over 1990–94. Naturally the validity of this figure depends not only on the realism of the econometric macromodel, but also on global developments, such as oil prices and interest rates.

Although Mexico's Brady deal implied a fairly limited external debt (service) reduction, significantly smaller than the 55 per cent Mexico had initially requested, it did seem to provide enough additional foreign exchange to sustain meaningful growth, given certain assumptions. Debt service reduction was relatively limited, representing only around 6 per cent of the country's exports and only around 20 per cent of average interest payments on medium- and long-term debt in the 1983–8 period. Indirect positive effects, linked to the removal of uncertainty and restoration of confidence generated by a deal implying no amortizations until the one payment in 2019, have been more important, at least in the short term. Soon after the announcement of the Mexican Brady package domestic interest rates fell by almost 20 per cent, presumably because of reduced pressure on the exchange rate. They remained low for a very long period. As the government's domestic debt reached $54 billion, domestic interest payments were reduced by over $9 billion (around 4.5 per cent of GDP). Van Wijnbergen (1991) estimated the additional positive effect on GDP growth at around 1 per cent initially, increasing to more than 2 per cent by 1994. A note of caution is needed;

there is room for debate about the extent to which it was just the debt deal which pushed interest rates down.

Finally an extremely important indirect positive effect is increased foreign private flows, especially FDI, and the substantial return of flight capital. By 1991 private capital flows to Mexico reached a massive $16.1 billion, according to a study by Salomon Brothers, a sharp contrast with the mere $0.7 billion in 1989. The debt deal was thus a very important factor helping to catalyse new flows and return previously fled capital. However, as pointed out above, other factors, such as NAFTA, prudent macroeconomic policies, successful export performance and the large differential between Mexican and very low US short-term interest rates, also played an important role (see Griffith-Jones *et al.*, 1992). Though clearly very welcome and valuable, these latter indirect beneficial effects will not necessarily continue. Regarding other, especially smaller and poorer countries that may sign similar debt deals, some doubts must remain as to whether these indirect positive effects would be as important as in Mexico.

Venezuela's and Uruguay's Brady deals seem to follow roughly the Mexican pattern. The Venezuelan deal had some interesting innovations, such as a new instrument called 'step-down, step-up bonds' designed to provide debt service relief in the medium term by temporarily reducing interest to below-market fixed rates in the first five years after the deal. Venezuela's cash flow relief seems even less favourable than Mexico's. The World Bank estimated it would reach only $460 million for 1990–94, or only 2.5 per cent of the country's exports. There is evidence, however, that there has been a positive effect at least on new private capital inflows to Venezuela estimated to have increased from $1 billion (1989) to $4.8 billion (1991).

The Costa Rican debt deal, even though in the context of the Brady Plan, was significantly different from the Mexican, Venezuelan and other packages. The two main features are that the deal has only the options of debt (service) reduction and no new money option, and that the level of debt relief is very large, estimated at around two-thirds of contractual obligations. It should be stressed that cash flow savings on interest payments are very close to zero (the World Bank estimates an average yearly net reduction of $0.07 billion for 1990–94) because the country had *not* been servicing its debt in full for several years. However the major reduction achieved seems to have improved both domestic and foreign private-sector expectations and also eliminated a highly demanding and time-consuming activity, external debt negotiations, particularly costly for small countries (see Rodriguez, 1988), from senior policy makers' agenda.

The interesting deal achieved by Costa Rica, its bargaining tactics (including large arrears accompanied by a permanently conciliatory approach to bargaining with creditors) and simultaneous sustained efforts at carrying out prudent macroeconomic policies seem to offer other small country debtors interesting lessons. Indeed, as Devlin and Guerguil (1991); correctly point out (see also Griffith-Jones, 1988b), unilateral action to reduce or stop debt servicing is likely to yield better results if it is seen as a step towards reaching a consensual and definitive deal with creditors, if accompanied by a coherent macroeconomic programme and if a conciliatory attitude is adopted with creditors, including commercial banks. Costa Rica skilfully met these preconditions, which seems to have helped it achieve a successful definitive deal. It should perhaps be mentioned that Costa Rica had at the time of the deal certain specific geopolitical features, which made the US government wish to maintain friendly relations.

Outside the Brady context more traditional reschedulings of commercial debt slowed down. An important exception was Chile's rescheduling in September 1990. The unique approach by the Chilean authorities was largely explained by certain particularly favourable features of Chile's recent economic evolution. Chile has had prudent macroeconomic policies for several years; its export growth has been extremely dynamic since 1985, which was one important factor why the debt service ratio fell. The other factor was that Chile had drastically reduced its commercial debt before the Brady Plan, mainly through an active programme of DES and debt buybacks. According to 1989 data Chile's debt indicators had improved enough for the World Bank to take Chile out of the severely indebted country category!

Chile's rescheduling deal was special, not only because it merely postponed amortization, but also because of the different mechanism to raise 'new money'. Instead of obtaining so-called 'involuntary new money', Chile placed bonds ($320 million) amongst a small number of large creditor banks with a long-term commitment to funding the country. It is interesting that Chile's debt deal (like Mexico's) contributed to triggering off very important private capital inflows which, together with other factors, had led by mid-1992 to a sharp increase in foreign exchange reserves. Another indicator of this return to creditworthiness is of course the secondary price of debt, over 90 per cent of face value. Sachs and Kneer (1990) define full re-establishment of creditworthiness as debt once again trading at 100 per cent. Chile seems very close to that aim. The overcoming of the debt crisis in Chile is naturally not only measured by balance of payments indicators. More important is the economy's ability to grow at a fairly rapid pace in recent years.

The recent experiences of Chile, Mexico, Venezuela and Costa Rica seem to show that there was perhaps no single optimum way for debtors to return to creditworthiness and growth in Latin America. Different paths are better suited to different countries. However common features of countries apparently returning to creditworthiness and growth are their fairly prudent macroeconomic policies and their relative clarity and consistency as to the way they wish to handle their external debt problems.

There is a group of other countries in the region where neither condition is yet fully met, though significant efforts are being made. This is particularly well illustrated by Brazil, where there are still serious fiscal and macroeconomic imbalances at the time of writing *and* an agreement on debt has not yet been reached with creditor banks, even though negotiations are progressing towards a Brady-type agreement (see World Bank, 1992) and a preliminary agreement to clear Brazil's arrears with commercial banks has already been reached. Even if Brazil were to reach an agreement with its creditor banks for debt (service) reduction of Mexico's or Venezuela's type and magnitude, it is not yet clear if this would be by itself sufficient to restore creditworthiness and growth. Parallel efforts would be required on the domestic front to reduce macroeconomic imbalances. It is encouraging that there has already been a general increase in private flows to Brazil in 1991 (though of a fairly short-term nature) in spite of difficult macroeconomic and political conditions and the unresolved debt situation.

Extra-Brady techniques
Even before the Brady Plan several commercial debt reduction operations had been fairly successfully launched. One of the most interesting ones, especially in an SSA context, was the Bolivian buyback. Since mid-1984, Bolivia had unilaterally suspended debt service. After rescheduling its Paris Club debt in 1986, Bolivia started to negotiate a buyback of its commercial debt, around $670 million (excluding interest on arrears) or about 15 per cent of the country's total public foreign debt. The secondary market price had been around 6 cents per dollar, but news of the buyback drove it up to 11–12 cents.

In 1987, Bolivia obtained waivers of restrictive clauses on debt reduction introduced in a previous rescheduling. Conditions for the buyback included the following: resources for the purchase had to come from third party donors, had to be placed in an IMF Trust Fund, and the same price had to be offered to all banks. Banks also obtained the option of receiving 25-year collateralized peso-denominated zero-coupon bonds indexed to the US dollar and eligible for conversion into local equity at a 50 per cent premium instead of cash. The buyback was announced in January 1988 with an offer price of 11 cents on the dollar. In March 1988 outstanding debt was reduced by half; nearly $270 million was exchanged for cash and $64 million for notes.

This buyback clearly illustrated how assistance from the international public sector could accelerate a sharp reduction of outstanding bank debt. In fact what made the operation feasible was resources provided by government donors and the IMF's good offices. There were, however, some short-comings. Only over 40 per cent of the country's creditor banks participated, even though the price offered was nearly double that prevalent in the secondary market (see Devlin, 1990, on the banks' reasons). Another shortcoming was the rise in the secondary market price itself. At 6 cents on the dollar, Bolivia's $670 million debt had a value of $40 million. At a price of 11 cents the remaining debt ($336 million) had a market value of $37 million. Thus $37 million of cash and Bolivian notes had bought only $3 million of reduction in market value of outstanding obligations. However the fact that donor foreign exchange resources were solely earmarked for the buyback and would not have been otherwise available made this operation particularly attractive. Furthermore later operations (including one being finalized with International Development Agency (IDA) support) further diminished the stock of Bolivian commercial debt. Obviously the fact that the face value of Bolivia's commercial debt had previously been reduced facilitated such operations.

IV Application of debt conversion techniques to official bilateral debt

A number of debt reduction measures have been implemented as regards official bilateral debt. These debt reduction techniques are simpler to implement technically for official bilateral than for commercial debt, as they mainly depend on political decisions of creditor governments not requiring complex interactions between governments and private actors needed to achieve 'voluntary' commercial debt reduction. Differential regulations, especially of an accounting and budgetary nature (see Mistry and Griffith-Jones, 1992), and particularly differential political commitment make it harder to reach agreement on sufficient official bilateral debt reduction.

An interesting new opportunity is opening up to achieve debt reduction via debt conversion for bilateral official debt in ways that parallel commercial debt. Such measures are currently only available for SILICs and SILMICs. They are very relevant for these countries (many of them in SSA), because of the very high proportion of official bilateral debt. Both for SILICs and SILMICs the Paris Club has agreed to introduce this debt conversion clause:

> creditor countries can, on a voluntary basis, swap part of the claims for DESs, debt-for-nature swaps and debt-for-development swaps for up to 10 per cent of bilateral official or officially guaranteed non-concessional loans, and (where relevant) for up to 100 per cent of ODA loans; there is also a value limit ($10 million or $20 million, depending on the case), which can be used if it is higher than the 10 per cent of non-concessional bilateral debt.

This clause has been granted, if requested, to SILMICs since September 1990 and to SILICs since December 1991 (see Griffith-Jones, 1992; also

Mistry and Griffith-Jones, 1992). Initially debt conversion of official bilateral debt was practically non-existent. There were indeed limitations on creditor governments selling their debt. Such operations potentially open debt conversions for these categories of countries for deals whose scale could be large, and which could be negotiated more easily and quickly with creditor governments. By early 1992, Benin, Congo, Côte d'Ivoire, Ecuador, Egypt, El Salvador, Honduras, Jamaica, Morocco, Nicaragua, Nigeria, Peru, Philippines, Poland and Senegal were among the countries that had already had this clause approved.

At present relatively limited activity has actually taken place in finalizing official debt conversions in the framework of the '10 per cent clause'. However a number of transactions are reportedly being considered or about to be implemented, including the following:

- Poland has presented a detailed request for funding a $3 billion Environment Fund. This was discussed at a large conference with creditor governments in mid-1991. Reportedly the USA and France have made commitments.
- Egypt: France is reported to have agreed to convert up to $10 million, using it for cofinancing (with the World Bank) the Social Emergency Fund. France and other creditor governments are reportedly considering a programme of official debt–equity conversions.
- Morocco: the Netherlands and other creditors are considering DES.
- Nigeria: different creditor governments are reportedly considering using official DES to support privatization.

It should be noted that certain European and North American governments had been selling (or converting) their Paris club debt even before September 1990 to improve the balance sheet of their export credit agencies. Because these operations were not allowed in the Paris Club framework, they were not publicized. However they are interesting because they pioneered DES with official debt, showing that it is feasible for an export credit agency both to take equity in LDC companies and to sell official debt to private investors. Furthermore a number of individual creditor governments – including, for example, Switzerland, Germany, France and Canada – have recently launched initiatives relating mainly to their ODA bilateral debt, which imply either debt reduction and/or debt conversion. Such initiatives open new and interesting opportunities for heavily indebted countries. They require agile action by their governments to maximize developmental benefits from such opportunities and to press for further opportunities.

V   Conclusions

The need for additional debt (service) reduction remains a major issue, particularly for the severely indebted countries in SSA, where large debt overhangs continue to be major obstacles to growth and development. A number of debt (service) reduction and debt conversion techniques have been developed since the mid-1980s, particularly, but not only, for Latin American commercial debt. Many of these techniques can be applied and are slowly beginning to be applied to the reduction of commercial debt in SSA; they include buybacks and collateralization of commercial debt with funds from creditor governments or international financial institutions.

It is also important that debt conversion techniques (either debt-for-equity or debt-for-development) can now increasingly be applied to official bilateral debt. Such transactions are particularly attractive to debtor governments if they imply, as is likely, additionality to the debt reduction that would have otherwise been obtained and direct efficiency gains for the debtor economy, which may be obtained via facilitating privatization or funding high-priority social and environmental spending. Furthermore such debt conversions (and indeed some other forms of debt reduction) may help encourage new private flows.

Naturally care must be taken in the case of debt conversions to avoid any undesirable negative effects, such as increasing the potential for future inflation. However the lessons from Latin America, especially Chile, show that negative effects can be fairly easily neutralized by appropriate macroeconomic policies. More broadly, it is hoped that the lessons from Latin America's too slow but fortunately fairly steady progress towards the reduction of its debt overhang and return to creditworthiness, contributing to the apparent restoration of favourable growth prospects, can offer relevant lessons for other still severely debt-distressed countries. These lessons do not only relate to the debt reduction techniques described above, but also to broader policy stances, such as prudent macroeconomic policies and emphasis on export diversification, which indirectly play an important role in the reduction of debt overhangs too.

Bibliography

Aspe, P. (1990), 'The Renegotiation of Mexico's External Debt' in Faber and Griffith-Jones (eds).

Devlin, R. (1990), 'Development vs. Debt: Past and Future', in Faber and Griffith-Jones (eds).

Devlin, R. and M. Guerguil (1991), 'America Latina y las nuevas corrientes financieras y comerciales', *Revista de la CEPAL*, **43**.

Faber, M. and S. Griffith-Jones (eds) (1990), 'Approaches to Third World Debt Reduction', *IDS Bulletin*, **21** (2).

Griffith-Jones, S. (ed.) (1988a), *Managing World Debt*, Brighton/New York/Mexico: Wheatsheaf/St Martin's Press/FCE.

Griffith-Jones, S. (1988b), 'Conclusions', in Griffith-Jones (ed.) (1988a).

Griffith-Jones, S. (1992a), 'Conversion of Official Bilateral Debt: the Opportunities and the Issues', World Bank Annual Conference on Development Economics, Proceedings (mimeo).

Griffith-Jones, S. with A. Marr and A. Rodriguez (1992), 'The Return of Private Capital to Latin America: the Facts, an Analytical Framework and some Policy Issues', in J.J. Teunissen (ed.), *Fragile Finance*, The Hague: FONDAD.

Mistry, P. (1992), *African Debt Revisited*, The Hague: FONDAD.

Mistry, P. and S. Griffith-Jones (1992), 'Conversion of Official Bilateral Debt', report prepared for UNCTAD (mimeo).

Rodriquez, E. (1988), 'Costa Rica: A Quest for Survival', in Griffith-Jones (ed.) (1988a).

Sachs, J. and J. Kneer (1990), 'Debt reduction: The Basis and Shape of a New Strategy', *Intereconomics*, January/February.

UNCTC (1990), *Debt Equity Conversions, A Guide for Decision-Makers*, New York: UN.

Van Wijnbergen, S. van (1991), 'Mexico and the Brady Plan', *Economic Policy*, April.

World Bank (Debt and International Finance Division) (1992), *Financial Flows to Developing Countries, Quarterly Review*, June.

World Bank (WDT) *World Debt Tables*, various issues, Washington DC.

10 International financial institutions and accountability: the need for drastic change

Kunibert Raffer

I Introduction

The dramatically increased leverage of international financial institutions (IFIs) on political decisions by debtor countries is a major result of the debt crisis. Before 1982, when finance was readily available from private banks, IFI influence and leverage had declined considerably. In 1981, for example, India even preferred the IMF to private sources, using the Fund as a 'lender of first resort', much to the discontent of the USA. This changed drastically after 1982. The debt crisis and their role of 'debt managers' gave IFIs new and increased leverage. During the 1985 IMF/IBRD meeting in Seoul the US Treasury Secretary, James Baker, expressly called on IFIs to support comprehensive macroeconomic and structural policies in Southern countries (SCs), demanding a continued central role for the IMF, together with multilateral development banks, and more intensive IMF and IBRD collaboration.

In 1989, Nicholas Brady reaffirmed and strengthened the role of the IMF and the IBRD as debt managers and promoters of 'sound policies' through advice and financial support. Paris Club debt reschedulings and debt reductions depend on an IFI 'seal of approval'. Prior agreement with the Bretton Woods twins is a condition for debt reduction under the Enterprise of the Americas Initiative. The EC considers SCs with IFI-supported adjustment programmes as automatically, although not exclusively, eligible for Community adjustment resources. Occasionally even domestic laws in the North, such as the US International Lending Supervision Act, base legal consequences on the IMF's judgement on a debtor country. Finally the dramatic changes in Eastern Europe and the former Soviet Union have increased the number of IFI clients.

In odd contrast to the strong leverage conferred on IFIs, particularly the IBRD and the IMF, by their major shareholders and to their growing importance neither the economic efficiency of their actions nor the problem of financial accountability for their errors seems to have received perceptible attention from Northern governments. This is all the more surprising as efficiency, accountability and the market mechanism rank high in the rhetoric of these governments, and official institutions such as the European Parliament have criticized IFIs quite strongly. The latter's *Report of the*

Committee on Development and Cooperation on Structural Adjustment (1992, p. 8) notes 'the substantial overall failure of the "first generation" structural adjustment policies proposed by the IBRD and the IMF', a fact meanwhile also conceded by IFI employees. It called on the IMF to reconsider the very foundations of its structural adjustment (SA) policies in the light of the obvious inadequacy of its proposals, and even demanded a new 'European approach' to SA different from the Bretton Woods variety.

The question whether IFI programmes and projects actually work has received relatively much attention in academic literature so far. But the problem of accountability as well as the link between accountability and economic efficiency have not received due attention. This is all the more inexplicable as these are two crucial elements of successful market economies. The most basic rule of a market system demands that decision making be inseparably linked with risk. This link promotes economic efficiency and makes those taking decisions accountable. It was severed in the countries of the former Eastern bloc where decisions were taken by bureaucrats not held accountable for the outcome of their actions.

In the case of IFIs, decisions are not linked to financial responsibilities: while IFIs determine or at least codetermine the policies of their clients, they refuse to share the risks involved. They insist on full repayment, even if damages caused by their staffs occur. Such damages have to be paid for by their borrowers. IFIs can even gain financially from their own errors by extending new loans necessary to repair damages done by prior loans. This kind of riskless decision making is certainly not a sound incentive system and is absolutely at odds with Western market systems.

This chapter discusses the problem of efficiency and accountability. First the high degree of IFI interference into debtor economies will be documented briefly. Stating the obvious appears necessary because Bank and Fund often try to play down, if not deny, their leverage, for example by claiming that they only finance a country's own programme, and by using phrases like 'Fund'- or 'Bank-supported programmes'. Next the problem of failures by IFIs will be discussed. Particularly with regard to SA this is an important issue because measures that hurt but help may be economically justifiable in contrast to those that hurt without helping. Finally proposals are presented as to how to link decisions and risks to make IFIs financially accountable and thus – according to the logic of market economies – more efficient.

II   Leverage and economic decision making

In the words of J.J. Polak (1991, p. 12), a leading theoretician of the IMF, 'The purpose of the Fund's conditionality is to make as sure as possible that a country drawing on the Fund's resources pursues a set of policies that are, in the Fund's view, appropriate to its economic situation in general and its payments situation in particular.'

Interestingly conditionality did not exist in the original IMF Articles of Agreement. It was introduced later and has been strengthened over time. The strengthening of conditionality can be best illustrated by the example of the Compensatory Financing Facility. Initially introduced to compensate shortfalls in export earnings beyond the control of SCs, its

> conditionality was limited to an obligatory statement by the member to 'co-operate with the Fund ... to find, *where required*, appropriate solutions for its balance of payments difficulties'.
> ...
> Over the years, however, the Fund has increasingly come to the realization that *even though a country's export shortfall was both 'temporary' and largely beyond its control the country might still have balance-of-payments difficulties attributable to inappropriate policies and that large amounts of unconditional credit might cause the country to delay adopting needed policy adjustments.* (Polak, 1991, p. 9; emphasis added)

Even if the country's economic policy is not at all the reason for the temporary problem, the country still has to change it if the Fund wishes so. From a logical point of view this is quite strange, unless the real reason is increased leverage rather than the elimination of economic inefficiencies.

To assess the influence of the Fund appropriately prior actions, which means changing policies in accordance with the Fund's views before receiving money, must not be forgotten. Reliance on prior actions has become more common in recent years. Polak suggests that this can be used to the country's advantage 'to minimize the policy commitments it must make in its letter of intent and thus to *present itself as opting for adjustment on its own rather than under pressure from the Fund*' (1991, p. 13, emphasis added). In plain English: a distressed country may chose whether to accept the IMF's conditions openly or by 'cleverly' disguising them as its own free choice.

The IBRD has never made unconditional loans either; even when financing concrete projects some conditions required policy changes (see Mosley *et al.*, 1991, I, p. 27). When starting programme lending conditionality was increased. 'The Bank felt that it needed a place at the top policy-making table' (ibid., p. 34) beyond what it could expect from mere project monitoring. This view can be corroborated by the description of structural adjustment lending (SAL) by Ernest Stern (1983), an IBRD top executive, praising the 'comprehensiveness' of its 'coverage in terms of both macro and sector issues of policy reform; the exclusive focus on policy and institutional reform; and the detailed articulation of the precise modifications in policy necessary to adjust to a changed economic environment'(Stern, 1983 p. 91). As the availability of funds is entirely dependent on progress in implementing policy reform, SAL enables 'the Bank to address basic issues of economic management and of development strategy more directly and urgently' (ibid.). Briefly put, Stern (1983, p. 104) saw SAL as a 'unique opportunity to achieve a comprehensive and timely approach to policy reform' and as the response to a *'feasible ... call for increased sacrifices'* (1983, p. 91, my emphasis). Of course, Stern explains, there is a need for a 'firm understanding' of monitoring, a Letter of Development Policies is explicitly referred to in the loan agreement and tranching of disbursements allows preconditions for the release of the next tranche. Stern (1983, p. 99) concludes: 'While this procedure may be called "conditionality", it is in principle no different from the relationship involved in Bank sector or project lending.'

Quite naturally the structural adjustment facility (SAF) introduced in 1986 for poor countries shows a similarly stern understanding of conditionality. Administered jointly by Bank and Fund, the procedure of lending is described by the *IMF Survey* (Supplement on the Fund, September 1987, p. 15):

- a 'policy framework paper'(PFP) has to be developed 'with the assistance of both the Fund and the World Bank'. It contains the macroeconomic and structural policy priorities, objectives and measures for a three-year period, as well as a more detailed description of structural reforms and policies to be implemented in the first year;
- the PFP is updated annually, reviewed by the IMF's Executive Board and the IBRD's Executive Directors in the Committee of the Whole;
- the first instalment is made upon approval by the IMF: the SC is requested to present programmes based on the PFP for the three-year period and the first year;
- further instalments are made upon the IMF's approval of annual arrangements;
- performance is monitored by benchmarks, not all quantified.

Finally the enhanced SAF (ESAF) introduced soon after SAF is subject to even stricter conditionality (Polak, 1991, p. 7).

The Group of 24 criticized the increasing restrictiveness of Fund lending and the proliferation of performance criteria in number and scope 'under one pretext or another'(*IMF Survey*, Supplement, 19 August, 1987). During 1983–5, nearly 80 per cent of the arrangements contained, on average, more than eight performance criteria, sometimes as many as 14, a number dwarfed by the more than 100 conditions of the IBRD's second SAL to Thailand. Quite often they extended to microeconomic variables such as prices for specific products. Reviews have become standard for all except SAF programmes, to fill in performance criteria that could not be specified at the outset and to reset targets. Performance criteria are specified quarterly and semi-annually. The IMF may or may not pardon non-compliance by granting a waiver.

One more quotation may suffice to establish the claim that IFIs are at least co-responsible for the success of programmes and projects they fund. The IBRD's own Operations Evaluation Department (OED) concluded: 'Finally, borrower preferences are not always seen as important in supervision management, although the outcome often has a critical impact on the borrower' (IBRD, 1989, p. 26).

Not surprisingly IFIs have repeatedly complained about insufficient borrower commitment or have stressed the need for programmes to be clearly 'owned' by affected governments. Such phrases were absolutely inexplicable if IFIs simply supported the affected governments' own proposals.

III Efficiency, failures and their costs

Blaming IFIs for making any mistakes is not intended, nor would it be fair to do so. Even the most successful institutions have to put up with a certain failure rate. Important questions are whether a minimum level of efficiency of operations can be proved, whether organizational arrangements provide incentives to avoid the same errors in the future and who pays for these errors. Finally it is important to ask whether these prescriptions have a sound theoretical and logical basis.

It is important to note that SA policies do not follow from neoclassical theory (see Raffer, 1992a). Pure trade theory contends – as Reisen and van Trotsenburg (1988, p. 83) show – that 'in a transfer situation, import substitution is preferable to export promotion', or the opposite of IFI advice. Historically successful countries such as South Korea, Taiwan or Japan indeed have not opted for IFI-type liberalization, nor have they reduced the role of the state in the way advised by IFIs at present. Theoretical models, though, always state meticulously on what restrictive assumptions they depend. They never claim to be valid if these restrictions are not met. One quick look at a textbook will show that the necessary conditions for market optimality cannot be achieved in reality, particularly so if one can apply pressure to emulate the free market on the relatively smaller players only. Even more important, market optima cannot be approximated by eliminating some but not all imperfections – in that case the outcome might even make things worse, as any good introductory textbook will warn. Therefore it must be shown for each policy change that it is indeed able to bring about improvements (see Raffer, 1992a).

While it is common knowledge that unit costs change with output, the assumption that they do not is absolutely essential to defend comparative advantage and the case of beneficial free trade – routine justifications of IFI policies. If unit costs are assumed to be constant an inconsistency between trade theory and growth theory follows, as Chenery (1961) has pointed out. If not, comparative advantage specialization may lead to productivity losses (Raffer, 1992b).

Empirical evidence on the success of SA is, at best, inconclusive; often there is no statistically significant difference between programme and non-programme countries. Khan (1990) even finds significantly reduced growth in programme countries and, as Polak (1991, p. 42) points out, a predicted reduction in the growth rate of at least 0.7 per cent of GDP for each year a country had an IMF programme. Mosley *et al.* (1991) found adverse effects of SA on growth rates, particularly in countries with low slippage on conditionality (a very weak favourable impact – because of the inflow of money rather than policy conditionality, according to the authors – emerges if one changes periods and country groupings) and declining shares of investment in GDP. Attempts by IFIs to prove success were usually short-lived. Statistical methods such as the grouping of countries have been repeatedly attacked as purpose-serving. The IBRD's *Africa's Adjustment with Growth*, published together with UNDP in 1989, is the best known example, where bold statements such as 'Recovery has begun' (p. iii) had to be corrected quickly.

Compelling examples of alleged and proven failures and inefficiencies of IFIs abound in the literature. Mosley *et al.* (1991, p. 24) found that the IBRD 'now not only admits its mistakes, but has enshrined learning from them as part of their corporate philosophy'. The IBRD (1984 p. 24) for example, admits:

> Genuine mistakes and misfortunes cannot explain the excessive number of 'white elephants'. Too many projects have been selected either on the basis of political prestige or on the basis of inadequate regard for their likely economic and financial rate of return ... . External financial agencies have shared the responsibility for this inadequate discipline over the use of investment resources.

Financial responsibility, however, has not been shared by all. If IFIs have learned during the last decade, poor countries and vulnerable groups in particular have paid their tuition. Brazil's Polonoroeste illustrates this point perfectly. *Time* (12 December 1988) reported that a loan of $240 million had caused considerable environmental damage. Bank officials admitted that they had erred and lent another $200 million to repair the damage done by the first loan. Brazil's debts increased by $440 million; the IBRD increased its income stream. Such examples render the remark by the Bank's OED (IBRD, 1989, p. xiii) that a 100 per cent success rate, if ever achieved, 'would invite questions about whether an appropriate level of risk was being faced in development investments' particularly sarcastic.

The delinking of decisions and risk could explain economically suboptimal practices. In addition it is a strong incentive to yield to political influence. Country lending targets often put pressure on officials to disburse. Mosley *et al.* (1991, p. 72) present an extremely telling example. Although the whole division, including its chief, agreed that Bangladesh could not absorb any more money, the lending programme was not slowed. The division chief explained that, if he advised slowing down, he would be fired. This is by no means a singular case. Quoting examples of pressure to lend, the OED (IBRD, 1989, p. xvii) warns that the Bank 'needs to be more realistic about the borrowers' implementation capacities'. The problem is further exacerbated by an even greater inflexibility on the regional level, which means that funds that should ideally be switched from, say, Africa to Asia cannot be allocated this way. Rightly or wrongly, they have to go into the predestined region.

This structural rigidity is certainly one factor explaining grave shortcomings pointed out by the OED (IBRD, 1989), such as unrealistic scheduling and objectives at appraisal, excessive expectations leading to gaps between appraised and re-estimated economic rates of return of up to 20 percentage points(!) for regional averages. The OED calls the Bank's enduring errors in implementation rate forecasts embarrassing. Evaluation concluded that preparation was good or adequate in 21 per cent of projects, which means it was not in 79 per cent. Insufficiently detailed engineering prior to approval, inappropriate expertise in procurement – an issue the OED could not elaborate on because of inadequate statistics – and lack of training, will or motivation by 'most operations staff' were found as well. The OED's critique was not always heeded. In the water supply and waste disposal sector this had not been done since the earliest appraisal in 1970 – a 'sobering' result, as the OED correctly remarks.

To assess success rates of projects properly one must understand that the economic rate of return (ERR) depending on costs and benefits measured by shadow prices or even by incremental benefits thought to stem from the project is itself not the hardest concept. An indicator of performance inherent in the costs and benefits considered 'particularly important', such as 'progress in institution building', is certainly not a hard monetary figure and may be valued differently depending on whether the IBRD's own department or someone else assesses it. Furthermore success is often 'based on the accomplishment of the project objectives and achievements' (IBRD, 1989, p. 3). Projects with major shortcomings but 'still considered worthwhile' (by the Bank itself) qualify as 'marginally satisfactory' according to the OED's methodology newly introduced in 1985–6 for the precise purpose of 'adequate recognition' of these marginal projects. This 'less mechanical and somewhat subjective judgement as to performance ... posed its own problems, not the least of which was the *subjectivity of assessments*, which *increased the weight given to evaluators' perceptions, some of which were difficult to explain fully*' (ibid., pp. 15f; emphasis added). Nevertheless this new method, described in some detail in IBRD (1989), produced success stories. While 28 per cent of projects were unsatisfactory for the 1987 cohort according to the traditional method, the new technique found only 12 per cent to have an unsatisfactory or uncertain performance. 'Uncertain' is in itself a window-dressing euphemism. The OED defines this category as follows: 'Project achieves few objectives, if any, and has no foreseeable worthwhile results' (ibid., p. 15). In spite of such generous evaluation the share of satisfactory operations has declined perceptibly during recent years.

The Bank has shown a predilection for convenient vagueness for quite some time. In 1980, figures on people affected by or expected to benefit from projects had already been shown to be a bluff by Tetzlaff (1980, p. 438). Interestingly the OED often criticized very much the same points with regard to projects in the 1970s as it does today, which does not suggest an immense impact of its findings on actual practice. The question of success or failure of projects is also of some importance for SA, especially in poor SCs with sufficiently high shares of IFI activities. Their economic flops help to accumulate debts. A high rate of IFI failures might therefore necessitate SA, which in turn is administered by IFIs, just as failed SA programmes are likely to call for new SA programmes, as long as unconditional repayment to IFIs is upheld. This logical relation might be described somewhat cynically as IFI flops securing IFI jobs.

Regarding SA, the OED sometimes found dated technical expertise (in the area of public enterprise), overall outcomes on the macroeconomic front below expectations, or overly ambitious targets. One cannot but concur with the OED that 'SAL conditionalities should take into account the macroeconomic consequences of the policy prescriptions' (IBRD, 1989, p. 92) or with its call for an integrated analytical framework to understand better the links between a programme and its expected macroeconomic outcomes: 'Such a framework would also be useful for ex-post evaluations' (ibid., p. 6).

The OED also allows us a glimpse of the Bank's own understanding of a debatable performance: 'a zero rate of acceptable performance would indicate that Bank loans made borrowers worse off, an outcome that would raise serious questions about Bank performance' (ibid., p. 16) The fact that 'acceptable' is not strictly defined assumes totally unacceptable results over a year would not raise any questions at all in a well functioning market economy. Rather institutions with this performance record are immediately dissolved. Even in Centrally Planned Economies an absolutely zero rate of success would have done more than just raised questions.

Regarding the efficiency of Fund programmes, even IMF sources are occasionally quite frank. Goldstein (1986, p. 45) contends that, depending on how one measures the effects, markedly different results, with regard both to size and to direction of effects, are obtained. Not surprisingly 'the Fund has come to a rather different assessment of programme effects than some observers'. It appears that the Fund prefers methods producing positive results. Regarding the critique of the IMF's efficiency, it may be sufficient to refer to Spraos (1986), who is most outspoken. What appears to be particularly alarming is that SA is even prescribed in cases where it is not needed:

> As a consequence the Bank often succumbed to the temptation to prescribe policy reform even in markets where its own analysis had revealed no significant distortion and to ride into battle, like Don Quixote with his lance tilted, even in fields where there were no noble deeds to be done. In some cases the Bank's SAL conditionality even ran counter to the policy changes which its own staff were trying to bring in at the project level. (Mosley *et al.*, 1991, p. 300)

A similar problem has been created by so-called 'cross conditionality', or the unpleasant situation where two lenders, such as the IMF and the Bank, demand actions that cannot be reconciled and the borrower is therefore logically unable to fulfil both lists of conditions.

Vali Jamal (1992) presents the example of Somalia in the 1980s where absolutely inappropriate policies were prescribed by the IMF, apparently because of insufficient assessment of the country's economy. After detailed criticism, the author sums up: 'All in all, the spectacle is one of the IMF trying to impose the trappings of a free market economy on Somalia whereas one already exists in all but name.' The Republic of Trinidad and Tobago documented grave irregularities and deficiencies in the IMF's assessment of its economy, which created the impression of economic mismanagement and led to an SA programme. After the IMF became aware of these substantial errors no correction was published in spite of the importance of this to the country. Because of the government's need for the IMF's 'seal of approval', Trinidad's own expert advised them not to pick a fight with the IMF. It is of interest to note that no OECD country, which as a non-borrower could have done so without any fear of consequences, bothered to ask for a detailed enquiry, although this case became famous as the so-called 'Budhoo affair'.

IFIs have a long history of political lending. For example, the Bank did not lend to Brazil under Goulart, Algeria until 1973, Egypt under Nasser,

Chile under Allende, Indonesia under Sukarno, Ghana under Nkrumah, Argentina under Peron, Jamaica under Manley or Grenada under Bishop. On the other hand, the IBRD organized a consortium of donors to provide aid to Saigon shortly before the fall of the city, and lavished money on military juntas such as in Argentina and Chile under Pinochet. It is, of course, logically possible that all projects considered during the periods mentioned above were economically unsound, while a flood of economically sound projects came up after, for example, the coups of General Videla or General Pinochet. This possibility is, however, certainly slight. As shown by the famous example of the IBRD's loan to Argentina in 1988, quickly disbursed and allowing the country to pay US banks in time, the Bank is even prepared to antagonize the Fund to please one major shareholder.

This does not mean that political considerations are beyond the IMF. Shortly before the Sandinista victory in Nicaragua, for instance, the IMF made a sizeable loan to Somoza, just in time for it to be gratefully pocketed by the fleeing dictator. Naturally the country was supposed to pay this money back. Duvalier's Haiti provides a similar example. According to *Time* magazine (2 July 1984) $20 million disbursed to alleviate balance of payments problems vanished without a trace, although the movement of a similar amount into the Duvalier's palace account could be observed. *Time* also reported the IMF's reaction: it '*threatened* to *halt aid* to the country *until Haiti made sure more money would not disappear the same way*' (emphasis added). As this example shows, some debts to IFIs are in need of scrutiny. Comparison with other clients, such as Manley's Jamaica, where an agreement was suspended on a minor technicality, does not provide purely economic explanations.

Economic theory suggests that economic inefficiencies and political decisions are fostered by riskless deciding. Without financial risks other factors become more important, such as disbursing enough to meet targets or pleasing one or more big shareholder(s). Financial accountability would provide a disincentive to do so.

IV   The need for financial accountability
The idea of financial accountability or paying for one's errors is absolute anathema to IFIs. As both bilateral and private lenders have meanwhile accepted reductions of their claims, they remain the only exception. The main argument of the IBRD – debt reduction has been more often suggested for development banks than for the Fund – is that its own excellent rating as a borrower would suffer unless all loans were repaid to the last cent. If that were true all commercial banks would have enormously low ratings, as no bank ever gets all loans back. A certain number of lost loans are simply part

of the costs of running a bank. The understandable self-interest of any creditor apart, there exists no reason for preferential treatment.

It is true that IFIs charge interest rates below the debtor's market rate (although this difference is small) even in normal lending, which is too tough to qualify as ODA according to the DAC definition. Concessional money is not exclusively provided by IFIs and not necessarily cheaper than that coming from bilateral sources. But slightly better financial terms do not necessarily make a loan cheaper. If the country has to pay for wrong decisions by IFIs it may finally turn out to cost much more than money at market terms.

The strong participation in decision making by IFIs is the other difference, particularly in comparison with private banks. As shown above, IFIs have massively influenced the use of loans and the adoption of policies they thought appropriate to regain economic viability. The IBRD has been proud of its strict monitoring over decades, a pride not quite as perceptibly expressed in the recent past. All in all there is no reason for preferential treatment of IFIs. The systemic bias towards accommodating other goals discussed above, be they internal to the IFI or external political demands, rather than strict economic efficiency, strongly demands accountability. Protecting institutions from the results of their own decisions cannot be justified in a market economy.

Discussing the introduction of financial accountability, one needs to differentiate between programmes and projects. As it is practically impossible to determine an IFI's fair share in programmes that went wrong, a clear and simple solution emerges in the case of countries where other lenders grant debt reductions. IFIs should lose the same percentage of their claims as other creditors; they should be treated symmetrically. In SCs with high IFI involvement, which have been forced to orient their policies according to IFI 'advice' for some time, this solution is particularly justified. As the shares of multilateral debts are relatively higher in the poorest countries, protecting IFIs from losses is done at the expense of particularly poor clients, whose lack of experts has often made them extremely dependent on solutions elaborated by IFI staff. Using a term coined by Svendsen (1987, p. 27) for African debts, we may call these IFI debts 'creditor-determined' or (mainly) the result of creditors' decisions.

As there is no sufficient proof that SA or IMF programmes work, while there is substantial evidence of their extremely negative effects – even IFIs agree, for instance, that the poor are hurt, their effects on capital formation endanger future development – they should be discontinued. According to strict logic, it does not even matter whether programmes do not work because of failures and inconsistencies, which appears to be the case, or because IFIs cannot make them work in SCs. There is no economically valid point in funding something that does not work but harms. Discontinuing programmes would also have the doubly beneficial effect that aid at present used to repair damages done by them would be free to be used in an economically better way. As a consequence the IMF could be dissolved. Considering that proposals to melt the Bretton Woods twins into one institution have already been made, this is not a wholly new thought.

Present SA should be replaced by a solution wherein debtor countries' debt services are brought in line with their ability to pay under present, protectionist conditions. The fairest and economically most sensible way to do so would be the internationalization of Chapter 9 of US insolvency laws which, as it regulates the reorganization of debtors with governmental powers, so-called municipalities, could be internationalized quickly and with minor changes (see Raffer, 1990). Its introduction would also mean that lenders would lend money if repayments could be financed by proceeds. Debts which have to be serviced out of the budget would and should remain the exception. Lenders would stop lending if previous loans were not put to efficient use, as they would be sure to lose their money eventually. Briefly put, if international insolvency had existed in the 1970s the burden of debt would be much lower – maybe there would not even be a debt crisis now.

This close scrutiny of the way loans are used does not mean the end of concessional loans, as their debt service can be covered with relatively lower-income streams. Nor does it mean the end of financing social agenda or projects in the poorest countries. These, however, should be financed by grants. Institutional changes, such as the reorganization of the legal system within a country or reforms in the course of democratization, should not be financed by loans, particularly not on the expensive terms of 'development finance'. While such changes are no doubt important for a sound framework of future development they do not generate foreign exchange income directly and will have to be serviced out of the budget. In indebted countries where debt service already puts heavy strains on the budget, new loans that do not earn their own amortization and interest service are not unlikely to deteriorate the country's debt situation further. The fact that the evaluation of such activities is particularly dependent on what the OED called subjectivity of assessment or perceptions difficult to explain fully should be a further caveat. If democracy is actually as important to OECD governments as their present rhetoric suggests, they should be prepared to support the creation of democratic structures with grants.

Naturally the volume of IFI activities would decrease markedly, to fewer but economically more viable projects. This is desirable as no project at all is preferable to a costly flop – at least for those who have to pay for it. This brings us to the problem of financial accountability for projects. Economically viable projects, which means projects that earn their amortization and interest payments, pose no problem. But if a project goes wrong the need will arise to determine financial consequences. In the simplest case borrower and lender(s) agree on a fair sharing of costs. If they do not, the solution used between business partners or transnational firms and countries in cases of disagreement could be applied: the decision of a court of arbitration. This concept is well known in the field of international investments. If disagreements between transnational firms and host countries can be solved that way there is no reason why disputes between IFIs and borrowing countries could not be solved by this mechanism as well.

A permanent international court of arbitration would be ideal, where SCs and IFIs nominate the same amount of members, who elect one further member in order to reach an uneven number. If necessary, this court might consist of more than one panel established in the way proposed above. It decides on the percentage of the loan to be waived to cover damages for which the IFI is responsible. The right to file complaints should be conferred on NGOs, governments and international organizations. As NGOs are under less pressure from IFIs or member governments, their right to represent affected people is particularly important. The court of arbitrators would, of course, have the right and the duty to refuse to hear cases that are apparently ill-founded. The need to prepare a case meticulously would deter abuse. The possibility of being held financially accountable would act as an incentive for IFIs to perform better.

Financial accountability would thus also be beneficial to IFIs themselves. It would give their staff a good argument against pouring money into regions just because of lending targets as well as against political interference by important shareholders including demands to bail out other creditors. Projects and programmes actually financed under these conditions of accountability would therefore have a much better rate of success and much more positive impacts on development.

Looking at present evolutions this proposal might not be as revolutionary as it seems. Signs exist that IFIs are likely to face increased problems with repayments in the near future: since 1982, IFIs have substituted a large part of private loans in debtor countries, thereby bailing out private banks but deteriorating their own exposure. IFIs have already started to give loans to allow debtors to honour repayments to themselves as due. To keep up appearances third parties had to be involved repeatedly. This rather recalls the situation of private banks in the early days of the debt debacle. Mounting problems with debt service and arrears, and even calls upon Northern governments for help, are clear signs of alarm. The IBRD (1988, p. xxxvii) asked bilateral donors for money to help finance repayments of IBRD loans by countries now in the IDA-only category. The total amount of debt outstanding was a mere $3 billion and its service could be covered neither by

IDA nor by the revenues of these IBRD-financed activities. While calls for bail-outs hardly inspire confidence in IFI management, they also show that the stage where an increasing number of SCs are simply unable to service IFI debts may be near unless Northern governments are prepared for a bail-out.

Economically it would make sense to look for a solution before such a bail-out becomes necessary. This solution should also eliminate the root of the problem, which is non-accountability and the systemic failures it causes. Naturally it would cost IFI shareholders something to clean up the failures of the past, but there is no more reason to spare IFI owners than any other shareholders of a firm. Furthermore a big bail-out would cost money as well. If development banks cannot survive being financially accountable, dissolving them totally would be the economically indicated solution. Considering the increasing involvement of IFIs in Eastern Europe and the former Soviet Union, the problem of efficiency and accountability becomes even more important. Pouring money there just to meet regional targets would certainly not be indicated.

References

Chenery, H.B. (1961), 'Comparative Advantage and Development Policy', *American Economic Review*, **51** (1).

European Parliament (1992), *Report of the Committee on Development and Cooperation on Structural Adjustment in the Developing Countries*, 4 February, Rapporteur: Mr Eugenio Melandri, PE 155.077/fin.

Goldstein, Morris (1986), *The Global Effects of Fund-Supported Adjustment Programs*, IMF Occasional Paper no. 42, Washington DC: IMF.

IBRD (1984), *Toward Sustained Development in Sub-Saharan Africa, A Program of Action*, Washington DC: IBRD.

IBRD (1988), *World Debt Tables 1988–89, External Debt of Developing Countries*, vol. I, *Analysis and Summary Tables*, Washington DC: IBRD.

IBRD, (OED) (1989), *Project Performance Results for 1987*, Washington DC: IBRD/OED.

Jamal, Vali (1992), 'Somalia: The Gulf Link and Adjustment', in Raffer and Salih (eds).

Khan, Moshin S. (1990), 'The Macroeconomic Effects of Fund-Supported Adjustment Programs', *IMF Staff Papers*, **37** (2).

Mosley, Paul, Jane Harrigan and John Toye (1991), *Aid and Power, The World Bank and Policy Based Lending*, vol. I, London, New York: Routledge.

Polak Jaques, J. (1991), *The Changing Nature of Conditionality*, Essays in International Finance No. 184, International Finance Section, Department of Economics, Princeton University, NJ.

Raffer, Kunibert (1990), 'Applying Chapter 9 Insolvency to International Debts: An Economically Efficient Solution with a Human Face', *World Development*, **18** (2).

Raffer, Kunibert (1992a), '"Structural Adjustment" or Debt Relief: The Case of Arab LLDCs', in K. Raffer and M.A. Salih (eds).

Raffer, Kunibert (1992b), 'Disadvantaging Comparative Advantages: The Problem of Decreasing Returns', in F. Stewart, R. Prendergast and D. Marsden (eds), *Market Forces and World Development*, London: Macmillan (forthcoming).

Raffer K. and M.A. Salih (eds) (1992), *The Least-Developed and the Oil-Rich Arab Countries*, London: Macmillan.

Reisen, H. and A. van Trotsenburg (1988), *Developing Country Debt: The Budgetary and Transfer Problem*, Paris: OECD.

Republic of Trinidad and Tobago, Ministry of Finance and the Economy (1989), 'Trinidad and Tobago's Government's Relationship with the International Monetary Fund 1988', January (mimeo).

Spraos, John (1986), *IMF Conditionality: Inefficient, Ineffective, Mistargeted*, Essays in International Finance No. 166, International Finance Section, Department of Economics, Princeton University, NJ.

Stern, Ernest (1983), 'World Bank Financing and Structural Adjustment', in John Williamson (ed.), *IMF Conditionality*, Washington DC: Institute of International Finance and MIT Press

Svendsen, Knud Erik (1987), *The Failure of the International Debt Strategy*, CDR-Research Report no.13, Copenhagen.

Tetzlaff, Rainer (1980), *Die Weltbank: Machtinstrument der USA oder Hilfe für Entwicklungsländer?*, Munich: Weltforum.

11 Does the world still need the IMF?

Graham Bird

A feature of the 1980s and early 1990s has been the increasingly broad and vehement criticism of the IMF as a major international financial institution. The criticism has indeed frequently been sufficiently hostile to call into question the Fund's very existence. Of course, criticism of any large institution is to be expected; and the Fund has never been free from those commentators who have sought to challenge at least some part of its operations. During the 1960s, for example, the most common criticism was that it had failed to do enough to redress the perceived inadequacy of official international reserves. During the 1970s more systematic criticisms of its lending facilities began to emerge. Its role as an adjustment institution also began to receive closer critical examination and it was this aspect of the Fund's activities upon which critics focused at the beginning of the 1980s, with a number of important books recommending the reform of IMF conditionality. Criticism ranged from the more extreme view that IMF-supported programmes were always, or at least invariably, inappropriate, to the more moderate one that a richer mix of conditionality was needed to accommodate the different economic circumstances in member countries.

Such criticisms have persisted through to the beginning of the 1990s, with evidence on the impact of Fund-supported policies proving inconclusive. However these, almost conventional, criticisms of the Fund have been joined by others. Perhaps not surprisingly, given the reassertion of market economics during the 1980s, a criticism has been voiced that the Fund should not be involved in lending at all, and that this is better left to the private sector through commercial lending and private foreign direct and portfolio investment. Significantly, therefore, the Fund began to be criticized from both ends of the political spectrum. Those from the left argued that it imposed stagflationary and anti-development policies based on monetarist modes of thought, while those from the right argued that, certainly as a lending agency, it was not needed.

The mid-to-late 1980s saw criticism of the Fund taking on a somewhat different dimension. An argument now was that, within the context of the Third World debt crisis in particular, the Fund had become much too political, with lending decisions reflecting political modalities rather than economic realities. The claim was that some of the Fund's principal shareholders were more overtly using it as an arm of foreign policy. With political considerations taking precedence over economic ones, the criticism was that the Fund would quickly lose its credibility and reputation, characteristics that were fundamental to its successful operation. With confidence in it lacking, the Fund will find it impossible to exert meaningful influence over international monetary matters and, in these circumstances, it might just as well be abandoned. A related problem is that as far as developed countries are concerned the role of the IMF has been replaced by fora such as the G-3, G-7, G-10 or the OECD.

Should the IMF be replaced or reformed? If it is felt that there are functions for an institution to perform, a critical question is whether there are any reasons to believe that a new institution will perform them better than an old one. Where, for example, the shortcomings of an existing institution arise from the attitudes of its major shareholders, it is difficult to see how institutional changes alone, even if they can be brought about, will have much effect, unless attitudes change. Yet with a change in attitudes the shortcomings of the existing institution may, more easily, be corrected.

I   The IMF in retrospect: systemic marginalization
Discussion of the future needs to be placed in historical context. Looking forward is assisted by looking back. What does looking back tell us about the Fund? The IMF was originally established to encourage international cooperation to cope with recession and protectionism on a world scale and to discourage individual countries from pursuing policies that would beggar their neighbours and eventually themselves. The desire to improve on the international chaos of the 1930s led to the Bretton Woods conference in 1944 and an attempt to devise a system which would provide a more permanent and acceptable framework for international transactions. It was intended that the emerging Bretton Woods system would generate benefits for international trade in the form of stable (though not necessarily fixed) exchange rates, while, at the same time, avoiding the deflationary rigidities of the gold standard mechanism. The system was designed to ensure a world of full employment and economic growth.

Within the framework set by its terms of reference the Fund operated, first, as a balance of payments adjustment institution, encouraging payments correction by means other than the use of exchange rates (except in cases of fundamental disequilibrium) or protectionist trade measures; second, as a balance of payments-financing institution, providing temporary finance designed to support adjustment measures to cushion self-reversing payments instabilities; and third, as a focus for a system of rule-based international macroeconomic policy coordination, based essentially on the defence of established currency par values. The Fund thereby provided a linchpin for the centralized management of the international monetary system.

The Bretton Woods exchange rate regime did provide a code for the non-aggressive use of devaluation; the IMF did provide a consultative forum within which international financial reform was debated and implemented; the world economy did enjoy a period of sustained expansion; and world trade was liberalized and did grow (see Bird, 1985). So what went wrong? The answer is that the Bretton Woods system broke down and was replaced by a much looser set of international monetary arrangements. The move over to generalized flexible exchange rates took away the means by which macroeconomic policy had been internationally coordinated. Not until the Plaza Accord of 1985 was there a serious attempt to manage exchange rates. However such coordination was handled outside the IMF by the G-7 or G-3 countries. The activities of the Fund were also marginalized in terms of balance of payments financing. Although the oil price rise of 1973 and the related acceleration and diversity in rates of inflation dramatically increased the need for international financial intermediation, this largely took place through the private international banks. The late 1970s saw the privatization of balance of payments financing. Related to both the move to exchange rate flexibility and the private financing of balance of payments deficits, the Fund's importance as a source of official reserve creation also became marginalized during the 1970s.[1] Finally, the trend seemed to be to move away from international monetary arrangements and towards regional ones. Increasing regionalization was most dramatically illustrated by the establishment of the European Monetary System in 1979. It was now at the regional level that the management of exchange rates and the coordination of macroeconomic policy occurred.

II   Changing partners: the Fund's involvement with developing countries

The Fund ceased to be a source of finance for industrial countries during the 1980s. The picture contrasts sharply with that for earlier periods. In 1968–72, for example, 11 industrial countries, including most G-7 countries, drew on the Fund. With the legitimization of floating exchange rates through the amendment of the Fund's Articles of Agreement in 1978, the establishment of the European Monetary System in 1979 and the credit facilities which this provided for members of the system, and continuing innovation in international financial intermediation using private capital markets, industrial countries could now easily bypass the IMF.

This was clearly not the case for developing countries, particularly after the debt crisis had come to the fore in 1982. Prior to that date a limited number of the better off developing countries had enjoyed access to private capital in the form of loans from commercial banks. By late 1981 most Fund lending was to the LDCs. This is reflected by the relatively large amount of

Table 11.1 Total net resource flows to developing countries*

	1981	1982	1983	1984	1985	1986	1987	1988	1989
					Current $ billion				
I Official Development Finance (ODF)	45.5	44.2	42.4	47.7	48.9	56.3	61.6	66.0	69.0
II Total export credits	17.6	13.7	4.6	6.2	4.0	-0.7	-2.6	-0.5	1.2
III Private flows	74.3	58.2	47.9	31.7	31.4	28.2	34.5	40.4	40.2
Total net resource flows (I+II+III)	137.4	116.1	94.9	85.6	84.3	83.8	93.5	105.9	110.4
Memorandum items: Total net credits from IMF	6.6	6.4	12.5	5.4	0.8	-1.4	-4.7	-4.0	-3.2

Note: * Flows from all sources, i.e. including DAC, Eastern European Countries, Arab and other LDC donors; excluding Taiwan.

Source: Development Cooperation, 1990 Report, OECD, Paris, 1990.

net Fund credit to the developing countries of Africa and Asia observed in 1982 and by the relatively small amount of net credit to the less developed countries of the Western hemisphere. At this time a division of labour appeared to emerge between the Fund and the banks in terms of lending to developing countries. However the pattern was rudely disturbed in 1983 and beyond, as countries formerly deemed creditworthy by the banks found their access to commercial credit being cut off. Given the size of their adjustment problems, these countries were now forced to turn to the Fund for finance. While in 1982 Fund credit in African LDCs had been 33 per cent more than in the LDCs of the Western hemisphere, by 1983 it was 79 per cent less. The change in the pattern of Fund lending to developing countries was indeed dramatic. While there had been a steady increase in outstanding Fund credit in African LDCs during 1970–85, and a rather less steady increase in Asian LDCs, Fund credit outstanding in the LDCs of the Western hemisphere actually fell between 1976 and 1981, but then increased tenfold in the next five years.

Yet while the first half of the 1980s saw the Fund becoming quite heavily involved in providing credit to developing countries, by the second half of the 1980s the net transfer between the Fund and developing countries had become negative (see Table 11.1). If the negative net transfer that LDCs faced in terms of the banks was a problem, the Fund seemed to be adding to it rather than contributing to its resolution. On the other hand, the positive net flow of Fund resources in the earlier 1980s seen against a negative net flow of commercial loans had led to accusations that the Fund was bailing out the banks.

Whatever its cause, the changing pattern of Fund lending raised a series of questions concerning the role of the Fund. Should the Fund be lending exclusively to developing countries? Had it become, to all intents and purposes, a development agency? Did lending to developing countries not mean that there was considerable overlap between the Fund and the World Bank and, if so, how should this overlap be handled?

III   Criticisms of the fund: 1980s vintage

It is largely in the context of its dealings with developing countries that the Fund has come in for criticism over the last ten years or so. These criticisms may be considered under a number of headings.

IMF conditionality

Design deficiencies   Fund policies have been seen by some critics as reflecting deeply entrenched monetarist modes of thought. In this context Fund-supported programmes are viewed as being too heavily oriented to the demand side of the economy and as ignoring the supply side and fundamental structural characteristics. It is further claimed that the conventional IMF package of devaluation and demand deflation is stagflationary in developing countries where the macroeconomic system often differs significantly from that to be found in developed countries, (see Bird, 1983; Williamson, 1983). Even critics who have not gone this far nonetheless suggest that the macroeconomic analytical underpinning of Fund advice has failed to keep up with the rapid rate of technical advance in macroeconomic theory. While the 1980s have been dominated by the New Classical Macroeconomics, by rational expectations, by time consistency and by credibility, the Fund is apparently trapped in a time capsule along with the Polak model. Edwards (1989), for example, argues that recent statements of the Fund's underlying model differ only marginally, and largely inconsequentially, from much earlier versions.

If the Fund's basic model is seen as being deficient, so is its assessment of the role of the state. Here critics argue that the Fund has been too quick to accept the neo-classical liberalism of the 1980s. Even temperate studies have suggested that the state, in conjunction with the private sector, and often using market incentives, has a crucial role to play in helping to bring about both short-run stabilization and longer-term balance of payments correction and economic development. Again the Fund is accused of being much too simplistic in its approach (see Killick, 1989a). A specific illustration of this ill-measured attitude has, according to critics, been the proclivity of the Fund to encourage reduced fiscal deficits by means of cutting government expenditure rather than by seeking to widen the tax base and alter the structure of taxation in order to raise tax revenue.

A final argument is that policies supported by the Fund suffer from a 'fallacy of composition' (see Stewart and Sengupta, 1982). The Fund recommends policies in one country which are designed on the assumption that external factors remain constant. At the same time, because it is involved in a number of countries simultaneously, this assumption is invalid. Any country within the system can only strengthen its balance of payments if others are prepared to accommodate the improvement by allowing theirs to weaken.

Poor record of success All the above arguments, if valid, would lead one to expect that IMF-supported programmes will experience a high failure rate. Surely the proof of the policies is in their impact; and surely this is simply an empirical issue. An empirical issue it may be, but simple it assuredly is not (Khan, 1990). Edwards (1989), after studying both the compliance of governments with the programmes that they have negotiated with the Fund and the performance of ultimate target variables (as opposed to proximate policy ones), concludes that Fund-supported programmes have been increasingly unsuccessful in the period since 1983. While conceding that countries with IMF-supported programmes experienced an improvement in their current account balance of payments, he points out that countries without such programmes also experienced an improvement in their current accounts over the same period. Related claims about the failure of Fund-supported programmes are made by Sachs (1989).

Against this rather gloomy picture, and on the basis of a study which covers more countries (69), a longer time period (1973–88) and uses a different methodology designed to capture the counter-factual, Khan (1990) maintains that Fund-supported programmes have had an increasing success rate. However, even here success is patchy and modest. Moreover, while Khan's study is indeed more positive about IMF-supported programmes than previous studies, it fails to distinguish between those countries that did and did not implement the agreed programme.

It has already been noted that industrial countries can escape Fund conditionality by making use of other sources of finance. Even amongst developing countries econometric attempts to derive a demand function for Fund credits have been largely unsuccessful, and those functions that have been identified have been unstable and not useful for predictive purposes (see, for example, Cornelius, 1987; Joyce, 1990). Many developing countries whose economic characteristics would lead one to believe that they will turn to the Fund in fact do not. Their revealed preference to avoid the Fund if at all possible surely implies something about the perceived costs, economic or political, of IMF conditionality.

Developing country debt

Criticisms of the Fund's handling of developing country debt comprise a number of elements. First, critics argue that it has been in this context that the Fund has become more overtly political. According to this view, lending decisions have been forced through by creditor countries, in particular the USA, with the clear objective of preventing specific debtor countries from defaulting and thereby damaging the interests of the large commercial banks that still have significant loans outstanding to them. The claim that this was justified in order to ensure systemic stability became increasingly illegitimate as the banks themselves adjusted to the crisis by provisioning, by reducing their developing country exposures through the secondary market, and by expanding other lines of business. Even normally docile members of the Fund's own staff began to complain loudly that it was being politically manoeuvred. Without having to subscribe to this view, aggregate evidence drawn from the mid-1980s does suggest that positive net transfers from the Fund to indebted developing countries financed negative transfers with the banks. It requires only a short step to claim that the Fund was bailing out the banks.

The second criticism associated with its involvement in developing country debt has been that the Fund treated the debt problem as if it was one of illiquidity and inadequate cash flow, rather than, as was indeed the case, a more deep-rooted and longer-term one of structural adjustment (Edwards, 1989; Sachs, 1989). The Fund opted to support new financing which assisted countries in meeting their outstanding debt servicing obligations, but did little to restore medium-term viability to their balance of payments. The adjustment programmes favoured by the Fund called for the deflation of domestic demand in order to compress imports, and devaluation to strengthen the tradeables sector in general. Demand deflation might have been appropriate had the debt crisis been one of temporary illiquidity, but it was largely inappropriate in circumstances where the crisis was one of long-term adjustment and development. Demand deflation had an adverse effect on domestic investment and on the importation of capital goods. It therefore exerted a damaging effect on future economic growth which represented the best chance developing countries had for handling their debt in the long run without sacrificing living standards.[2] Given the lengthy lead time of investment over growth, policy mistakes in the 1980s will become increasingly evident during the 1990s.

The third criticism of the Fund in the context of debt has been its inability to devise incentives that positively encourage the pursuit of adjustment (see Berg and Sachs, 1988; Krugman, 1988; Edwards, 1989). The additional foreign exchange that adjustment creates has been largely used to repay commercial creditors abroad. The domestic rate of return has in many cases been low or even zero. Critics argue that it was this low domestic return which led to the problems of non-compliance discussed earlier. Governments found it difficult to muster domestic political support for programmes which seemed to imply heavy domestic costs but no readily discernible benefits. Such critics go on to argue that what was needed was debt relief in order to reduce the domestic adjustment burden and raise the incentive to adjust. In fact through its policy of 'assured financing' the Fund discouraged banks from granting relief. In this way the Fund postponed appropriate systemic reform (Sachs, 1989).

It is clear that the Fund has failed to achieve its own target of normalizing creditor–debtor relations and restoring country access to sustainable flows and spontaneous lending. At the end of the 1980s, creditor–debtor relations remained strained and far from normalized; access to spontaneous lending had not been restored – indeed the creditworthiness of the highly indebted countries, as proxied by the secondary market price of their debt, had continued to fall; net transfers were still significantly negative; a concerted cooperative approach to the debt problem had not emerged; most debt indicators failed to show any significant or sustained improvement; and macroeconomic performance in the indebted countries remained poor and often deteriorating. Even the IMF itself faced increasing arrears and had to make more and more use of waivers. Hardly, then, a picture of great success.

Low income countries
If the Fund's dealings with the highly indebted countries of the Western hemisphere have largely failed, what about its track record in the poorest countries of the world, in Africa and Asia? Some commentators suggest that it is likely to be bad. They argue that in low-income countries (LICs) more than anywhere else it is impossible to draw a distinction between the balance of payments and development. Payments deficits are of a structural type, reflecting the fact that LICs have undiversified product mixes, with a high concentration on products which generally have low price and income elasticities. Moreover, reliance on a few key exports makes LICs particularly vulnerable to external shocks and movements in the terms of trade. The resolution of these problems is a long-term process which needs to focus on the supply side of the economy. The short-run management of demand is important, but fails to capture the essence of the problem.[3] Moreover critics suggest that Fund-supported programmes which rely on changing behaviour by means of altering the domestic set of relative price incentives will be at their least effective where elasticities are low and where markets are not fully developed. Thus devaluation has been most commonly criticized in the context of LICs. With ill-developed financial markets, fiscal deficits are more likely to be monetized, with consequences for inflation and the balance of payments. Tax revenue may be insensitive to changes in tax policy and government expenditure may be difficult to cut. On top of this, to the extent that Fund-supported programmes have a contractionary effect on the countries that implement them, this may be deemed to be of particular concern in the poorest countries of the world.

The evidence seems to lend some support to these concerns. For a number of years researchers have argued that the elements of adjustment programmes do not appear to discriminate between LICs and other borrowers (Killick *et al.*, 1984). At the same time, programmes appear to be relatively less successful in LICs than elsewhere. Indeed some empirical studies have suggested that, even on the basis of methodologies used by the Fund, there are few significant differences to be found between those low-income countries that have adopted Fund-supported programmes and those that have not (Loxley, 1984; Zulu and Nsouli, 1985).

Lines of demarcation with other international institutions
Economic developments during the 1980s and perhaps in particular the Fund's involvement in developing countries have served to cloud the lines of demarcation between the Fund and other institutions, with this periodically leading to quite severe demarcation disputes. The Fund has seen others encroaching on areas that it previously saw as its own. The interlopers included the commercial banks and the World Bank. It should be noted that, at a systemic level, there has also been increasing overlap between the Fund and the groupings of industrial countries in the form of the OECD, G-10, G-7, G-3 and the European Community. Increasingly during the 1980s it has been these groupings that have assumed responsibility for the management of exchange rates and the international coordination of macroeconomic policy, functions which were previously associated with the Fund.

Demarcation disputes also arose between the Fund and the World Bank. The division of labour between the two Bretton Woods institutions which had begun to alter in the 1970s underwent still more fundamental change in the 1980s. Prior to the breakdown of the Bretton Woods system, the division of labour had been relatively straightforward. The Fund's orientation was towards the short run, the balance of payments, the demand side, the monetary sector, and programme support. The Bank's was towards the long run, economic development, the supply side, the real sector, and project support. The differences between the two institutions were nicely encapsulated in Keynes's observation that the Board of the Fund should comprise 'cautious bankers' whereas that of the Bank should comprise 'imaginative expansionists' (Moggridge, 1980).

In 1966, an internal memorandum clarified the division of labour by assigning 'primary responsibilities' to each agency. The Fund had jurisdiction 'for exchange rates and restrictive systems, for adjustment of temporary balance of payments disequilibria and for evaluating and assisting members to work out stabilisation programmes as a sound basis for economic advice'. The Bank's primary responsibility, in contrast, was 'for the composition and appropriateness of development programmes and project evaluation, including development priorities'.

Less than a decade later, the Fund had begun to accept that payments deficits could be of a structural nature for which correction required longer-term financial support. The Extended Fund Facility (EFF) was introduced to fill what was perceived as a gap in the range of the Fund's lending facilities. Although critics have argued that EFF programmes in practice were little different from normal stand-by programmes, and although the Fund's staff were rather unenthusiastic about the facility, its introduction clouded the distinction between the Fund and the Bank. The distinction was further blurred throughout the 1980s, first by the Bank's commencement of a programme of structural adjustment lending through structural adjustment loans (SALs) and sectoral adjustment loans (SECALs) which incorporated conditionality linked to the structural causation of balance of payments deficits, and second by the introduction by the Fund of the structural adjustment facility and then the enhanced structural adjustment facility. In both terminology and in areas of involvement, structural adjustment had served to create an important area of overlap between the Fund and the Bank (Feinberg, 1988).

The agencies themselves attempted to deal with these overlapping responsibilities by seeking to achieve greater cooperation and collaboration and, through this, consistency. The cooperation has been both formal, as incorporated in the mutual design of a policy framework paper (PFP) as part of the SAF, and informal, relying, as some observers have suggested, on the 'personal chemistry' of the relevant staff members. Clearly the overlap can bring with it both advantages and disadvantages. The former exist in terms of better informed analysis and judgement, the latter in terms of inefficiency caused by increasing labour input per unit of output, by delays and by institutional conflict.

IV   Lessons to draw: a rehabilitation of the Fund

What is the appropriate lesson to draw from this avalanche of criticism? It is hardly surprising that the suggestion is made that the Fund should cease operations and close down. But is the Fund a strong candidate for institutional euthanasia, or can it be rehabilitated? There are a number of points relevant to such rehabilitation and to the challenge of coming up with a more measured assessment of the Fund.

First, the list of criticisms presented above gives an artificial picture of reality since some of the individual criticisms conflict. Second, in any economic debate it is possible to strengthen one side of the argument by being selective in the issues and evidence quoted. As part of an ongoing study at the Overseas Development Institute (ODI), programme completions have been analysed as an indicator of compliance. This evidence suggests that, in the mid-1980s and in contradiction to the claim made by Edwards (1989), compliance actually improved slightly. However in the following period 1987–90, not covered by Edwards, there was a dramatic deterioration, with 57 per cent of IMF-supported programmes remaining uncompleted as compared with 41 per cent in 1984–6. The ODI evidence, however, confirms Edwards's claim that IMF-supported programmes have encountered a lower rate of compliance in the severely indebted countries than elsewhere. It also confirms the absence of incontrovertible evidence relating to the success of Fund-supported programmes.

Third, however, success is judged against the benchmark of expectations. As the Fund's defenders have maintained in the past, it may be unreasonable to expect too much of the Fund, given the array of factors which influence economic performance (Nowzad, 1981). The theory behind Fund-supported adjustment programmes might lead one to expect that, while the short-run impact on the balance of payments would be positive and that on output would be negative, the longer-run impact on output would be positive (IMF, 1987). The available evidence is not totally inconsistent with this expectation. Having said this, the theory of economic policy confirms that countries experiencing apparently similar macroeconomic problems may actually require rather different policy remedies (see Bird, 1987a).

Underpinning the 'strong' argument for Fund closure is a misplaced confidence in the efficiency of private international capital markets. Without reviewing the evidence on efficient markets which in fact provides little that is conclusive upon which to base such confidence, the experiences of the 1970s and early 1980s surely provide enough evidence to call into question the claim that markets know best. And who would have provided balance of payments support to low-income countries if the Fund had not existed? Would the economic performance of these economies really have been better had such support not been forthcoming?

Looking to the future, another specific problem will be the continued emergence of the economies of Eastern and Central Europe, which have until now been essentially excluded from the world economy. Their emergence will create additional demands for international finance, but will also require balance of payments accommodation in the rest of the world. A more general problem is the changing structure of power amongst the world's leading economies. In the field of international political economy this is seen as a continuing decline in the hegemony of the USA, although it is premature to say what structure may replace this. Some have argued that it will be replaced by a tri-polar structure based on the USA, Japan and a more fully integrated Europe (Bergsten, 1990). Others have argued that a more fragmentary, variegated and mutable 'mosaic' will emerge (Cohen, 1991). Whatever form change in fact takes, it will create difficulties which could threaten the continued growth of global output and world trade. The thawing of the Cold War which, at its coolest, served to unite Western industrial nations will, it is argued, exacerbate economic tensions; as also will the rapid shift in the status of the USA from being a creditor to being a debtor nation. Ensuring that such tensions do not lead to outright economic warfare is seen as the principal challenge facing the world economy. Avoiding competitive balance of payments policy and seeking to provide an orderly mechanism for the correction of balance of payments policy was where the IMF started. Again drawing on the international political economists' analysis of regime types, one alternative would be to move away from the 'hegemony' that previously gave the world stability to 'supranationality'. The IMF would be an appropriate institution under which to achieve this transition.

However one does not have to subscribe to any particular vision of the future to see that the international monetary regime is moving in a direction that recreates a potential systemic and regulatory role for the Fund. It is now accepted that flexible exchange rates are not the panacea that some of their original and more outspoken advocates believed. They exhibit volatility and do not guarantee the maintenance of equilibrium real exchange rates. Since the mid-1980s the trend has been towards the greater management of exchange rates. Related to changing views about exchange rates, it has also become increasingly accepted that internationally uncoordinated macroeconomic policies can create problems for the world economy in terms of both growth and stability.

Moreover it is more widely recognized that the world economy is not necessarily intrinsically stable. Shocks do occur and these shocks are usually asymmetric in their effects, requiring adjustments in real exchange rates. If there is no orderly mechanism for bringing such adjustment about, there is a danger of global recession and rising protectionism. There is the need to redesign the so-called 'multilateral debt strategy', which has failed to work for the indebted countries, but which may now have reached a stage where private banks are prepared to make concessions. The world economy needs an institution such as the IMF more, rather than less.

V   Concluding remarks

Although the IMF as an international institution has encountered severe problems during the 1980s it may yet be premature to start writing its obituary. The problems that have buffeted the Fund are not easy ones with which to deal and there seems little reason to believe that simply closing down the Fund will make things better. Institutional euthanasia is not warranted. Indeed international monetary developments and changes in the world economy suggest that the rationale of the Fund's existence will be re-emphasized during the 1990s and beyond. If we did not already have the IMF, we would have to invent it. To reject the extreme argument for closing down the Fund does not imply that there is no need for change. This should take the form of either significant modification to the Fund's operations or a more radical reorganization of the Fund's role vis-à-vis that of the World Bank. What is clear is that nothing much will happen without a political commitment on behalf of the governments of the major economies of the world.

Notes

1. Some analysts have argued strongly that the adequacy of international reserves was never as important an issue as it was thought to be in the 1960s, and that the so-called 'Triffin dilemma' associated with the key role of the dollar was not a dilemma at all, see Chrystal (1990).
2. On the basis of a study of 34 developing countries, Khan and Knight (1988) identify a strong positive correlation between the availability of imports and export volumes. Moreover Otani and Villanueva (1990) find strong quantitative support for the view that export performance has a dominant influence on economic growth in developing countries.
3. For examples of this literature, see Killick *et al.* (1984) and Helleiner (1983). Helleiner identifies many differences between African and Latin American economies, characterizing the typical African economy as 'smaller, poorer, more trade-dependent, less urbanised, and less socially stratified than its Latin-American counterpart. Its agricultural sector weighs more heavily in overall output and is based much more upon small-holder production; the urban work force is not only relatively smaller and politically weaker, but also usually enjoys close links to rural families. Its financial institutions are weaker and more rudimentary. Despite the dramatic acceleration and education programmes in the post-independence period, levels of literacy and educational achievement are still relatively low in Africa. The ability to govern is limited by severe shortages of appropriate skills, not least in the area of economic analysis.' He notes that 'these intercontinental differences play upon the politics and economics of alternative stabilisation or adjustment programmes'. Low–income countries in Asia and the Pacific encounter similar problems.

Bibliography

Berg, A. and J. Sachs (1988), 'The Debt Crisis, Structural Explanations of Country Performance', *Journal of Development Economics*, **29**.

Bergsten, C. Fred (1990), 'From Cold War to Trade War', *International Economic Insights*, July/August.

Bird, Graham (1978), *The International Monetary System and the Less Developed Countries*, London: Macmillan.

Bird, Graham (1983), 'Should Developing Countries Use Currency Depreciation as a Tool of Balance of Payments Adjustments? A Review of the Theory and Evidence and a Guide for the Policy Maker', *Journal of Development Studies*, July.

Bird, Graham (1985), *World Finance and Adjustment: An Agenda for Reform*, ch. 2, London: Macmillan.

Bird, Graham (1987a), 'The International Monetary Fund and Stabilisation Policy in Small Open Economies', ch. 10 of *International Macroeconomics: Theory and Application*, London: Macmillan.

Bird, Graham (1987b), *International Financial Policy and Economic Development*, London: Macmillan.

Bird, Graham (1988), 'The Changing International Economic Order and the Interests of Developing Countries', ch. 12 of *Managing Global Money*, London: Macmillan.

Chrystal, K. Alec (1990), 'International Reserves and International Liquidity: A Solution in Search of a Problem', in Graham Bird (ed.), *The International Financial Regime*, Surrey University Press with Academic Press.

Cohen, Benjamin J. (1977), *Organizing the World's Money*, New York: Basic Books.

Cohen, Benjamin J. (1991), 'Towards a Mosaic Economy: Economic Relations in the Post-Cold War Era', *The Fletcher Forum of World Affairs*, **15**, (2), Summer, pp. 39–54.

Cornelius, Peter (1987), 'The Demand for IMF Credits by Sub-Saharan African Countries', *Economic Letters*, **23**, pp. 99–102.

Edwards, Sebastian (1989), 'The International Monetary Fund and the Developing Countries: A Critical Evaluation', *Carnegie Rochester Conference Series on Public Policy*, **31**.

Feinberg, Richard E. (1988) 'The Changing Relationship Between the World Bank and the International Monetary Fund', *International Organization*, Summer.

Helleiner, G.K. (1983), 'The IMF and Africa in the 1980s', *Essays in International Finance*, Princeton University, no. 152, July.

IMF (1987), *Theoretical Aspects of the Design of Fund-Supported Adjustment Programmes*, Occasional Paper, no. 55, Washington: IMF.

Joyce, Joseph P. (1990), 'The Economic Characteristics of IMF Programme Countries', Wellesley College Working Paper, no 118.

Khan, M. (1990), 'The Macroeconomic Effects of Fund Supported Programmes', *IMF Staff Papers*, June.

Khan, Mohsin S. and M.D. Knight (1988), 'Import Compression and Export Peformance in Developing Countries', *Review of Economics and Statistics*, May.

Killick, Tony (1989a), *A Reaction Too Far: Economic Theory and the Role of the State in Developing Countries*, London: Overseas Development Institute.

Killick, Tony (1989b), 'Issues Arising from the Spread of Obligatory Adjustment', in Graham Bird (ed.), *Third World Debt: The Search for a Solution*, Aldershot: Edward Elgar.

Killick, Tony *et al.* (1984), *The Quest for Economic Stabilisation: The IMF and the Third World*, London: Overseas Development Institute.

Krugman, Paul (1988), 'Financing versus Forgiving a Debt Overhang', *Journal of Development Economics*, **29**.

Loxley, John (1984), *The IMF and the Poorest Countries*, Ottawa: North–South Institute.

Moggridge, Donald (ed.) (1980), *The Collected Writings of John Maynard Keynes, Vol. XXVI, Activities 1941–46*, London: Macmillan.

Nowzad, Bahram (1981), 'The IMF and its Critics', *Princetown Essays in International Finance*, no 146.

Otani, Ichiro and D. Villanueva (1990), 'Determining Long Term Growth Performance in Developing Countries', *World Development*.

Sachs, Jeffrey D. (1989), 'Strengthening IMF Programmes in Highly Indebted Countries', in R. Gwin and C. Feinberg (eds), *The International Monetary Fund in a Multipolar World, US–Third World Policy Perspectives*, no. 13, Washington, DC: Overseas Development Council.

Stewart, F. and A. Sengupta (1982), *International Financial Co-operation: A Framework for Change*, London: Frances Pinter.

Williamson, John (ed.) (1983), *IMF Conditionality*, Washington, DC: Institute for International Economics.

Zulu, Justin B. and Saleh M. Nsouli (1985), 'Adjustment Programmes in Africa: The Recent Experience', *IMF Occasional Paper* no. 34, April.

12 International trade policy and the developing world

Sheila Page

I Introduction

The last two decades have seen a remarkable reversal of positions between the developed and developing countries in world trade negotiations. In the 1970s, the developed countries started extending, reintroducing and inventing non-tariff barriers to trade. Since the 1950s these had been recognized as contrary to GATT principles (if not always to the letter of the rules) and had in fact been avoided, except in a limited range of activities. Even in areas where such intervention was common, like agriculture, it was accepted that this was an undesirable relic, perhaps needed until a sector or population could fully adapt to international trade. In the 1980s, the reversal went further, with the EC and the USA, at least, seeming at times even to be turning away from the principle of multilateral negotiations as a basically beneficial activity. In contrast, developing countries were moving from recognition, during the 1970s, that import substitution, usually behind tariff and non-tariff barriers, was at least not the only and not a complete path to development, towards (with outside pressure in the 1980s) an absolute commitment to opening their economies to imports and putting their emphasis on exports. The NICs gave examples of an alternative road. In the second half of the 1980s, this led logically to growing faith and participation in multilateral negotiations.

The purpose of this chapter is to analyse first where these changes in direction have left the world environment of trade policies and trade negotiations which developing countries must now face. What effect have these changes had on their apparent prospects for trade and on the appropriateness of different approaches to trade policy? But as well as these absolute changes, it is also necessary to explore briefly how the even greater change in their policies relative to those of the developed countries will affect the trade and investment relationships between them.

II Multilateral trade policy

The Uruguay Round of trade negotiations began in 1986, with a target for completion of December 1990. This was later extended repeatedly, to various dates in, first, 1991, then 1992 and now late 1993. This was the first of the eight rounds since the formation of GATT to attract substantial interest and participation by the developing countries, and in which they in turn were major targets for liberalization requests from the industrial countries. In all the major 'negotiating groups' into which the issues under negotiation were divided, demands both by and on the developing countries were on the table. In the past many of the most important developing countries, notably in Latin America, had chosen to remain outside GATT. During the round, countries like Mexico and Venezuela joined, and officials from developing countries, especially the Latin American (not only Uruguay, but also Brazil and Colombia) played leading parts.

There are three types of explanation for this. The first is actual economic weight: the trade of developing countries had become a major force at world level, and no longer just in primary or other non-competing products; it had increased from 21 per cent in 1973, the beginning of the previous round, to 26 per cent by 1986, and in manufactures it had doubled to 15 per cent of the total. Developing countries had become major markets, and competitors for the developed countries in the products which had traditionally been the core of negotiations. On their side, trade was a higher share of their income and output, and within this the traditional GATT-type goods, manufactures, had by 1986 become more than 50 per cent of their total exports.

The second explanation was the extension of this round into new areas. Both developed and developing countries wanted to bring agriculture, textiles and clothing more fully under GATT rules; services were also added. All these were areas in which developing countries have a strong interest or a potential advantage through their low labour costs. The third was the nature of trade policy. Partly because of the growth of protection in the industrial countries and partly because of the central importance assigned to trade and trade policy in analyses of the success of NICs in the 1970s, developing countries had to take more interest in influencing the trade policies which affect their exports.

The Round has already had some identifiable outcomes and the pattern, if not the details, of a final settlement (if there is one) is now clear. The new developing country members of GATT were compelled to accept not merely a commitment in principle to international constraints on their trade policy, as earlier developing members had been able to do, but immediate reductions in their tariff and non-tariff barriers, and in their freedom to alter them. This reflected the growing doubts, on both sides, about the benefits of giving developing countries their traditional 'special and differential treatment', and also the growing interest of industrial countries in penetrating their markets. GATT has introduced regular 'Trade Review' missions and published reports, spelling out the actual trading practices of each member.

While not in themselves condemning any restrictive actions, the reports place any interventions before GATT Council for discussion.

If the proposed settlement is accepted, many of the remaining (small) restrictions on tropical products such as coffee will be removed. On these, however, and on all other commodities, the problem of 'tariff escalation' (tariffs on more processed goods are normally higher) would remain. For the EC, for example, tariffs on raw materials are on average close to 0; on semi-processed about 4 per cent; on finished goods almost 7 per cent. The tariff reductions proposed are about a third for all goods. Although there are slightly greater reductions for tariffs now above 30 per cent, and all those above 40 per cent should come down to 20 per cent, the preference for less processed goods would remain, and would continue to discourage processing in the country of origin. The effective reductions in all tariffs would also be much less for exports by developing countries benefiting from GSP (generalized system of preferences). As most GSP tariffs are already below the proposed new levels, their access would not be eased. GSP would, indeed, indirectly damage such countries by reducing or removing their margin of preference relative to normal tariffs. On the other hand, tariffs imposed by developing countries (particularly the more advanced) would be reduced by the same formulas and, as they do not offer GSP, these reductions would be effectively greater, and, cover all suppliers.

The proposed settlement on 'temperate' agriculture would reduce subsidized EC exports and therefore raise world prices and reduce the quantities exported from industrial countries. (If it includes rice, it will increase rice exports to Japan and perhaps South Korea.) All these effects would benefit developing country producers of grains and meat, again with the principal benefit going to primary exports. The proposed settlement would end the current system of tight country-to-country and product-specific quotas on textile and clothing trade under the Multi-Fibre Arrangement (MFA). This (with its predecessor schemes) dates from 1961, and the objective of the Uruguay Round negotiations was to bring restrictions on these commodities back into normal GATT channels, in particular ending discrimination among suppliers and rigid quotas, and leaving only regulation by tariff. The settlement would do this by increasing quotas in three stages, and removing them after ten years, while simultaneously removing an increasing proportion of goods from the quota system. It is structured to be loaded heavily to the end of the period, and tariffs in the sector are and would remain among the highest, with the usual structure, biased against more processed goods (clothing relative to fabric, and fabric relative to fibres). It would be of most benefit to the countries with large supplies of low-cost labour (and, among them, those with their own supplies of the raw materials).

On both temperate agriculture and textiles and clothing, strong and coordinated intervention by the developing countries (on agriculture, in association with the efficient developed exporters like Australia) has made the likely Uruguay settlement one which goes well beyond most expectations at the beginning of the Round, and thus success would offer a convincing vindication of the decision to participate fully in the Round. Failure of the Round would have the opposite effect.

Services offer a different lesson. Attaining more open markets on these was the principal reason (although closely followed by the reduction of subsidies to agriculture) for US advocacy of holding the Round. Other developed countries had much less enthusiasm for a Round. Both the EC and Japan had a few minor objectives (market access to NICs; greater protection of patents and copyright), but greater fears of having to make concessions (on agriculture or clothing) and the EC in particular had more urgent trade negotiations within itself for the implementation of the Single European Market (SEM). Initially the developing countries were in most cases not interested in, and in a few opposed to, the inclusion of services. The principal practical outcome of the services negotiations has been a massive expansion of data and understanding of services trade, and the result of this has been recognition on the part of the USA and the developing countries that the advantages of the USA were seriously overestimated, and those of the developing countries were underestimated. (They have low labour costs and new, more modern structures: air, shipping and construction services are the most obvious examples.) The USA, like the EC, has therefore now become less enthusiastic about the potential gains from multilateral negotiations, while the developing countries (potentially) have another piece of evidence for their benefits.

A successful conclusion of the Round would have a final implicit benefit: it would mark a return to order in the regulation of international trade and away from unilateral interventions. The latter have been used increasingly by the most developed countries: the increase in protection in the 1970s, because of their economic difficulties; the choice of GATT-illegal measures, because countries' range of action on tariffs is more restricted under GATT; their use of their economic strength to discourage their suppliers from complaining to GATT, thus securing 'voluntary' restraint, or to ignore adverse rulings by GATT, when discouragement fails. Although there are some large developing countries and some weak industrial, in general, this provides another argument in favour of multilateral methods for the developing countries.

The principal weakness of a Uruguay Round settlement (other than its failure to go far or fast enough) would be the bias against industrialization. This failing, combined with the fear that no settlement at all will be reached, helps to explain developing countries' interest in other types of trade negotiation.

III   Regional negotiations and organizations

EC 1992
Up to now, the only regional groups which have had discernible effects on trade, among their members or between the members and the rest of the world, have been those among the industrial countries, in particular the EC, other European groups and the long-standing USA–Canada car industry agreement. Traditional analysis emphasizes the effect of diverting trade from non-members to members because of lower (or 0) tariffs for goods from the latter. In principle, any identifiable losses require compensation under GATT rules, but the EC rarely gave this, even to developed countries, as it moved to a common external tariff and attracted new members. It is even harder to prove damage resulting from the Single European Market exercise. This is a change in relative position (the EC members have freer access to each other) rather than direct action against others (the EC is not actually raising barriers to the rest of the world).

The EC has argued that there are also beneficial demand effects, both immediate and dynamic. Competition will lead to increased efficiency within the EC, and thus higher and faster growing income, which will in turn lead to higher imports from the rest of the world. (The contrary argument, that adjustment to new competition will lead to a temporary slump, has rarely been heard within Europe.) In the case of the EC's move to a single market, which goes well beyond simple trade measures, there are additional effects from the package of measures intended to improve the efficiency of all economic activities involving more than one country, through harmonization or mutual recognition of regulations, on services, standards, capital and labour movements, and some taxes. Not only do they reduce barriers within the EC relative to those to outsiders (like direct trade measures), but they also ensure that large elements of the trading environment are subject to regulations set in accordance with the interests of the 12 members, not on a multilateral basis, thus giving rise to unintentional discrimination and diversion. Because the structure, direction and quantity of their exports are more likely to be changing rapidly, developing countries also face more acutely than excluded industrial countries the problem that compensation for damage can only be for actual exports, not those which they might have introduced or increased. The SEM has also had the effect, noted above in the discussion of GATT, of providing an alternative negotiating interest, reducing GATT and other worldwide negotiations' relative, if not absolute, weight in EC trade policy.

Trade effects will again favour primary products. These are less likely to face competition from the member countries and therefore will lose little from diversion and make any available gains from the income effect. Manufactures, especially those standard low-technology, highly labour-intensive products in which the poorer members of the Community compete with the more advanced developing countries, are more likely to suffer diversion, leading to negative effects on developing countries, or at least greatly reduced positive ones. The EC is different from other actual or potential groupings among industrial countries (the USA–Canada, for example) in having a NIC-type area within it.

NAFTA

The admission of Mexico to the North American Free Trade Area (NAFTA), and the possibility of its further extension to other Latin American countries clearly has consequences for both Mexico and other developing countries. The initial NAFTA, the USA–Canada agreement, had little effect (even on the participants) because the economies were already integrated in some major products (notably cars) and the scope of the Agreement was much more limited than that of the EC, or even the European Free Trade Association. The extended NAFTA, however, has attracted great enthusiasm in Mexico and fears in areas such as South-east Asia and the Caribbean which see themselves as relatively disadvantaged.

The first observation which must be made is that, for Mexico as well as for the USA, negotiating NAFTA was a move away from multilateralism: from using the rules of GATT and the collective power of developing countries to obtain concessions from all industrial countries and to diversify export markets and products, back to using individual political and geographical leverage to extract concessions from the principal trading partner. Unlike the EC, it is not and is not intended to become a common market with completely free movement of labour and capital as well as goods, or common conditions for operating. Its intentions are even more modest than those of the various regional groups which have been formed among developing countries, as these in general have at least the intention of moving to a common external tariff, and some (the Andean Pact in its 1970s origins; SADC – Southern African Development Community – today) include provisions for common industrial or infrastructure projects. But NAFTA does increase relative barriers against the rest of the world, although over an exceptionally long transition period (15 years to full removal of tariffs, with the goods to be chosen by the individual countries) and by varying amounts, as Mexico's average external tariff remains higher than those of the USA and Canada. The effects and the difference are much less than they would have been a few years ago, as Mexico has already lowered its tariffs substantially.

For Mexico itself, as 45 per cent of its exports already enter the USA duty-free under GSP, the immediate effect on its exports of allowing 50 per cent to enter on both sides is not large. But on imports, although the effects are lower than they would have been when tariffs were higher, US exports do make more immediate gains, especially on cars (tariffs to be halved from the start; quotas eliminated over ten years). The estimated effects on Mexico's exports are thus much less than those on US exports. Although its national income gains from the cheaper imports, the hoped-for gains on output, investment and the balance of payments come from expected rises in US investment and the apparent expectation of stability from long-term integration into the US economy. In particular gains on manufactured exports will come slowly as these will await the lowering of tariffs in the later stages of opening.

It is not clear what the explanation for the expectations of higher investment is. In the EC, higher investment (and diversion of investment from the rest of the world) was expected as a result of higher growth, which in turn results from higher intra-EC trade and efficiency. (There is preliminary evidence supporting this.) If neither trade nor efficiency changes are expected to be large (especially in the short term), investment cannot be caused by them, or replace them as a source of growth. Investment in export processing is already unrestricted in Mexico, and the products of this do not face barriers in the USA, so NAFTA does not affect this type of investment.

The protracted negotiations for NAFTA and continuing uncertainty over whether it will be ratified suggest that it cannot be assumed that the USA will automatically extend it to other Latin American countries (The Enterprise for the Americas). Latin American countries will therefore share any adverse effects on 'outsiders': these could be large for those exporting to Mexico, but smaller for those exporting to the USA, in line with the expected effects on the members.

Regional groups of developing countries
Some of these groups date from the 1960s (notably in Latin America) or the early 1980s (in Africa), but the last two years have seen a strong revival of interest, which has finally extended also to South-east Asia. This revival is surprising in terms of economic calculations as it comes at a time when the reductions in tariffs by developing countries have greatly reduced the potential gains from preferences or free trade among them, and when the clearest successes at promoting exports, the original Asian NICs and their southeastern successors, have come about through increasing their exports to industrial countries first. Then, as they themselves became major and fast-

growing markets, trade grew among them, without any preference areas. The data suggest that, once normal explanations for trade are allowed for, regional flows are not significantly higher than extra-regional flows (and are frequently lower, including those among the Asian). Lower tariffs also have the practical disadvantage that they reduce the potential pool of customs revenue which such groups normally rely on to compensate the poorer or less successful members. All groups formed of developing countries face potentially more difficult problems because the structural changes which they are undergoing make necessary more frequent adjustments in the initial assumptions of which countries will specialize in which goods, and in trading arrangements generally, than would be seen among mature economies. A few of the most active are described to give an indication of the nature of those which are appearing.

In Africa, the potential emergence of South Africa as a regional power has led to a rethinking of its arrangements with its fellow members of the Southern African Customs Union, and of its future relationship with the SADC (Southern African Development Community) and therefore of the relationships of these with other groups, both subsets and the larger PTA (Preferential Trading Area) with some East African members as well). The pattern that seems to be emerging is a variety of small groups of countries coming together for specific purposes (some in trade, but others in currency unions, for common transport or energy arrangements, or for more diffuse economic coordination). These are the normal arrangements neighbouring countries make with each other and it is principally the intellectual fashion of the 1990s that groups them under the rubric of 'regionalism'.

In Latin America, groups like the Andean Pact and the Central American Common Market (CACM) (which date from the 1960s) have revived, and been joined by new groups: Mercosur is the largest and potentially most important because it includes Argentina, Brazil, Paraguay and Uruguay. But these are then cross-linked, with arrangements between one or two members of each and members of another, or none: Mexico, Colombia and Venezuela; Argentina, Chile and Venezuela; Bolivia to Mercosur; the CACM to the Caribbeans, and some countries have further links to various outside countries, not just Mexico in NAFTA, but the Caribbean to the USA under the Caribbean Basin Initiative (CBI) and to the EC under Lomé arrangements; some Andean Pact members with special privileges have links to the USA and the EC; Chile to the USA; and so on. Unlike the African groups, all these are trade-based links, offering different degrees of preference and reciprocity, and many with no obvious geographic logic (Mercosur is the only one arising out of strong existing trading links, previously impeded by lack of economic cooperation). The impulse may be more that lowering tariffs (combined with improving popular support for governments) has lowered the costs of offering concessions, while the memory of previous barriers perhaps produces an exaggerated perception of the benefits. The large number of arrangements has clearly also fed on itself by producing a fear of being left out. All have programmes of staged reductions of tariffs, with targets between two and six years ahead for full liberalization. All have already suffered temporary withdrawals of some countries or deferrals of concessions.

The ASEAN Free Trade Association, the first Asian manifestation, is perhaps most blatantly a simple reaction to others' groups. As trade is already extensive among members, and they are mainly open or opening economies, the practical effects on trade are small (Toh and Low, 1992, give a good recent summary of the evidence). But the feeling that the multilateral institutions are failing to provide new opportunities, and that regionalism in other areas could be closing existing ones, has inspired a political commitment to cooperate.

The apparent 'growth of regionalism' thus appears to be on the one hand a preference for using economic power rather than negotiating on the part of the EC and the USA, and on the other a manifestation of frustration at lack of progress in multilateral negotiations on the part of the developing countries which had placed a new faith in them. It is true that in Latin America and Africa intra-region trade has tended to be less concentrated on primary products than exports to the industrial countries, but this has not been true of the NICs, so this is not a strong argument for promoting it, and it does not in fact appear to be the motive of policy makers, despite its appearance in some economists' arguments. Given the range of linkages which are appearing, many with only the most tenuous geographical or traditional basis – the Pacific or Black Sea rims, for example – segmentation or clubbing together might be more accurate descriptions than regionalism. This is clearly not a stable basis for long-term organizations. A revived GATT would return them to their 1970s existence as secretariats with some data collection and research arms. But a breakdown of the multilateral system is more likely to lead also to breakdown of many of the groups which implicitly depend on a 'peaceful' external trade environment following known rules; they offer little protection against more economically powerful trading partners.

IV   Bilateral trade policies

The growth of protection

Until the early 1970s, it was clear that bilateral protection was falling. Although some developing countries had restrictive or import-substituting policies, their share of world trade was low, and these were treated by developing and developed countries as temporary measures, not permanent strategies of trade. The developed countries reduced exchange controls and negotiated down average tariffs during a series of GATT trade rounds, and simultaneously accelerated this process within areas like the EC or EFTA, or between neighbours, with arrangements like those between the US and Canadian car industries. From 1974, the regional groups made no further progress; the pace of tariff reduction slowed; the industrial countries, faced with a series of shocks and recessions, introduced quotas and other restrictions, first extending controls on traditionally sensitive areas such as agriculture, coal, steel, and textiles and clothing, and then extending these to other energy, electric and electronic goods, and cars. This brought not only direct effects on trade, but a change in the assumption that trade was inexorably becoming freer.

Most of the new barriers were in manufactures (partly, it is true, because controls on agriculture were already about as extensive as possible), while even the cuts that did continue in tariffs did not reduce the problem of tariff escalation. This continued in the 1980s when the increase in the share of manufactures controlled was (by UNCTAD estimates) twice that for all goods. These trends can be identified in the 1970s, by the discussion of individual measures in IMF studies of the period, and some independent ones, and from the 1980s by more formal indices devised by UNCTAD and modified by the World Bank. Although there may be doubts about the details of the calculations, the consensus view, and the one which developing countries on the whole accepted, was that bilateral interventions were moving in the direction of more control. Further they confirmed the impression of bias against developing country exports both because the traditional industries which the industrial countries protected were the developing countries' new industries and because it was easier to impose barriers on countries not linked by groups such as the EC, and particularly against their manufactures. These measures would have damaged developing countries' interests at any time, but provoked particularly strong reactions in the late 1970s and 1980s. Not only were an increasing number of countries becoming dependent on manufactured exports, but there was also a conviction (thanks to the multiplying studies of the NICs and their experience) that exports were a, if not the, key to industrial success and material progress. The only offsetting influences to the growth of protection were the periodic liberalizations in GATT rounds or those within regional groups, and, in the 1970s, special treatment for developing countries.

Preferences for developing countries
Under the GSP individual developed countries (or the EC as a unit) offered lower or 0 tariffs to most developing countries. Its history has been one of erosion of the size of the preference margins, of the goods covered and of

the 'general' nature of its country coverage. Although both its concessional nature and its 'generality' were intended to preclude negotiation, the result has been that obtaining or retaining the preferences has required developing countries to negotiate with the donors. The first exclusions were of the OPEC countries (by the USA after the 1973–4 rise in oil prices) and other countries have had privileges withdrawn (or withdrawal threatened) for non-economic reasons. There have also been extensions or increases in prefer-ences for special cases (most recently the Eastern European, for political reasons, and some Latin American countries to discourage overdependence on illegal drug exports). Among developing countries, the most advanced have been excluded, completely or as regards their most competitive prod-ucts. At the same time, both the extension of non-tariff barriers (which override GSP) and the reduction of standard tariffs (in many cases to below the GSP level) have eroded the benefit of GSP.

The EC's associated countries of Africa, the Caribbean and Pacific (ACP) have received more extensive preference under the Lomé convention (as well as other forms of assistance). They have also faced erosion from lower-ing of other tariffs (including those stemming from extension of the GSP to new countries, and increased privileges for some GSP recipients) and, al-though nominally free from quotas and other non-tariff barriers, the most sensitive exports have faced 'understandings' or 'surveillance'.

Effects of current changes in trade policy
If the Uruguay Round produces a settlement, it will have its largest effects on exports of textiles and clothing (because it is here that there is a clear path to non-quota trade), increasing particularly the exports of the South Asian countries, followed by the NICs, with smaller benefits to other areas for which these sectors are less important. The other major beneficiaries will be the producers of temperate agricultural products, in particular in Latin America, and perhaps some rice producers. The total identifiable impact at about 3 per cent of the value of developing country exports is significant, but not overwhelming (in the context of growth of 7–8 per cent a year for their exports) but the most important result would be the signal that multilateral negotiations could produce results, and that exports can rise in more open markets, an impulse to improving the competitiveness of exports.

But even in the context of a successful outcome, the way in which the negotiations became tied into bargaining between the two economic powers, the EC and the USA, over their own agricultural difficulties has indicated the risk to multilateral solutions from having three powerful industrial mem-bers, rather than one very powerful (the USA), one slightly less powerful and much less interested (Japan), and several middle-ranking European coun-tries. The dynamics of the negotiations in this Round compared to earlier ones have been altered by this, although the inability of the EC to behave consistently as either one country or 12 has acted as a partial offset. In a future round, or in other international institutions if the EC extends Community competence to these, the threat would be greater.

As planned at present, the EC 1992 exercise, by preserving the privileges of the ACP countries, avoiding offending the most powerful non-associated countries (especially the USA) and gradually admitting the other European countries (both EFTA and eastern) to more favoured status, reinforces the traditional habit of the EC of differentiation among suppliers according to political and other criteria which have little to do with economic competitiveness. It will also reinforce the position of the EC as a market less open to manufactures from the developing countries (except under special arrangements) than the USA.

The risk from NAFTA is that, if the assessment given here that its effects will be small is wrong, the effects on developing countries other than Mexico would be in the same direction as those of 1992, of disadvantaging non-members and hurting the least associated and most competitive non-members most.

V   Competitiveness or rent seeking
The reactions of some developing countries to EC 1992 and NAFTA (and also to innovations like the new trading links with the Eastern European countries), that these are potentially damaging to their exports because of the effect on their margins of preference, indicate how important considerations of trading partners' policy have become to developing countries' assessments of their own prospects. The trends that we have noted in terms of increased bilateral protection, more differentiated use even of general measures, and loss of interest on the part of the industrial countries in multilateral organizations and negotiations offer strong reasons for such an approach. But it also stems from a reactive, demand-based approach to trade, one of responding to external changes (whether negative or opportunities). The question which the more successful export performers have put is different: how do changes like 1992 or NAFTA alter the set of external conditions within which their export and industrialization strategy must evolve? While the empirical answers on trade creation or diversion are obviously the same, it is notable that initial reactions have shown greatest concern from the countries like those of the ACP which habitually behave most 'dependently' with respect to the EC (lobbying for preferences and not participating in multilateral negotiations), even though they are the least likely to be negatively affected (because their exports tend to be non-competing primary products). The successful exporters, the Asians, both NICs and the new South-east Asian economies, have shown least concern, although on paper

they lose most from 1992 (as exporters of competing manufactures), with the Latin Americans falling in between on both concern and success.

There is a serious risk that a failure of multilateral negotiations could alter the balance of rewards to concession seeking relative to competitiveness, both actual and as perceived by developing countries. This is a parallel at international level to the choice between unproductively seeking protection through lobbying and improving productivity. In turn, it is probably not independent of it because producers within developing countries will also perceive the choices facing their governments and alter their own behaviour appropriately. If the perception is wrong, acting according to it will be wasteful and unsuccessful. The fact that over the last 20 years it has been the Asian countries with fewest preferential links, either with industrial countries or among themselves, and lowest access to even the general preferences which have been most successful, while the ACP have been the least successful, suggests that at least in the past the perception has been wrong. Rapid increases in exports have not depended on special access to markets; they have not come from concentration on improving access to just one market; they have led to high regional intra-trade only after success has been achieved at world level. Countries with special privileges, like the Lomé countries, have shown worse, not better, performance than average and the successes from GSP have tended to be only at very limited points in countries' development.

If it is now right to switch to a more bargaining approach, and clearly the shifts identified here suggest that it is increasingly likely that it is, then the results will be seriously distorting at both international and national level. Regional trading groups would represent a further substitution of bargaining for efficiency as a criterion for success, and one which the evidence suggests would have a very much poorer return.

VI Relative protection

A different set of consequences follows from the coincidence of increasing protection among the industrial countries and decreasing protection in the developing countries (if the latter do not reverse their opening in disillusionment or frustration). Much of the literature on the direction of both trade and capital movements assumes that it is the industrial countries which are open, or moving in that direction, and the developing which are relatively closed. It also tends to assume that growth rates are higher in the developing, and therefore that capital is more likely to be attracted from the industrial, and that it is more mobile from there. But now developing countries have reduced their tariffs, removed their capital controls and seen their growth rates reduced by trade diversion in the industrial countries. They face industrial countries with their relative growth and protection correspondingly increased.

The first consequence has already been discussed: it is now the developing countries which are most interested in multilateral trade negotiations. The pressure for special relationships like NAFTA or regional groupings is only seen as second-best to multilateral free trade, and the diversion of GATT negotiations to the US–EC differences has been resisted as far as possible.

It is too early to see strong evidence of a response of investment flows or trading patterns, but there are indications. Among the expected consequences would be lower trade flows overall, as protection-leaping investment moved into the USA and the EC to replace imports (this would not yet be balanced by greater imports into the developing countries, both because the magnitudes are likely to be smaller, given the size of the economies, and because the shift to developing country openness followed that to industrial country protection by about ten years). Trade flows have been lower relative to output or income in the 1980s than in the past. This fall should particularly hit manufactures, as they are more likely to be competing goods: the traditional differential in world trade growth in favour of manufactured exports appears to have diminished. Investment by developed countries in developing (relative to investment in other developed) declined sharply in the early 1980s (although general loss of confidence clearly contributed as well as more identifiable growth or market factors). In the last three to four years, investment by developing countries in developed countries, and in manufacturing rather than the traditional property, has increased, with a higher than usual move into the EC. The purpose of some investment has been explicitly stated to be to replace a firm's exports, or as an alternative strategy to starting to export.

In themselves, such responses are as rational for a firm (if as inefficient for world economic welfare) as the reverse movements when the protection was in the developing countries and the investors in the developed. But from a more long-term development-strategic point of view, they may be more questionable. While the investing country makes a gain (or at least avoids a loss) in national income from the export-replacing investment, its output and its industrialization clearly do not benefit as much from foreign investment as from producing manufactures for export. (This is especially true if it is simultaneously facing more stimulus to its primary exports from various trade policy changes, as discussed earlier.) Attracting investment by raising the return to capital through policy in the industrial country relative to the developing country seems unlikely to encourage an efficient reallocation of capital between capital-abundant and capital-scarce countries. The effects on income distribution of an increase in the returns to capital and (at least relative) reduction in those to labour should also be considered, although in principle, of course, these could be offset by intervention. The combination of accepting an extreme form of the 'conservative welfare function', of preventing losses to existing industries and interest groups, in the developed countries, with rejecting any belief in an 'infant industry' or 'structural weakness' argument for protection in developing countries seems likely to produce the least efficient possible allocation of resources internationally.

Bibliography

Commission of the European Communities (1988), *Research on the 'Cost of Non-Europe', Basic Findings*, vol. 1: *Basic Studies: Executive Summaries*; vol. 2: *Studies on the Economics of Integration*, Brussels.

Erzan, Refiq, Junichi Goto and Paula Holmes (1990), 'Effects of the Multi-Fibre Arrangement on Developing Countries' Trade: An Empirical Investigation', in Carl B. Hamilton (ed.), *Textiles Trade and the Developing Countries*, Washington DC: World Bank.

Langhammer, Rolf J. (1992), 'The NAFTA: Another Futile Trade Area (AFTA) or a Serious Approach Towards Regionalism?', *Kiel Discussion Papers*, Institut für Weltwirtschaft, Kiel.

Page, Sheila (1987), 'The Rise in Protection since 1974', *Oxford Review of Economic Policy*, **3** (1).

Page, Sheila (1992), 'Some Implications of Europe 1992 for Developing Countries', *OECD Technical Papers*, no. 60, Paris.

Page, Sheila with Michael Davenport and Adrian Hewitt (1991), 'The GATT Uruguay Round: Effects on Developing Countries', *ODI Special Report*, London: Overseas Development Institute.

Toh Mun Heng and Linda Low (1992), 'Is the ASEAN Free Trade Area a second best option?', National University of Singapore (mimeo).

UNCTAD (1985), *Data Base on Trade Measures, Introductory Note*, Geneva: UNCTAD.

UNCTAD (1986), *Restrictions on Trade and Structural Adjustment*, Geneva: UNCTAD.

13 The Europe Agreements: with a little help from our friends

L. Alan Winters[1]

The Europe Agreements (EAs) negotiated over 1991 and signed early in 1992 define the future economic relationships between the European Communities (EC) on the one hand and Czechoslovakia, Hungary and Poland (CHP) on the other. It is intended that they should become operative in March 1992. Although there are three independent agreements, they differ only in detail and are therefore best treated as a group.

This chapter sketches the principal components of the Europe Agreements, as defined by their economic effects, and introduces some of the policy issues which they raise. In summary, while it is constructive to establish EC–CHP relations firmly in legal form, the agreements are disappointing in the degree of support and encouragement they guarantee to CHP. Indeed they sometimes appear to be designed as much to minimize the adjustment that the revolutions of 1989 cause in the EC than to maximize the benefits that accrue to CHP. The issue is not so much that the Agreements are directly restrictive – although they are in certain areas – but that they leave a large number of opportunities for future restrictiveness in their implementation. Such opportunities are potentially harmful if they are exercised and actually harmful in that their existence undermines confidence in the EC's willingness and ability to aid the transition process. The fundamental policy issue, then, is not rewriting the Agreements, but minimizing the resort to the restrictions that they currently permit.

In the words of their preambles, the EAs aim to create a new climate for economic relations between the EC and CHP, and in particular for the development of trade and investment, instruments which are indispensable for economic restructuring and technological modernization; they aim to promote the expansion of trade and the harmonious economic relations between the Community and CHP and so to foster dynamic economic development and prosperity in CHP.

The Agreements recognize that ultimately CHP wish to become full members of the EC. The Eastern partners negotiated hard for this objective to be made explicit, probably at the expense of more immediate and concrete benefits, but they felt that the commitment to membership lent a necessary element of credibility to their reform programmes.

The Agreements contain five substantive elements: Title III, free movements of goods; Title IV, movement of workers, establishment and the supply of services; Title V, payments, competition and the approximation of laws; Title VI, economic cooperation; and Title VIII, financial cooperation.

I   Title III: free movement of goods

This aims at establishing trade areas between the EC and each (separately) of CHP over a period of ten years. By common consent this is the most important element of the EAs and within it the critical issue is the access to EC markets granted to CHP.

Buoyant sales provide incomes for consumers, funds for investment and incentives for work and for change. With the collapse of intra-bloc trade, sales means for Eastern Europe exports to the market economies, the dominant among these are sales to the EC, which accounted for over 30 per cent of each of CHP's exports in 1990 (CEC, 1991). Such exports offer not only the stimuli noted above, but also contact with more advanced consumers, firms and technologies, all of which enhance the rate and direction of technical change.

International trade between the EC and Eastern Europe shows a huge potential for growth. Wang and Winters (1991) suggest that, even at the low levels of incomes of 1985, Polish and Hungarian exports to the EC would have been five times higher and Czech exports ten times higher if those countries had been fully integrated into the world economy. In absolute terms the scope for increasing exports (and imports) is of the order of ECU 10 billion per year for Czechoslovakia, ECU 4 billion for Hungary and ECU 8 billion for Poland. Even assuming that half of the value of exports came from imported inputs – a rather pessimistic view – these amounts are far more important in their income-generation effects than any likely inflow of aid or investment.

But trade will not grow unless it is encouraged by a commitment to open markets, and long-run benefits will not come unless CHP can stimulate economic activity and sustain their reform programmes over the short run. The EAs aim to abolish all tariffs and non-tariff barriers (NTBs) on CHP–EC trade, but they maintain anti-dumping and safeguard clauses and, in critical sectors, offer only a gradual approach to free trade. In addition they impose a restrictive definition of local origin which will reduce the volume of exports to which the negotiated concessions apply.

Coverage
For most products defined in the international trade classifications the EAs offer access to EC markets free of tariffs and quantitative restrictions (QR) within one year. For certain metal products, however tariffs will be reduced

Table 13.1 Schematic schedule of liberalization of EC access for CHP products

Products	Notes and definitions	Mar 92	Jan 93	Jan 94	Jan 95	Jan 96	Jan 97	Jan 98
(A) Agriculture								
Annex VIIIa (tariff-quotas)	a							
quota level	i	110	119	128	137	146	146	146
levy within quota	ii	50	50	50	50	50	50	50
tariff within quota		100	100	100	100	100	100	100
duties beyond quota		100	100	100	100	100	100	100
Annex VIIIb	b							
tariffs	ii, iii	70	70	70	70	70	0	0
Minimum price agreements	c				no change			
Regulation 3420/83	d							
QRs	e	abolished	none	none	none	none	none	none
Annex Xb (tariff quotas)								
quota level	i, iv	110	119	128	137	146	146	146
levy within quota	ii	80	60	40	40	40	40	40
beyond quota		100	100	100	100	100	100	100
Annex XI (tariff quotas and tariff only)	f							
quota level	i, v	110	125	140	155	170	170	170
tariff (within quota where applicable)	ii, vi	90	80	70	60	49	49	49
variable levy		100	100	100	100	100	100	100
Other products								
quotas, tariffs and levies					no change			
(B) Industrial products								
Standard products	g							
tariff	ii, vii	0	0	0	0	0	0	0
Certain metal products								
tariff	ii	80	60	40	20	0	0	0

		unspecified rate of reduction to 0						
Sensitive products								
within tariff quota								
tariff	ii	85	70	55	40	25	10	0
quota level	viii	100	120	140	160	180		
outside tariff quota								
tariff	ii	80	60	40	20	0	0	0
QRs		abolished	none	none	none	none	none	none
Iron and steel (ECSC products)								
tariff	ii	abolished						
QRs		none	none	none	none	none	none	none
Textiles and clothing (MFA products)								
tariff	ii	71	71	57	43	29	14	0
QRs		unspecified relaxation until abolition						

h

Notes

i) as percentage of quota in 1990; estimated increase for 1992 comes from CEC (1991).

ii) as percentage of levy/tariff in 1991.

iii) values representative of a range over commodities, including abolition of some tariffs.

iv) representative values; actual range is increases from 8.3% to 37.5% p.a.

v) representative values; actual range is increases from 0% t0 15% p.a.

vi) representative values; actual range includes tariffs with no change to those halving over five years.

vii) for some products abolition of duties are halved in 1992 and abolished in 1993.

viii) measured relative to quotas in 1992.

Definitions:

a) Duck and goose meat.

b) Live horses, pork, poultry (some), rabbits, some fruit and fruit products, cut flowers.

c) Certain soft fruit for processing.

d) Vegetables and fruit, dairy products, animal and vegetable oil or fat. Vermouth and other wine of fresh grapes, spirits, cigars, cigarettes and tobacco.

e) Meat of domestic swine, some diary products (mainly eggs, cheese, milk), wheat flour.

f) Cheese, live plants, some vegetables, fruit and nuts, animal or vegetable oils and fats, preparations of meat and vegetables, fruit.

g) Products not elsewhere specified.

h) Textile (not MFA products), footwear, iron and steel (not ECSC products), glassware, motor vehicles, furniture.

over four years and for 'sensitive' products, including some items of chemicals, steel products, furniture, leather goods, footwear, glass and vehicles, tariffs will persist for up to five years. In agriculture, the most sensitive area of all, concessions are restricted to a subset of commodities, and then only to quantities inside quota limits. The latter will grow by only about 10 per cent per annum from 1990, and although some tariffs fall to zero within one year, variable levies are only ever to fall by 60 per cent (30 per cent in some cases) and that over three years. Outside the quota limits full tariffs and levies remain.

Special protocols govern the liberalization of processed agricultural goods, textiles and clothing, iron and steel and coal. For textiles and clothing import duties on CHP output will be abolished over six years and those on outward processing trade immediately. Quantitative restrictions will be removed in not less than five years and not more than half the time agreed in the Uruguay Round for the abolition of the MFA (if such an agreement is reached), but the precise schedule for relaxing the QRs is yet to be settled. In iron and steel duties will be abolished over six years and QRs immediately, while for coal duties will be abolished in four years and QRs in one, except for special restrictions on exports to Spain and Germany, which will persist for four years.

Table 13. 1 gives a schematic representation of the liberalization schedule. It shows clearly the delays and derogations involved. The list of items in the slow liberalization lane is precisely the set of goods which CHP currently export most successfully: see Table 13.2, where 33–45 per cent of exports fall in the most restricted groups. Thus, while large numbers of EC trade headings are to be liberalized almost immediately, the effective liberalization for CHP is much slower. Since near-term export growth must depend on the goods which CHP can currently produce to Western standards, these remaining restrictions seriously constrain the speed with which foreign exchange earnings can expand. Moreover, while it is true that many of the QRs

Table 13.2   The commodity composition of CHP exports to the EC, 1989

	Czechoslovakia	Hungary	Poland	CHP
Food and agriculture	8.6	29.3	23.2	20.4
Textiles and clothing	9.9	14.7	10.3	11.6
Iron and steel	14.1	7.2	8.9	10.3
Total of above	32.6	51.2	42.4	42.3
Chemicals	8.9	10.4	6.6	8.6

Sources: CEC (1991); Mobius and Schumacher (1990).

on CHP did not bind prior to 1990 – that is, CHP exports fell short of the amounts permitted under the QRs – this observation offers little guidance about their restrictiveness under reformed production conditions. In particular foreign direct investment could dramatically increase output and potential exports. Even under the uncertainty ruling before the EAs, and with all the supply-side difficulties experienced in CHP, these countries increased their exports to OECD countries by 18 per cent, 30 per cent and 44 per cent respectively over the two-year period 1988–90.

Anti-dumping and safeguard
The EAs offer rapid liberalization in iron and steel, but even before they become operative EC producers are threatening anti-dumping (AD) actions against their CHP competitors. Under a fair AD regime this would hardly matter but, as is well-known (see, for example, Messerlin, 1989) EC AD practices are heavily biased against exporters. Hence there is always a significant probability of a positive finding. The EAs specify that AD actions must accord with Article VI of the GATT, but most EC practice is GATT-consistent, so that is little comfort. It is true, however that, immediately after signature of the EAs, the EC committed itself to treating CHP as market rather than non-market economies. This is a considerable concession – especially given that they are not really market economies yet – but it still leaves CHP trade potentially subject to the same tender mercies as accorded to Korean or Japanese trade.

AD action is also important for chemicals – another sector of export significance to CHP – see Table 13.2. GATT (1991) shows that over 40 per cent of 'successful' EC AD actions over the 1980s concerned this sector.

Safeguards offer another loophole. Unspecified safeguard measures are permitted if imports from any of CHP causes either 'serious injury to domestic producers of like or directly competitive products' or 'serious disturbances ... or difficulties which *could* bring about serious deterioration in the economic situation of a region' (emphasis added). The former accords with regular safeguards law and has been little used in the past (AD is simpler), but the latter is ominously innovative. There is no case law or convention defining 'serious deterioration' or 'region' in this context, and 'could' certainly suggests pre-emptive action. In addition, special safeguard provisions are to be developed for the textile and clothing trade.

The AD and safeguards clauses can only undermine the confidence of potential investors – domestic and foreign – in EC-oriented production in CHP. As noted above, at least for the next few years EC orientation is the biggest if not the only game in town. Moreover subsequent progress has not been encouraging. In August 1992 the EC reintroduced QRs on Czech exports of steel pipes to Germany and Italy, and rumours abound of Eastern producers being approached by Eurofer – the EC producers' organization – to raise their prices.

Rules of origin

To qualify for concessions under the EAs, products must originate in CHP. Origin is formally defined in terms of the location of the last major transformation of the product (change in its four-digit trade heading), but for many products it is operationalized in terms of the value of imports. To qualify for 'originating status' in these cases, no more than 40 per cent (sometimes 50 per cent) of the value of the output must be accounted for by imported materials excluding those imported from the EC. Rephrased, this is a 60 per cent local content requirement, which is rather strict. It precludes CHP from many relatively light processing tasks applied to non-EC materials, and thus further discourages (non-EC) foreign direct investment.

CHP liberalization

The EAs provide for mutual market access. In general CHP have slower liberalization and more exceptions than the EC, being allowed up to ten years before free access is established. This gradualism is consistent with their desire not to subject their already traumatized economies to further shocks, but we should not be blind to temptations that it offers to postpone adjustment and exploit consumers. CHP generally had rather liberal trade regimes at first, and so probably did not face major trade diversion as a result of the EAs. Since negotiation, however, Polish external tariffs have been increased, raising the EC's margin of preference. Thus trade diversion has become more of an issue. At least one Article, Article 29, explicitly requires CHP to maintain an element of preferences for EC suppliers in the event of tariffs being increased.

The implications

The delays in removing EC trade restrictions on CHP will curtail these countries' short-term recoveries; the possibilities of AD and safeguards actions will have additional longer-run effects. The consequences for CHP incomes – both directly and via reduced investment inflows – are obvious enough, and the threat to their reform programmes hardly bears thinking about. Indeed some would argue that the prospect of substantial profits through exports to the West is not only necessary but also sufficient to sweep away the supply-side and institutional problems of the transitional economies: if the opportunities are great enough the pressure on the factors preventing their realization becomes irresistible. On this view the access restrictions would be little short of catastrophic.

Delay also imposes costs on the West. EC firms, while favoured by the rules of origin, may still feel it safer to pass up profitable investment opportunities if they depend on EC access. EC exporters, including services industries, will face weaker markets. EC consumers will be denied the benefits of free trade, which can be quite large: for example, Winters and Brenton (1991) suggest that UK import restrictions on imports of men's leather footwear from Poland could have cost up to £60 million per year in the mid-1980s.

Of course, admitting CHP goods will involve some industrial adjustment in the EC, but that adjustment could be exaggerated, and what is not is unavoidable. I have argued elsewhere – CEPR (1990), Hamilton and Winters (1992) – that CHP's longer-term comparative advantage, especially Hungary's, probably lies in more sophisticated goods and services than those protected by the EAs. Hence the short-run import pressure in these sectors might not be as great as suspected. But to the extent that the emergence of CHP economies implies permanent changes in comparative advantage, these will have to be accommodated eventually. Moreover, while the necessary adjustments may tend to fall on older and less skilled EC workers, it should be recalled that EC governments are rich enough, and the benefits of free trade large enough, to allow compensation to be paid, and all EC workers are substantially better off than their Eastern brothers.

II Title IV: workers, establishment and services

The EAs guarantee CHP workers non-discrimination and certain rights in the EC so long as they are 'legally employed'. No special definition of that term is offered, however, and so CHP workers are subject to EC member states' existing, and generally highly restrictive, laws on the employment of aliens. The best on offer is that, subject to a member state's labour market situation and its labour legislation and rules, existing access to employment for CHP workers should be preserved and improved (Article 41). The caveats are clear and no modalities for improvement are specified. The conclusion is that, little as the EC desires CHP goods, it desires their workers even less. This position implicitly recognizes that, having once excluded CHP labour-intensive exports from its markets, the EC will come under intense pressure to accept their workers directly and that, to maintain the effects of protection for EC workers in the protected sectors, it must keep closed its immigration gates as well.

In theory the provisions over workers are symmetric. EC workers generally have no special advantages in CHP. However, in practice this is not quite correct. The EC rightly offers training to CHP residents, but as studies of the US market reveal – see Ulph and Winters (1989) – training is frequently the precursor to work and residence for the better trainees, and the training process provides an excellent means of sorting out the better workers. In addition, the EA Articles on establishment permit the mobility of key personnel between the CHP and EC arms of a company. Key personnel include managers, supervisors, personnel staff, highly qualified workers and professionals. While this provision is a perfectly sensible adjunct to establishment rights, it entails two de facto assymetries in the labour market: first, it allows the EC to exploit its relatively abundant factor in CHP; second, it offers highly skilled CHP workers close contact with their corresponding EC labour markets, thus making it easier for them to be poached by EC firms. At least in the UK, high levels of skill are the most common reason for granting work permits to aliens. The implications for brain drain are obvious.

The EAs seek to facilitate the establishment of CHP and EC firms in each other's territories. This is a means of increasing economic integration and, to the extent that it reduces uncertainty, a useful stimulus to the foreign direct investment that CHP need. The EAs guarantee national treatment for each other's firms and, in Title V payments, guarantee the free mobility of capital (including disinvestment) and the repatriation of earnings for companies established under the terms of the agreements.

CHP may exclude sectors from the mutual establishment rules for new companies where restructuring or the emergence of a new industry is occurring, where the indigenous producers come under extreme pressure, or where social problems are caused. In addition a number of sectors and activities are exempt for five or ten years. These differ slightly by country but include defence industries, financial services and the acquisition of natural resources and real estate in Czechoslovakia and Poland. In addition foreign companies might be treated specially under the privatization laws. These temporary exemptions reflect the restrictions on foreign ownership of industry found in many Western countries. Their economic rationale is not entirely clear, except perhaps for the privatization case, but their political role in avoiding nationalistic backlashes may be significant.

Mutual service trade by non-established companies is a stated objective of the EAs; the means of bringing it about are not spelt out, however, and it is subject to 'the development of the service sector in the Parties'. Service providers may have temporary mobility between the Parties, but only within the scope of all existing migration and labour laws. No new rights of service are established. Again one suspects that, while professionals will encounter little difficulty, manually skilled and less skilled workers will not find it easy to gain business legally.[2]

The EAs also cover transport services. Agreements on air and inland transport will be negotiated later (a slight liberalization of the former has been arranged with Czechoslovakia). In the meantime CHP will progressively adapt its legislation to the ruling EC position in so far as doing so 'serves the liberalization process'. One might characterize the convergence of legislation to the current EC position as a rather modest objective for a liberalization programme, but it is conceivable that matters will improve under the Single Market programme. Observe that, if the adaptation intention means anything at all, CHP have agreed to adapt to future legislation about which they know nothing and over which they have no influence. This observation leads usefully on to the next Title.

III   Title V: payments, competition and the approximation of laws
As noted above, payments related to foreign investment under the EAs are guaranteed free from restrictions, as are all current account transactions stemming from liberalization. This ensures a limited convertibility and to the extent that full convertibility is not yet feasible probably concentrates it in the right places. Longer-term objectives include the free movement of capital and the absence of foreign exchange restrictions along the lines of intra-EC arrangements. CHP have escape clauses, however, in the event of severe balance of payments difficulties, but these must not interfere with the guarantees noted at the beginning of this paragraph.

The arguments for convertibility and free capital mobility have been well aired within the EC and also in the CHP context. They presuppose a degree of macroeconomic stabilization and convergence between partners that is not yet evident. Much depends on the policies adopted by the CHP governments, and the EA objective of open payments offers a valuable landmark for them to aim at. On the other hand, too great a focus on these goals might induce more short-term austerity than these economies' long-run health demands, especially if their short-run export earnings are constrained by Western trade policies.

CHP are obliged to adopt within three years almost the full panoply of EC competition law; the only exception is for state aids, which *may* be deemed acceptable on the grounds that they are designed to aid the development of an exceptionally poor region or one of high unemployment. This derogation is for five years and may be extended to ten. Its precise import is unclear, however, for it is only permissive. It appears not to alter the requirement that CHP must ensure that state monopolies act in a commercial fashion, inducing no distortion in competition between CHP and the EC.

Intellectual property protection in CHP is to be brought into line with EC practice and international conventions within five years, and best endeavours are called for to approximate CHP to EC law in all other areas. The EAs make particular note of customs law, company law, banking law, company accounts and taxes, intellectual property, protection of workers at the workplace, financial services, rules on competition, protection of health and life of humans, animals and plants, consumer protection, indirect taxation, technical rules and standards, transport and the environment.

It is clear that CHP need the legal framework – the soft infrastructure – to establish a market economy, and that they need it quickly; off-the-shelf institutions seem to make sense in these circumstances and in many cases the EC model is as good as any other. Moreover, given their aspiration to join the EC, it seems better to adopt the necessary institutions *ab initio*. The difficulties, however, are twofold. First, CHP have no discretion about the final goal, harmonization, and no influence on the ways in which the EC might move the goalposts either through new legislation or through the interpretation of existing legislation. Second, the timetable for approximation looks unduly short – see Rollo's (1991) excellent paper. In particular it appears to be intended that approximation precede CHP–EC free trade, which is not due for ten years. This reverses the normal order of integration and leaves a distinct impression that the EC is willing to trade freely only on its own terms. By requiring CHP to adopt the same legal restrictions on economic activity as it has itself, the EC undermines many of the advantages of mutual trade. If CHP feel happy with, say, lower worker protection, it makes sense for the EC to buy from them those goods for which this offers significant cost reductions. It is far from clear that EC conventions, developed for countries such as France and Germany, are ideally suited to the needs of the poorer transitional economies, and yet the EAs appear to offer the latter no alternative, even temporarily.

The asymmetry in approximation is starkest in the area of competition law and AD. The ostensible justification for AD is to prevent predatory pricing, a practice which is dealt with domestically by competition law. The EAs impose EC competition law on CHP, implying a degree of control from Brussels even over the three year transitional phase, but they also allow the EC to maintain quite unfettered AD regulations just in case that is not sufficient. It is true that the Treaty of Rome allowed the coexistence of competition law and AD action during the original transition period, but since then both policies have become more powerful: competition law is better able to cope and AD is in much greater danger of overkill. Thus, as currently positioned, CHP producers suffer a potential double-jeopardy – if competition law doesn't get them, anti-dumping will.

IV Title VI: economic cooperation

This title aims to 'back-up CHP's achievements and strengthen economic links'. It makes few concrete commitments, but promises cooperation and technical assistance over a wide range of areas of the economy, including industry, services, agriculture, education and training, the environment, transport, telecommunications, financial services and tourism. Particular emphasis is to be given to the establishment of private-sector activity.

The need for cooperation and assistance is palpable, but this is not pure, disinterested, charity. Tucked away in the details are some EC concerns about the CHP competitiveness – regarding agriculture: 'to promote complementarity in agriculture'; the environment (an 'agreed priority'): 'approximation of laws (Community standards)'; and transport: 'the setting-up of consistent transport policies compatible with the transport policies applicable in the Community'. If 'complementarity' in agriculture entails advising CHP not to export goods in excess supply in the EC or to buy EC surpluses (World Bank, 1990), it is little short of criminal. The second item appears intended to ensure that CHP cannot out-compete EC producers by virtue of a more relaxed attitude to the environment.

V   Title VIII: financial cooperation

'CHP will benefit from temporary financial assistance ... in the form of grants and loans.' Grants will initially be made under the PHARE programme, whose 1992 budget provides ECU 1 billion to be spread over six countries. Although this is significant relative to the EC's own budget, relative to capital requirements it is very small: CEPR (1990) suggested total capital needs in the Eastern bloc of $1000 billion over ten years; Hungary's debt service is likely to be around $4 billion per annum until 1995 (Riecke, 1992) and Poland's $10 billion per annum for five years (Rollo, 1991). It is also small compared with the potential trade flows noted above.

Loans will be available from the European Investment Bank (EIB), but the total entitlement is yet to be negotiated according to the EAs. Moreover, while EIB loans are on top-class terms, they are not concessionary and they offer only part finance, making it difficult for fiscally constrained governments to take them up. In the pre-accession Association Agreement with Greece, some $125 million of loans were planned – not a large amount – but in the event only around half were take up (Swann, 1978).

The EC may also offer temporary financial assistance for stabilization or restructuring purposes against an approved IMF programme, and will cooperate with other donors/lenders in the development of an overall financial package. The former may increase the general funding available to CHP, but ties them into IMF conditionality. Some such constraints on borrowing countries are probably necessary, not least for domestic political reasons, but conditionality does not have a perfect track record.

VI   Conclusion

The year 1991 offered the EC the chance to make a major and imaginative contribution to the emergence of the transitional economies from their years of economic twilight. Having been in the forefront of the supporters of the revolutions of 1989, having taken upon itself the leading role in coordinating the G-24 response to those events, being geographically and culturally the closest major economic bloc to Eastern Europe and being the world's largest trading bloc, the EC had, perhaps, the greatest responsibilities in this regard. These have been recognized in the detail and formality of the EAs, but not, unfortunately, in their content.

Throughout the EAs one finds the stamp of the EC's powerful internal enemies of change. Despite the parlous state of the CHP economies, the EC will maintain agricultural protection, keep quantitative import restrictions on textiles and clothing for six years, leave chemicals and iron and steel producers free to harass CHP suppliers through anti-dumping law, keep tariffs on sensitive labour-intensive products for five years and discourage CHP processing of inputs from other countries. In the meantime it will impose its competition and intellectual property laws on CHP and encourage explicitly and implicitly (through technical assistance programmes) CHP to adopt all the rest of the EC's commercial infrastructure. It will ensure its rights to establish firms and provide services in CHP; it will permit highly skilled residents of CHP to move westwards, if only temporarily, but will equally effectively ensure that CHP's currently abundant factor – labour – can neither be efficiently utilized in producing exports for the EC nor improve its productivity by moving directly to the EC.

The restrictions in the EAs threaten the recovery of the CHP economies and ultimately even their reform programmes. They also penalize EC citizens: new generations of workers will be drawn into low-tech dead-end jobs, exporters will face weaker markets, investors will miss profitable opportunities and, above all, EC consumers will be denied cheap supplies from CHP. The EAs are a missed opportunity for doing well out of doing good. A clear commitment to liberalism would have benefited both sides. Indeed it is not yet too late: the EC should unilaterally renounce the permitted restrictions in the EAs and replace some of its current QRs and immigration restrictions. Moreover it should do so not only in the name of bilateral EC–CHP relations but for broader reasons. Great though the EC's responsibilities are towards Eastern Europe, they are not unique. In particular the USA and EFTA have considerable commercial opportunities in that region (Wang and Winters, 1991; Hamilton and Winters, 1992). Both they and Japan should aim to reach cooperation agreements with the transitional economies quickly. One hopes that such agreements will be more liberal than the EAs, for it would be a double tragedy if the EAs succoured other countries' conservatism and timidity.

Notes

1. I am grateful to Zhen Kun Wang for assistance in preparing this chapter, and to Tina Attwell for typing.
2. There is some uncertainty over the interpretation of this part of the EAs. Article 56.2 (or 55.2 for Poland) requires that, eventually, free temporary movement for the providers of service be granted, but only 'subject to the provisions of Article 59.1 (58.1)'. The latter asserts the primacy of the Parties' labour law, except where it is applied in such a way as to nullify or impair a specific provision of the EA. Article 56.2 seems specific (if rather vague on timing), but its caveat suggests its subservience to Article 59.1

References

CEPR (1990), *Monitoring European Integration: The Impact of Eastern Europe* London: CEPR.

Commission of the European Communities (CEC) (1991), 'EC Trade with Eastern and Central Europe: Trade rather than Aid?, Brussels: Commission of the European Communities (mimeo).

GATT (1991), *Trade Policy Review: European Communities, Vol I and II*, Geneva: GATT.

Hamilton, C.B. and L.A. Winters (1992), 'Opening up trade in Eastern Europe', *Economic Policy*, no.14, forthcoming.

Messerlin, P.A. (1989), 'The EC anti-dumping regulations: a first economic appraisal 1980–85', *Weltwirtschaftliches Archiv*, vol. 125, pp. 563–87.

Mobius, U. and D. Schumacher (1990), 'Eastern Europe and the EC: trade relations and trade policy with regards to industrial products', Berlin: German Institute for Economic Research (DIW) (mimeo).

O'Brien, R. (1991), *Finance in the International Economy, AMEX Bank Review Prize Essays 5*, London: Oxford University Press.

Riecke, W. (1992), 'Managing foreign debts and monetary policy during transformation', paper given to a conference on *Hungary: An Economy in Transition*, London: CEPR, February.

Rollo, J.M.C. (1991), 'Integrating Eastern Europe into a wider Europe', ch. 6 of O'Brien (ed.), pp. 81–92.

Swann, D. (1978), *The Common Market*, 4th edn, Harmondsworth: Penguin.

Ulph, D.T. and L.A. Winters (1989), 'Strategic manpower policy and international trade', presented at Empirical Models of Strategic Trade Policy, Boston: NBER, September.

Wang, Z.K. and L.A. Winters (1991), 'The trading potential of Eastern Europe', discussion paper no. 610, London: Centre for Economic Policy Research.

Winters, L.A. and P.A. Brenton (1991), 'Quantifying the economic effects of non-tariff barriers: the case of UK footwear', *Kyklos*, **44**, pp. 71–92.

World Bank (1990), *An Agricultural Strategy for Poland*, Washington DC: World Bank.

14 Trade policy reform in developing countries: problems and prospects

David Greenaway and Oliver Morrissey

I Introduction

Throughout the post-war period there has been enormous and sustained interest in trade policy in developing countries. Analysts have addressed three sets of issues: should developing countries follow inward or outward-oriented trade strategies; what are the consequences of a particular trade strategy for the structure of protection and overall economic performance; and what has been the experience of developing countries which have undertaken reform programmes? The first two of these questions have been very intensively studied (for a review see Rodrik 1993; Greenaway and Reed, 1990). Although they remain controversial, some kind of consensus has been reached – the costs of indiscriminate intervention have been well documented, and a positive association between growth of exports and growth of output has gained a lot of empirical support, although the strength and direction of causality remains problematic (see, for example, Jung and Marshall, 1985; Salvatore and Hatcher 1991). Indeed a greater consensus on these issues has in part been responsible for the extensive reforms we have observed in the last decade. This is the third issue alluded to above, and the one on which we focus in this chapter.

A large number of developing countries have initiated and implemented trade policy reform programmes over the last 15 years or so, some unilaterally, many as part of a package of conditionality for securing adjustment finance from the World Bank. We examine the rationale for trade policy reform, the nature of the reforms themselves and the lessons which can be learned from the reform programmes.

II What is liberalization?

The regime changes which we shall be discussing are programmes aimed at more open policies – programmes which are often referred to as 'liberalization'. But what is liberalization? In a simple two-sector trade model this is a trivial question which is easily answered. In Figure 14.1 the free trade (production) equilibrium is at a where the terms of trade line or world price line P_w is tangential to the production frontier. Point b represents a tariff-distorted equilibrium. If the import tariff is the only distortion in place, its

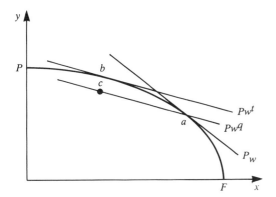

Figure 14.1   Import distortions

removal constitutes a clear act of liberalization – returning the economy to point *a*. Theory gives us a clear lead on what constitutes liberalization and on the potential benefits of such a policy change.

There are however, a number of obvious problems in operationalizing this concept. First, we may have a range of imported inputs and final products rather than one. Although theory is more ambiguous in its guidance here, we can develop rules for liberalization (reducing the mean) and harmonization (reducing the variance) which are consistent with welfare gains in a wide range of circumstances (see Ennew, Greenaway and Reed, 1993). Indeed this has clearly been the way in which liberalization has been pursued in the Kennedy, Tokyo and (probably) Uruguay Rounds of multilateral trade negotiations. Frequently liberalization is defined (implicitly) in this narrow sense of reducing the average level of protection. This is a rather inadequate approach, as we could envisage reforms which reduced the mean tariff, for example, but increased the variance and therefore increased domestic price distortions.

A second complication is that intervention may be aimed at exports as well as imports. Using the Lerner symmetry theorem, for a given tariff we can always find an equivalent export subsidy – where equivalence is defined in relative price terms. Referring again to Figure 14.1, point *a* could be consistent with a relative price ratio $P_w = P_m/P_x$ or $P_w{}^q = P_m(1+t)/P_x (1+s)$ where $t = s$, *m* stands for imports and *x* for exports. We can think of P_w as a *neutral* set of relative prices. Whether it is secured by free trade, or by the introduction of equivalent taxes and subsidies, relative prices are neutral in the sense that they do not provide a net incentive to agents to invest in one sector rather than another. When some analysts are discussing liberalization, they clearly have in mind this notion of neutrality. In a recent study of 36 liberalization episodes in 19 countries, Papageorgiou *et al.* (1991) define liberalization as 'any act that would make the trade regime more neutral' (vol. 7, p. 13). In another multi-country study, Krueger (1978) measures changes in trade policy by reference to a bias index where

$$B = \frac{\sum_{i=1}^{k} w_i \left(\dfrac{P_{mi}}{Q_{mi}} \right)}{\sum_{j=1}^{n} w_j \left(\dfrac{P_{xj}}{Q_{xj}} \right)} \tag{14.1}$$

where P and Q refer to domestic and international prices respectively, m and x refer to importables and exportables, w refers to trade share weights, and i and j are product groups. A value of 1 denotes neutrality; that is, incentives to importables are exactly offset by incentives to exportables. If B is greater than 1 the incentive regime favours importables, if less than 1, exportables.

The notion of neutrality has obvious intuitive attractions. In relative price terms it is equivalent to free trade and, in that sense, policy actions which move the economy towards neutrality would superficially appear to be liberalizing. The great difficulty with the concept is, however, that although we can identify equivalence in relative price terms across an infinite set of tariffs and offsetting subsidies, the resource allocation effects will only be equivalent at one unique set of relative prices, when $t = s = 0$; that is, free trade. This is so in part because as t and s increase it is likely that they become more distortive, and partly because once we introduce a non-tradeables sector we have to allow for a second set of relative prices and, as Greenaway and Milner (1987) show, what happens to the price of non-tradeables relative to tradeables has a profound effect on resource allocation. For example, Hong Kong and South Korea would have had similar computed values for Krueger's bias index in the early 1970s, but these numbers came from quite different trade regimes which had different allocative effects.

A third complication of trying to operationalize the simple notion of liberalization outlined in Figure 14.1 is that tariffs are not the only instrument of import protection, nor in many developing countries are they even the most important instrument. Since Bhagwati (1969), equivalences and non-equivalences between tariff and non-tariff barriers have been extensively analysed. What theory shows us is that, although we can always identify the tariff equivalent of a given non-tariff distortion in relative price terms, there are clear (static and dynamic) non-equivalences in allocative and distributional terms. The proposition that a tariff is generally more efficient than an equivalent quota is well established and needs no detailed elaboration here. In the context of Figure 14.1 the excess costs of the quota (due to rent seeking for example), may mean that we end up at a point *c* rather than point *b*. For this reason many analysts view the substitution of more efficient for less efficient instruments of protection as liberalization. Indeed, as we shall see later, this particular policy change has been a key ingredient in policy-based lending programmes.

Thus, in framing reform programmes, it is not a straightforward matter to map from the simple unambiguous notion of liberalization that comes out of the two-sector trade model to an operational measure. In practice 'liberalization' could refer to import liberalization and/or a move towards neutrality in the structure of relative prices and/or the substitution of less distorting for more distorting forms of intervention. As we shall see in Section III, World Bank-sponsored reform programmes often incorporate ingredients of all three. Table 14.1 summarizes the policy reforms associated with the liberalizations evaluated by Papageorgiou *et al.* (1991). This illustrates nicely the menu of reforms which can be construed as comprising 'liberalization'. It is clear from Table 14.1 that the majority of the reforms fall within the import liberalization or instrument substitution definitions. In six of the 17 cases export promotion measures were included, which is potentially consistent with the 'neutrality' approach. It is worth noting that most cases also included exchange rate adjustments, usually devaluation. This would not normally be considered a trade reform although it has important trade effects. In particular, exchange rate adjustments alter relative price incentives between importables and exportables. We will return to this issue in the next section.

III Why liberalize?

Trade policy reforms are a key ingredient of programmes in World Bank structural adjustment lending (SAL) conditionality. Since the inception of the SAL programme in 1980, some 70 developing countries have implemented, to some degree or other, trade policy reforms. In addition, a large number of countries, in particular the Asian and Latin American NICs, have implemented reforms either unilaterally or under GATT auspices. Why was liberalization such a prominent feature of the 1980s? There are a number of factors which have been at work.

First, and perhaps most obviously, has been the advent of policy-based lending itself. If 80 per cent of all SAL conditions are trade policy-related, and if the disbursement of funds is conditional upon acceptance of those conditions, then it should not be surprising to find that the conditions have been accepted. There is no doubt that this must have been an important influence, with the implication being that many developing countries have

Table 14.1   *Components of liberalization episodes: the Papageorgiou* et al.
study

Country	Features of liberalization episode
Argentina 1967–70 1976–80	Average tariff reduced from 94% to 49% Increased variance of tariffs Increase in effective exchange rate Exchange rate devaluation Export promotion
Brazil 1965–73	Tariff reductions Duty drawback scheme Tax exemptions and subsidies for exports Exchange rate devaluation
Colombia 1964–6 1968–82	Tariff reductions Prohibited import list abolished Reduced variance of tariffs Differential export subsidies
Peru 1979–80	Maximum tariff reduced from 355% to 60% Some increase in tariff escalation Most imports go on quota free list
Uruguay 1974–82	Tariff reductions QRs eliminated Unification of foreign exchange market
Indonesia 1950–1 1966–72	Rationalized tariff structure Elimination of import licence restrictions Reduced use of QRs, but pervasive controls remained Simplification of export restrictions Exchange rate devaluation and unification of foreign exchange market
South Korea 1965–7 1978–9	Reduced tariffs to average of 22% Reduced use of QRs, but 1200 items remained controlled Export incentives Exchange rate adjustment
New Zealand 1951–6 1964–81 1982–4	Tariff reductions Import licence reductions Tariff compensation Greater exchange rate flexibility

Country	Features of liberalization episode
Pakistan 1959–65 1972–8	Exchange rate devaluation Abolition of export bonus scheme
Philippines 1960–65 1970–74	Liberalized foreign exchange system Reduction in peak tariffs Piecemeal reductions in import controls Increase in effective tariffs
Singapore 1968–73	Tariff reductions QR liberalization
Sri Lanka 1968–70 1977–9	Removal of import licences Increased tariffs Increased export taxes Greater exchange rate flexibility Free trade zone incentives
Turkey 1970–73 1980–84	Tariff reduction QR reduction Export incentives Exchange rate devaluation
Israel 1952–5 1962–8 1969–77	Replacement of QRs with tariffs Some tariff reduction to hit target effective protection rate Exchange rate adjustment
Spain 1960–66 1970–74 1977–80	Tariff reductions Export incentives Exchange rate adjustment
Yugoslavia 1965–7	Average tariffs reduced from 23% to 10.5% Shift of products from restricted to liberal lists Abolition of export subsidies Exchange rate devaluation
Chile 1956–61 1974–81	QRs largely eliminated Tariffs reduced to uniform rate of 10% Exemptions reduced

Source: Adapted from Greenaway (1993).

been 'bribed' into liberalizing. Things are not quite so simple. We still need to explain what the attractions of liberalization were to the key lending agency – after all, that has not always been the advice which the Bank has offered (see Little, 1982). In addition we need to explain the sudden attraction to countries which unilaterally liberalized. Moreover, we also need to explain why many SAL recipients went beyond the acceptance of conditionality to its actual implementation.

A key factor was the rise of what Toye (1987) refers to as 'neo-conservative' ideas. In the formative years following independence for many LDCs, in the 1960s and 1970s, structuralist ideas were very influential. This philosophy is admirably encapsulated by Little (1982, p. 20) as follows:

> The structuralist sees the world as inflexible. Change is inhibited by obstacles, bottlenecks and constraints. People find it hard to move or adapt, and resources tend to be stuck. In economic terms, the supply of most things is inelastic ... Peasants were hardly economic men and were stuck in the mud; people were ruled by custom and authority; entrepreneurs were lacking; and communications were poor. There was little choice as to what to produce from the land. As a result of poverty, demands too were inflexible, especially for food. If there was to be any development, the demand for imports would be highly inelastic, since capital goods must come from abroad. Demands also were inelastic, especially for food, for imports into developing countries, and for their exports.

This provided the justification for pervasive intervention, especially in the traded goods sectors. In the 1970s, this perception of developing countries altered to one where it was believed that markets could work, if only they were allowed to do so. This point of view is put most stridently by Lal (1984). It was certainly a view which was sympathetically held by the technocrats within the World Bank in the late 1970s and 1980s.

Related to the previous point is the influence of a growing body of evidence on trade orientation, exports and growth (for a review, see Greenaway and Reed, 1990). A range of multi-country studies (for example, Balassa, 1982; Krueger, 1981), cross-country comparisons (for example, Donges, 1976; Greenaway and Nam, 1988) and a very large number of country case studies seemed to suggest that industralization programmes based on import substitution had been less successful than those founded on some kind of outward orientation. This is often caricatured by contrasting the performance of the 'Gang of Four' with that of older industrializing economies like India, Pakistan and Argentina. The empirical literature is not decisive, but suggests the following. First, although it is not always clear that outward-oriented trade strategies can actually deliver growth, it does seem to be the case that, in general, inward-oriented trade regimes have features which are limited to growth. In particular inward orientation has tended to be associated with distortions that reduce the relative returns on exporting activity.

Second, theory leads us to believe that there are deadweight losses of protection; evidence on rent seeking and directly unproductive activity suggests that these deadweight losses substantially understate the true costs of protection. Third, it appears to be the case that countries pursuing outward-oriented strategies are more resilient in responding to trade shocks than inward-oriented economies. Finally, exports and growth appear to be positively, and causally, correlated. There is some dispute about the direction of causality but, from the standpoint of underpinning a strategy designed to stimulate exports and growth, that is irrelevant – to be successful, any strategy needs to result in more outward orientation. It is fair to emphasize that outward orientation is not identical to free trade. In fact it suggests a trade regime distorted in favour of exports. In this sense, trade liberalization can be interpreted as any reforms that serve to reduce the degree of inward orientation (which will include exchange rate devaluation).

The essence of the 'neo-conservative' philosophy, as accepted in the World Bank by the late 1970s, was to remove any distortions on incentives to produce goods for domestic or foreign markets. This was interpreted as free trade and promulgated as structural adjustment (to remove internal price distortions) with trade liberalization (to correct domestic versus foreign price distortions). Evidence that inward orientation constrained growth potential was adduced in support of this commitment to liberalization. Thus a combination of a change in the prevailing philosophy, a growing body of empirical evidence and a lending agency committed to liberalization stimulated pervasive and, in some instances, profound reform.

IV   What form has liberalization taken?

We saw in Section II that there are complications in translating the simple theoretical concept of liberalization into a practical equivalent. In a world where there are multiple instruments of intervention, and self-interested agencies to defend their use, policy reform tends to be incrementalist rather than comprehensive. Bold across-the-board liberalizations like those in Chile in the 1970s are the exception rather than the rule. In practice, liberalization tends to be broadly defined as discussed in Section II. Papageorgiou *et al.* (1991) define an episode of liberalization as commencing 'at a point at which a significant policy change towards liberalisation was implemented. It ends with a reversal or when no further policy trend in either direction is apparent' (vol. 7, p. 29). The project team use this criterion to define 36 liberalization episodes across 19 countries. This study is a particularly ambitious one since, as well as identifying the episodes, the authors also attempt to evaluate various characteristics such as speed, intensity and duration.

The ingredients of the liberalization episodes in their sample are listed in Table 14.1. Inspection of that table reveals that tariff reductions are a recurring component, as is liberalization/reduction of quantitative restrictions. Such acts would, *ceteris paribus*, be consistent with a rotation of P_w' towards Pw in Figure 14.1. Note also, however, that some form of export support is also common – export promotion, export subsidies, duty drawback arrangements and so on. Other things being equal, these kinds of policy innovations would result in greater neutrality in relative prices. Note also that, in a number of cases, the replacement of quotas with tariffs is mentioned.

Whalley (1991) reports the results of an evaluation of liberalization in 11 developing countries. He acknowledges the difficulties of identifying a liberalization episode and refrains from making any attempt to do so. Instead he infers that liberalization has occurred from the scale and intensity of reforms. The components for his sample are listed in Table 14.2. There is some overlap in country coverage between Tables 14.1 and 14.2 but it should be noted that, even where this occurs, the liberalization episodes are actually different. Table 14.1 effectively ends in 1984, whilst for the most part Table 14.2 begins around then. What is clear, however, is that the ingredients taken by Whalley as signalling liberalization are, with the exception of export promotion measures, similar to those of Papageorgiou *et al*. Although both studies have some difficulty in defining liberalization, they seem to be able to recognize it when it occurs.

The same can be said of the World Bank evaluations. We noted earlier that the advent of policy-based lending was a crucial ingredient in explaining liberalization in developing countries – around four-fifths of SALs incorporate trade policy conditions. This conditionality has resulted in actual or intended trade policy reforms of a liberalizing nature in some 60 or so developing countries. The type of reforms which are typically proposed are outlined in Table 14.3, which is drawn from a detailed analysis of 40 SALs. The pattern which one observes in Tables 14.1 and 14.2 is repeated here. Some reform proposals have been directed at 'pure' liberalization, others are directed at moving relative prices towards neutrality and some are aimed at replacing more costly with less costly instruments.

V What are the effects of liberalization?

Trade policy reform in developing countries over the last 20 years or so has been pervasive. Although, as we shall see, we need to qualify this statement somewhat to acknowledge the fact that not all intended liberalizations are implemented and, moreover, many of those which are implemented subsequently collapse. Despite these qualifications, we have observed widespread liberalization. Has it been successful in some sense? Has it 'worked'? Theory leads us to believe there are gains to be realized from successful liberalization. Have these gains been reaped?

Table 14.2   *Components of liberalization in 11 developing countries: the Whalley study*

Country	Features of Liberalization Episode
Argentina 1987–8	Coverage of QRs reduced Reduction in import licensing Reduction in average tariffs Reduction in variance of tariffs
Brazil 1988	Lowered tariff rates Elimination of tariff exemptions Reduction of non-tariff measures
China 1978–87	Creation of export processing zones Reduced taxes on exports
Costa Rica 1982–3	Reform of foreign exchange market Creation of export processing zones
India 1985–8	Reduced tariffs on agricultural items Auxiliary customs duty abolished Open General Licencing extended
Kenya 1980–86	Reduction in import duties Reduction in non-tariff barriers Exchange rate depreciation
Mexico 1985–8	QR liberalization Tariff reductions Reduced variance of tariffs Reformed customs valuations procedures
Nigeria 1986–7	Import licensing system abolished Import levy discontinued Cuts in import tariffs Import deposits abolished Exchange rate reforms
Philippines 1981–7	Import controls liberalized Reduction in tariffs
South Korea 1978–81 1989	Elimination of discretionary import licensing Reduction in tariffs
Tanzania 1984–9	Exchange rate adjustment Reduction in import restrictions Rationalization of tariffs Export promotion

Source: Adapted from Whalley (1991), Appendix 10.1.

Table 14.3   Trade policy reform proposals in 40 SAL countries

Item	Intensity of reforms[a]			Presence	
	Strong	Medium	Weak	Yes	No
Overall import policy	14	15	11		
Non-protective QRs	14	16	10		
Protective QRs[b]	14	15	11		
Tariff level[b]	7	21	12		
Schedule of future reduction	6	29	5		
Overall export policy	15	15	10		
Imports for exports	17	15	8		
Overall reduction in anti-export bias	17	12	11		
Exchange rate flexibility[c]				38	2
Export promotion measures[d]				33	7
Studies of effects of trade policy reform				28	12

Notes:

The assessments refer to proposals supported by the Bank. They do not refer to policy implementation (experience with which is very varied).

a   Totals are 40 in all cases.

b   Reforms which replaced QRs with tariffs are included in both lines.

c   Often these were not explicit conditions, but constituted understandings made under the programme, usually as part of a standby agreement.

d   Includes such schemes as export credits, insurance, guarantees and institutional development.

Source: Thomas and Nash (1991) Table 1.

Problems of evaluation

Evaluating this wave of liberalization is exceedingly demanding, for several reasons. First of all, one needs to have some reasonable counter-factual element – some picture of what the economy would have looked like in the absence of the reforms. One response to this may be to assume that the paths which various indicators were on would have continued in the absence of reform. The problem with this is that trade liberalization is not always implemented in the most auspicious of circumstances. Indeed, in the context of SAL-based reforms, the opposite is frequently the case – reform against the backcloth of difficult, and possibly unsustainable conditions. Related to this there is also the problem of disentangling the effects of trade policy reforms from other policy changes. Many of the liberalizations studied by Papageorgiou *et al.* (1991) were not accompanied by other major reforms, others were. The hallmark of the SALs is a package of reforms addressing several targets simultaneously. Thus, at the same time as tariffs are reduced, or QRs eliminated, agricultural prices may be reformed, privatization promoted, the financial sector reformed and so on. For obvious reasons it then becomes difficult to conduct anything that resembles a 'controlled experiment'!

A third complication is one of timing – how long should a liberalization programme have been in place before we evaluate its success? Theory gives us no clear guidance on this. It would depend, among other things, on the ingredients of the programme, the circumstances in which it was implemented, whether it was single-stage or multi-stage, whether other reforms were simultaneously implemented or not and so on.

Finally, there is the issue of performance criteria – what indicators do we use to evaluate success or failure? One possibility is to compare outcomes with targets. If the reform set out to reduce the average nominal tariff to 10 per cent, and its upper bound to 50 per cent, was this achieved? Superficially this is an attractive option because it focuses on the instruments of reform. In the case of policy-based lending reforms, it is also a relatively straightforward strategy to implement, since the World Bank uses compliance with conditionality as a performance criterion. However, one has to show some caution, in part because these criteria are inputs to the reform process rather than outputs from it, and in part because it is not unusual to find that instrument substitution occurs. In other words, the average nominal tariff may be reduced to the stated target; if at the same time, however, new anti-dumping or safeguard provisions are introduced, the overall impact on protection may be unchanged. Rather than inspecting the target indicators, one could try and evaluate the impact of reforms on overall economic performance – for example on exports, investment or growth. This is where the counter-factual problem can be seen most clearly. What would have happened to exports, investment and growth in the absence of the reforms? How do we disentangle the effects of trade policy changes from other reforms?

Evaluation of outcomes

Studies of the process of implementation outnumber studies of the impact of liberalization. This is partly a function of time – the liberalization experience is fairly recent – partly due to the problems of evaluation adumbrated in the previous paragraph. The most comprehensive study of outcomes is Papageorgiou *et al.* (1991), which supersedes Krueger (1978) in terms of coverage and breadth. In addition there have been a number of studies of the experience with SALs, notably World Bank (1988; 1990), Mosley, Harrigan and Toye (1991) and Thomas *et al.* (1992), as well as a series of individual country case studies. These however, are assessments of adjustment programmes overall and do not just consider the experience with trade policy reform.

As noted earlier, Papageorgiou *et al.* (1991) is a cross-country assessment of the process and outcomes of 31 liberalization episodes in 19 countries. In terms of scale, it is unrivalled. The methodology which the authors deploy involves detailed documentation of the experiences of 17 of their sample countries, the output of which then forms the raw material for a comparative analysis. The key conclusions reached are as follows:

1. Liberalization which is initiated at a time of crisis (as defined by the authors) tends to be radical and sustained. Moreover, liberalization which is launched as a bold step tends to be more sustainable than one which is staged.
2. Radical removal of quotas is conducive to sustainability.
3. Exchange rate devaluation is crucial to sustainability, but expansionary demand management is associated with abortion of liberalization.
4. Liberalization appears to have a favourable impact on the balance of payments.
5. The impact of liberalization on unemployment is minimal.
6. Liberalization tends not to lower production, nor to inhibit economic growth.
7. Liberalization leads to rapid and sustained export growth.

Thus the analysis provides insights on timing, sequencing and adjustment problems, as well as on 'performance indicators'. Timing/sequencing/adjust-ment lessons will be evaluated more fully in the next section. For the time being we will concentrate on performance indicators.

As we saw in Section II, the objective of liberalization is to 'get (relative) prices right' in the tradeable sector, with a view to improving efficiency in the allocation and utilization of resources, increasing exports and increasing growth. Judged in these terms, the Papageorgiou *et al.* (1991) evidence seems to suggest that liberalization has 'worked'. Tables 14.4 and 14.5 report the results for growth rates and exports before and after liberalization. In the case of the former it seems that average growth three years after liberalization was 35 per cent higher than the average for the three years prior to liberalization (6 per cent as opposed to 4.45 per cent). In some cases, the increases are quite spectacular, as with South Korea and Spain, for instance. The results for real export growth are even more impressive, with average real growth rates being 150 per cent higher for the three-year period following liberalization, than they were for the three years prior to liberali-zation (11 per cent rather than 4.4 per cent). Again the performance of some countries stands out as particularly striking, that of South Korea and Turkey, for example.

Table 14.4   Performance of gross domestic product (real annual rate of growth)

Episode	PtL	T	T+1	T+2	T+3	AVG-T	AVG
Argentina 1 (1967–70)	6.70	2.60	4.40	8.50	5.40	6.10	5.23
Argentina 2 (1976–80)	2.90	–0.60	6.50	–3.10	6.90	3.43	2.43
Brazil (1965–73)	3.23	2.70	5.10	4.80	9.30	6.40	5.48
Chile 1 (1956–61)	2.30	1.20	7.90	2.80	0.53	3.74	3.11
Chile 2 (1974–81)	–1.50	8.50	–12.90	3.50	9.86	0.15	2.24
Colombia 2 (1968–82)	3.87	2.67	4.93	6.59	6.50	6.04	5.17
Greece 1 (1953–5)	4.90	13.06	3.10	6.81	8.70	6.20	7.92
Greece 2 (1962–82)	6.13	0.58	10.07	7.54	9.25	8.95	6.86
Indonesia (1966–72)	0.80	2.72	1.41	10.89	6.83	6.38	5.46
Israel 2 (1962–8)	9.80	10.10	11.40	9.80	9.10	10.10	10.10
Israel 3 (1969–77)	5.77	12.60	7.90	11.00	12.60	10.40	10.95
New Zealand 2 (1962–81)	4.02	5.84	6.57	5.54	–2.16	3.32	3.95
New Zealand 3 (1982–4)	4.32	4.66	0.48	2.78	3.29	2.18	2.80
Pakistan 1 (1959–65)	2.15	1.47	4.34	5.23	5.92	5.16	4.24
Pakistan 2 (1972–8)	0.30	3.78	3.07	3.14	0.74	2.32	2.68
Peru (1979–80)	0.30	3.78	3.07	3.14	0.74	2.32	2.68
Philippines 1 (1960–65)	5.88	7.55	6.39	9.49	11.48	9.12	8.73
Philippines 2 (1977–80)	5.32	4.84	5.72	5.23	8.48	6.48	6.07
Portugal 1 (1970–74)	5.88	7.55	6.39	9.49	11.48	9.12	8.73
Portugal 2 (1977–80)	16.0	5.30	3.20	4.50	4.90	4.20	4.48
Singapore (1968–73)	10.10	14.27	13.50	13.65	12.61	13.25	13.51
South Korea 1 (1965–77)	6.97	5.80	12.70	6.60	11.30	10.20	9.10
South Korea 2 (1978–9)	13.80	3.31	6.36	–6.20	6.36	2.17	2.46
Spain 2 (1970–74)	6.67	4.89	5.54	8.59	8.06	7.40	6.77
Spain 3 (1977–80)	3.30	3.72	2.50	0.16	1.48	1.38	1.97
Sri Lanka 1 (1968–70)	3.57	7.57	4.25	3.50	–0.52	2.41	3.70
Sri Lanka 2 (1977–9)	2.80	4.87	8.69	6.28	5.47	6.81	6.33
Turkey 1 (1970–73)	5.69	5.28	9.00	6.00	4.10	6.37	6.10
Turkey 2 (1980–84)	2.90	–1.07	4.10	4.61	3.25	4.00	2.73
Uruguay (1974–82)	–4.69	3.37	5.28	1.62	2.75	3.22	3.26
Yugoslavia (1965–7)	7.90	1.40	5.00	0.90	3.50	3.13	2.70
Average	4.45	4.69	5.45	5.26	6.00	5.57	5.35

Notes:
PtL: average of three years up to liberalization: *T*: year of liberalization; *T*+1: one year after liberalization; *T*+2: two years after liberalization; *T*+3: three years after liberalization; *AVG-T*: average of three years after trade liberalization; *AVG*: average of *T* plus three years after liberalizations.

Source: Papageorgiou *et al.* (1991) vol. 7, Table 12.4.

Table 14.5 Export performance (annual real rate of growth)

Episodes	T-3	T-2	T-1	PtL	T	T+1	T+2	T+3	AVG	AVG-T
Argentina 1 (1967–70)	-6.4	9.8	6.8	4.4	-1.2	-1.4	16.1	7.2	5.2	7.3
Argentina 2 (1976–80)	16.8	2.2	-22.7	-1.2	-31.5	42.2	5.2	0.7	19.9	1.6
Brazil (1965–73)	-7.2	28.8	-14.1	2.5	4.0	11.7	-2.9	15.2	7.0	8.0
Chile 1 (1956–61)	-23.6	15.3	13.3	1.7	-7.3	1.9	0.7	16.4	3.0	6.4
Chile 2 (1974–81)	8.6	-13.0	-0.4	-1.6	49.4	7.9	25.4	7.4	22.5	13.6
Colombia 2 (1968–82)	6.5	-1.7	8.7	4.5	8.3	4.7	0.9	-0.2	3.4	1.8
Greece 1 (1953–5)	-21.7	13.3	17.6	3.1	7.5	17.8	20.4	3.8	12.4	14.0
Greece 2 (1962–82)	-3.5	1.7	9.3	2.5	8.2	2.5	7.7	8.8	6.8	6.3
Indonesia 2 (1962–8)	-6.0	11.9	3.1	3.0	-1.1	-0.2	10.5	14.0	5.8	8.1
Israel 2 (1962–8)	44.4	23.1	15.5	56.7	15.3	20.5	6.0	10.4	13.0	12.3
Israel 3 (1969–77)	12.2	9.0	26.9	16.0	7.6	7.5	19.0	14.9	12.2	13.8
New Zealand 2 (1962–81)	17.4	3.1	-6.4	4.7	0.6	14.0	18.1	-6.3	6.6	8.6
New Zealand 3 (1982–4)	-7.7	13.1	6.8	4.1	3.3	-1.1	9.3	9.7	5.3	6.0
Pakistan 1 (1959–65)	26.3	-13.2	-20.0	-2.3	10.0	49.1	-23.8	4.8	10.0	10.0
Pakistan 2 (1972–8)	-3.3	13.9	-3.4	-6.4	-21.6	-5.3	17.8	-3.9	-3.0	
Peru (1979–80)	-14.4	17.0	19.6	7.4	44.7	-2.7	-9.8	16.0	12.0	1.2
Philippines 1 (1960–65)	-6.2	9.9	-1.0	0.9	8.1	-3.7	9.7	23.8	9.5	9.9
Philippines 2 (1977–80)	-1.5	-3.9	-3.5	-3.0	23.1	9.0	-13.5	11.6	7.5	2.4
Portugal 1 (1970–74)	8.9	5.0	10.0	-3.0	12.0	1.2	5.9	7.8	6.7	5.0
Portugal 2 (1977–80)	1.7	-22.8	-0.7	-7.9	9.0	3.0	21.4	10.1	10.8	11.5
South Korea 1 (1965–77)	12.6	7.4	23.6	14.5	40.6	52.3	35.7	41.6	42.6	43.2
South Korea 2 (1978–9)	10.6	35.5	27.9	24.7	13.8	-0.3	10.0	19.0	10.6	9.6

	T-3	T-2	T-1	T	T+1	T+2	T+3	AVG	AVG-T	PtL
Spain 1 (1960–66)	1.0	3.1	11.0	5.0	51.4	1.2	-7.1	-0.6	11.2	-2.2
Spain 2 (1970–74)	1.5	-3.9	-3.5	-3.0	23.1	9.0	-13.5	11.6	7.5	5.4
Spain 3 (1977–80)	0.9	-1.4	10.0	3.2	8.5	10.7	6.4	0.6	6.6	5.9
Sri Lanka 1 (1968–70)	6.1	-6.0	6.2	2.1	2.1	-2.6	3.1	0.1	0.7	0.2
Sri Lanka 2 (1977–9)	-13.4	20.1	2.2	3.0	-13.3	9.5	13.8	3.6	3.4	8.9
Turkey 1 (1970–73)	9.3	-1.8	8.1	5.2	8.0	7.4	29.7	15.6	15.2	17.6
Turkey 2 (1980–84)	-17.7	14.1	-9.6	-4.4	4.2	85.5	10.0	13.7	35.8	46.4
Uruguay (1974–80)	-12.9	-19.5	-1.3	-11.3	20.4	13.9	28.2	6.8	17.3	16.3
Yugoslavia (1965–7)	17.0	15.0	8.4	13.5	11.1	12.6	5.2	4.9	8.4	7.6
Average	1.6	6.5	5.1	4.4	12.6	11.8	9.6	9.9	11.0	10.5

Notes:
T-3: three years prior to liberalization; T-2: two years prior to liberalization; T-1: one year prior to liberalization; PtL: average of the three years prior to liberalization; T: year of liberalization; T+1: one year after liberalization; T+2: two years after liberalization; T+3: three years after liberalization; AVG: average of the three years after liberalization; AVG-T: average of T plus the three years after liberalization.

Source: Papageorgiou *et al.* (1991) vol. 7, Table 12.4.

These results appear to be very favourable to the case for liberalization, not only because of the absolute magnitude of the changes, but also because they appear to reflect the experience of a large number of countries with different initial conditions, different programmes and so on. There are, however, problems with the evidence. In particular there are some fairly fundamental problems with the way in which liberalization episodes are identified and measured. These are discussed at length in Greenaway (1993) and need not detain us here. The point which comes out of that evaluation is that it is not always clear that 'liberalization' in any of the various senses discussed above has occurred. In some instances it is only stabilization combined with devaluation which has been implemented. This is important because these may be key causal ingredients in stimulating export and output growth. Thus, for example, Whalley (1988) has argued that an ability to stabilize quickly when faced with exogenous shocks is a crucial element in explaining South Korean growth in the 1960s and 1970s.

Related to the previous point, as we noted at the start of this section, trade liberalization may be only one of a number of factors which has an impact on growth. To 'strip out' the effect of trade policy reform is complicated, but the starting-point is some explicit counter-factual model. This is not the methodology adopted by Papageorgiou *et al.* (1991). They simply compare performance before and after liberalization, and attribute the differences to trade policy reforms. The changes may indeed be attributable to trade policy reforms, but then again they may not. In the absence of an explicit model and rigorous statistical testing, we cannot be entirely certain. In fact, given the authors' vague definition of liberalization, we can barely accept the evidence as a test of the effect of trade liberalization.

World Bank (1988; 1990) and Mosley *et al.* (1991) use similar performance indicators to evaluate the impact of policy-based lending programmes overall. The problem here is that, although trade policy conditions figure very prominently in SALs (accounting for around 80 per cent of all conditions), they are typically not the only reforms which are implemented. When we observe a particular set of results, therefore, we cannot be sure of the precise contribution of trade policy reform. Nevertheless the results are interesting, and are reported in Table 14.6. The methodology used is 'with–without': a comparison of the performance of adjustment lending with non-adjustment lending countries. The studies suggest that adjustment lending may improve real export performance and also lead to an improvement in the current account. On the other hand, they also suggest that the impact on real GDP growth is more or less neutral, whilst the impact on real investment is adverse. There is some consistency with the Papageorgiou *et al.* results, for example on real export growth, but not so on others, such as real output growth and investment.

Table 14.6   Comparison of results on effectiveness of SALs.

Study	Percentage of SAL countries which outperformed non-SAL countries			
	Growth of real GDP	Investment % GDP	Growth of real exports	Current Account % of GDP
World Bank (1988)	53	37	57	70
Mosley *et al.* (1991)	50	36	65	79

	Effect of SAL on variable*		Effect of compliance*	
	Growth of real GDP	Growth of real exports	Growth of real GDP	Growth of real exports
All (19)	−	−	+	+
SSA (8)		−	+	?
MIC (14)	−	−	+	+

Notes:
* Summary of econometric results in Mosley *et al.* (1991, Vol. 1, pp. 212–14); only those coefficients estimated as statistically significant are reported.
Numbers in parentheses are number of countries in Sub-Saharan Africa (SSA) sample and middle-income countries (MIC) sample.
Both SAL and compliance variables were lagged – the one case where lags gave conflicting significant estimates is denoted '?'.

What can we make of these results? The stock of cross-country evidence is unfortunately limited and the studies which we have evaluated use different methodologies and methodologies which are not free of problems. They suggest that successful liberalization may have encouraged real export growth, and may be associated with real output growth. If so, this is not only consistent with what theory would predict but also potentially encouraging to policy-based lending which has a strong element of trade policy reform. However, alongside this evidence, we also have to recognize that many liberalization attempts have failed, and failed liberalization may be more damaging than no liberalization. A number of the failed cases are analysed in Thomas *et al.* (1992) and Mosley *et al.* (1991). The final questions we need to address are what factors result in failure, and what lessons can we learn from both successful and failed liberalizations?

VI   What lessons can we draw?
We have shown that trade liberalization is difficult to define and that, owing to the absence of a consistent definition and methodology, the Papageorgiou *et al.* (1991) study fails to offer unambiguous evidence on its effects. How-

ever, there are a number of lessons that can be drawn from the studies referred to in the previous section. First we need to clarify further what trade liberalization means. This can most easily be achieved, for our present purposes, by reference to outputs. What are the intended effects of trade liberalization? What features did successful reform programmes share, and what features distinguished them from unsuccessful programmes? The fundamental objective of trade liberalization is to remove distortions favouring importables, thereby facilitating the growth of real exports which should contribute to enhanced overall economic growth. The basic questions then, are did real exports increase and, if so, what factors contributed to this increase?

The evidence in Tables 14.5 and 14.6 shows that real exports did tend to increase following liberalization, although in a third of the episodes listed in Table 14.5 this was not the case. We cannot distinguish the factors contributing to success and failure in all cases but can draw some broad conclusions. It does appear that the order in which reforms are implemented, the sequencing, is important. A realistic exchange rate, which nearly always means devaluation in the cases we are considering, is a first step as it increases the relative returns to exporters (Colombia and Peru in Table 14.5 are two cases where a failed episode followed a failure to devalue). Once the country has a realistic exchange rate, preferably one rather than multiple rates, it can then proceed with conventional trade liberalization. Reducing protection, and so removing many price distortions, will encourage exports as it reduces the input costs facing exporters and the incentives for resources to go into import-competing industries. For reform to succeed, however, it is important that exporting becomes attractive so that resources are released by import-competing sectors and are absorbed by exporting industries. Many reform programmes will include export promotion measures to facilitate this transition (this worked well for South Korea in the 1960s and Turkey in the 1980s).

The evidence suggests that macroeconomic stabilization, in particular devaluation to a realistic (and maintained) exchange rate and control of the fiscal deficit, should precede liberalization. Failure to stabilize the macroeconomy retarded trade liberalization in Morocco and the Philippines, and reversed the reform process in Argentina and Zambia (Thomas and Nash, 1991). Once the macroeconomy is stable a country should find it easier to liberalize its trade regime. Converting QRs to tariffs is a useful first move, both because tariffs are generally less distortionary and because this can generate tax revenue for the government. Such tax revenue can offset losses which could be incurred when the government commences tariff reduction. Experience suggests that this is rather important as maintaining government revenues makes it easier to sustain the reform programme. The general principle guiding tariff liberalization is to reduce all tariffs in proportion. Economic theory is less clear about the welfare effects of differential tariff reductions although, if goods are net substitutes, it is generally beneficial to reduce the highest tariffs and increase the lowest tariffs. This procedure of increasing low and zero tariffs will also offset revenue losses from tariff reductions. Finally, if one doubts the ability of exporting industries to respond quickly to the reforms, export promotion measures could be used, not least because they help build commitment to the reforms. Sequencing is perhaps a necessary condition but it is by no means sufficient for successful liberalization; the reform process must be supported by political and administrative capacity.

If agents are to respond to reform they must believe the reforms are permanent. This need for credibility requires that the government be committed to the reforms and signal its commitment. It appears that 'new' governments have an advantage in establishing credibility. In 14 of the 36 cases evaluated in Papageorgiou *et al.* (1991) liberalization followed a change of political regime. It is not necessarily the regime change itself that is of importance, however. Rather, as the existence of distortions creates rent seeking and political lobbies opposed to change, what is required is a regime with the administrative capacity to implement reform and the political strength to take on the vested interests (see Mosley *et al.* 1991; Thomas and Nash, 1991). A new regime may have an advantage in this respect. The point is that greater care must be taken in designing a reform programme for an established regime, especially if it has a record of failed reforms.

Given the existence of political and administrative constraints, programme design is of vital importance. Policy reforms should reinforce each other and, in so far as is possible, should generate political support for the reforms. For example, export promotion measures create a lobby favouring exports that may counteract the protection lobby. This suggests that, in sequencing, export promotion measures should coincide with, if not precede, tariff reductions. Devaluation should also encourage an export lobby. Furthermore, as devaluation renders imports more expensive in domestic prices, reducing tariffs may be politically appealing. As another example, replacing quotas with tariffs can be defended on distributional grounds as internalizing the rents of source-specific quotas. A common feature of liberalization is that governments are trying to reduce the fiscal deficit while also cutting tariffs; an additional benefit of converting quotas to tariffs is in bridging any revenue shortfall. This reduces the pressure often faced by liberalizing governments to cut recurrent expenditure, which tends to be quite costly politically.

Having taken a decision to liberalize, should the programme be implemented rapidly or gradually? Economic theory would suggest that, in the absence of distortions and with full factor mobility, liberalization should be rapid. Rapid reform gives strong signals to economic agents who will respond quickly and does not provide the political opposition with time to mobilize. Papageorgiou *et al.* (1991) argue that the evidence favours abrupt liberalizations, although the length of an abrupt episode is not well defined (and extends to a few years in some cases). On the other hand, a number of arguments can be raised to favour gradualism. First, adjustment costs, notably unemployment, are likely to be higher if reform is rapid; while commentators interpret the evidence in different ways, there are ample cases of high unemployment associated with rapid liberalization. Sector-specific unemployment following liberalization provides a case for gradualism: it allows time for sector-specific labour to retrain and permits sector-specific capital to be written-off at some 'optimal' rate. Second, opposition may be less vociferous if adjustment costs are mitigated, while gradualism allows time to build a political consensus in favour of the reform process. Finally there is a credibility argument for gradualism. If a government does not have a reputation for credible reform, then introducing a series of gradual reforms to which it demonstrates commitment can allow that government to build up a reputation for credibility. It is, of course, essential that the gradual reforms be successfully introduced in sequence.

There have been numerous attempts at trade liberalization in numerous countries over the last few decades. The rationale underlying GATT is liberalization on a global level. If successful trade liberalization is defined as achieving and sustaining an outward-oriented economy, which is taken to imply that the real growth of exports and the economy would both be higher than if the economy was inward-oriented, many attempts must be considered failures. Using a less stringent definition of liberalization, as do Papageorgiou *et al.* (1991), we will find more successful cases. Future research must tackle this issue more methodically than hitherto. If we cannot agree on a definition of trade liberalization we must at least identify which trade and macroeconomic policies are most conducive to sustained economic growth. We must also identify how governments can implement successful policy reform so that they can adopt the desired policy stance. A failed reform episode imposes very high costs, may make the economy worse off than before the reform and undermines future credibility. It may even be the case that no reform is preferable to failure; therefore it is essential to understand what features in the design of a reform programme will contribute to its successful implementation. We have tried to identify some of these.

The process of trade liberalization, as of any economic policy reform, must take into account the initial political and economic conditions of the country. Politically it is important whether the regime is a new regime or an old regime with little credibility, and whether the bureaucrats have technical competence and capability (are they adequately resourced and trained, for example?) Old regimes with a reputation for failures are well advised to undertake gradual reforms to build credibility; new regimes, with political commitment and administrative capability, are better placed for rapid reforms. In general, the speed at which reforms are introduced should be informed by political considerations. Economically one should first investigate the state of the balance of payments, exchange rate, fiscal deficit and inflation. Any of these, especially overvaluation, will affect trade liberalization. In many cases they will undermine or negate trade liberalization. When trade liberalization commences, the responsiveness of the economy (in redirecting resources towards producing for export) is often enhanced if export promotion measures are introduced in conjunction with import liberalization.

References

Balassa, B. (ed.) (1982), *Development Strategies in Semi-Industrialised Countries*, Baltimore: John Hopkins University Press.

Bhagwati, J. (1969), 'On the Equivalent of Tariffs and Quotas', in *Trade, Tariffs and Growth*, London: Weidenfeld and Nicolson.

Donges, J. (1976), 'A Comparative Study of Industrialisation Policies in Fifteen Semi-Industrialised Countries', *Weltwirtschaftliches Archiv*, **113**, pp. 626–59.

Ennew, C., D. Greenaway and G.V. Reed (1993), 'Tariff Liberalisation and Harmonisation: Do Trade Negotiators Get What They Want?', *Journal of International and Comparative Economics*, **2**, pp. 119–37.

Greenaway, D. (1993), 'Liberalising Foreign Trade Through Rose Tinted Glasses', *Economic Journal*, **103**, pp. 208–22.

Greenaway, D. and C.R. Milner (1987), 'True Protection Concepts and their Role in Evaluating Trade Policies in LDCs', *Journal of Development Studies*, **23**, pp. 39–58.

Greenaway, D. and C. Nam (1988), 'Industrialisation and Macroeconomic Performance in Developing Countries Under Alternative Trade Strategies', *Kyklos*, **41**, pp. 419-36.

Greenaway, D. and G.V. Reed (1990), 'Empirical Evidence of Trade Orientation and Economic Performance in Developing Countries', in C. Milner (ed.), *Export Promotion Strategies*, London: Harvester Wheatsheaf.

Jung, W.S. and P. Marshall (1985), 'Exports, Growth and Causality in Developing Countries', *Journal of Development Economics*, **18**, pp. 1–13.

Krueger, A. (1978), *Foreign Trade Regimes and Economic Development: Liberalisation Attempts and Consequences*, Cambridge, Mass.: MIT, NBER.

Krueger, A. (1981), *Trade and Employment in Developing Countries*, Chicago: University of Chicago Press.

Lal, D. (1984), *The Poverty of Development Economics*, London: Institute of Economic Affairs.

Little, I.M.D. (1982), *Economic Development*, New York: Basic Books.

Mosley, P., J. Harrigan and J. Toye (1991), *Aid and Power: The World Bank and Policy-based Lending. Volumes 1 and 2*, London: Routledge.

Papageorgiou, D., M. Michaely and A. Choksi (1991), *Liberalising Foreign Trade*, 7 vols, Oxford: Basil Blackwell.

Rodrik, D. (1993), 'Trade and Industrial Policy Reform in Developing Countries: A Review of Recent Theory and Evidence' (mimeo).

Salvatore, D. and R. Hatcher (1991), 'Inward Oriented and Outward Oriented Trade Strategies', *Journal of Development Studies*, **27**, pp. 7–25.

Thomas, V. and J. Nash (1991), 'Reform of Trade Policy: Recent Evidence from Theory and Practice', *World Bank Research Observer*, **6** (2), pp. 219–40.

Thomas, V., A. Chibber, M. Dailami and J. de Melo (1992), *Restructuring Economies in Distress*, Oxford: Oxford University Press.

Toye, J. (1987), *Dilemmas of Development*, Oxford: Basil Blackwell.

Whalley, J. (1988), Trade Policy and Growth in Korea, mimeo.

Whalley, J. (1991), 'Recent Trade Liberalisation in the Developing World: What is Behind it and Where is it Headed?' in D. Greenaway, R. Hine, A. O'Brien and R. Thornton (eds), *Global Protectionism*, London: Macmillan.

World Bank (1988), *Report on Adjustment Lending*, Document R88-199, Country Economics Department, Washington DC: World Bank.

World Bank (1990), *Report on Adjustment Lending II: Policies for the Recovery of Growth*, Document R90–99, Washington DC: World Bank.

15 Economic security and North–South relations

Saadet Deger and Somnath Sen*

Introduction

The decade of the 1980s was important in the history of international economic and political relations, for a number of reasons. At the close of the decade the Cold War ended, putting North–South relations on a new basis. It also proved to be a lost decade in terms of the economic crisis which engulfed many people in the developing world, particularly in Latin America and Sub-Saharan Africa. Official development finance increased by almost 30 per cent between 1980 and 1990 in constant prices, but aid–dependency ratios also increased, especially in Sub-Saharan Africa, threatening the smooth long-run tendency of aid helping to build self-sustaining economies. Examination of environmental crises showed that very high levels of growth in populous countries might have significant negative externalities for the world as a whole, yet the dynamics of population changes implied that rapid growth was essential for minimum levels of economic development. In the absence of a well defined security structure to replace bipolarity, inter-state political and military relations became more complex. At the same time, the 'protection' provided by superpower rivalry was removed, leading to the possibility of an anarchic world order. There was far greater awareness of the role of good governance in fostering economic development, but the attainment of higher standards of governance could require more intervention in the affairs of sovereign states. Taking all these effects together, North–South relations today are possibly the most complex to be found in the post-colonial period.

In spite of the ending of the Cold War, the claims that there is now a beginning of a 'new world order' under the auspices of the United Nations, and major developmental achievements in the so-called Third World, important unsolved problems remain in international relations and the advent of peace is not sufficient to solve them. In particular, economic insecurity threatens to engulf many countries, including the newly emerging countries of central and eastern Europe and, unless the threat of economic deprivation is removed, the prospects for conflict remain strong. In many regions of the

* The views presented in this chapter are those of the authors alone and do not represent those of the affiliated institutions.

Third World conflict resolution has made impressive progress, but the possibility of future conflict remains owing to environmental degradation and economic deprivation. It is clear that economic security is vital for a more durable peace.

All these factors have focused attention on the new dimensions of security which encompass economic, political and environmental aspects rather than traditional military security relations alone. These aspects are set to become more important in North–South relations as asymmetric development in the two regions produces economic insecurity as well as related threats to the environment. The main concern of this chapter is to analyse the interrelationships between security problems and economic crises both at individual country level and at the level of the North and South. The chapter tries to demonstrate that security issues can have an adverse economic impact which exacerbates developmental problems. On the other hand, developmental failures contribute to greater insecurity. The development dilemma is how to balance the contradictory claims of military and economic security.

The term 'economic security' is used to describe a state of affairs where the vulnerable are protected from economic threats such as poverty, famine, mass unemployment and so forth. Economic security is achieved when such threats are matched by countervailing economic capabilities – which essentially requires sustainable and equitable development. Such forms of security also needs resources – financial, human and economic. The world military sector is a vast repository of resources, therefore it is only natural to ask whether the change in the political structure at the end of West–East confrontation would reallocate and change the economic resource structure as well.

To focus attention on the foregoing interrelationships, the chapter discusses two issues which are particularly relevant in North–South relations, one to foreign aid and its role in fostering development, and the other to the peace dividend which could provide additional resources in the long run. The chapter is organized as follows. Section II discusses the relationship between development and military security and provides the framework for the overall analysis. Section III analyses foreign aid. Section IV discusses the possibility of the peace dividend but shows that the short-term impact of the ending of the Cold War has yet to release any significant rewards. Section V concludes briefly.

II Development and security

Development *economists* have been wary of discussing security issues, relegating them to the ranks of *ceteris paribus* issues which provide the given framework within which analysis can proceed on more substantive matters. Standard surveys or handbooks on development economics rarely analyse matters related to the military. This is a major omission, since the development and security aspects of a poor country's fortunes are often related. The security guarantees given to Western Europe after the Second World War were essential for its rapid growth, particularly for Germany which acted as a 'free-rider' within NATO until the mid-1960s (Sandler and Forbes, 1980) and therefore spent a very low proportion of GDP on defence. The miracle cases of the Far East – Japan, Taiwan and South Korea – all had explicit or implicit security guarantees from the USA as well as considerable foreign military presence and military assistance at early stages of development. Few countries in the developing world had such consistent cast iron and credible assurances as well as help regarding their military security.

Military-related spending generally has three forms of negative impact on the macroeconomy's growth performance. First, it reduces domestic savings which in turn could have an adverse impact on investment and growth. Higher defence spending clearly increases government budget deficits and contributes to dissaving by the government sector. It also reduces house-holds' propensity to save since in poor countries the reduction of government services causes the private sector to spend more on health and education. Foreign saving, manifested through the current account deficit, could also be adversely affected by arms imports. Thus importation of arms reduces the foreign exchange available for capital imports. This adverse resource allocation and mobilization effect may be strongest in developing countries. Second, there could be an impact on absorptive capacity, with the skilled labour force and productive capital being diverted towards a sector whose measured productivity impact is zero. In arms-producing economies there could be a shortage of scientists and engineers if the military sector utilizes the human capital for the production of arms. Third, there is a trade-off within government expenditure categories, with military expansion taking place at the expense of health and education expenditures. The latter contribute to human capital and could be the source of endogenous growth in poorer societies.

It has been claimed (see Benoit, 1978) by some that there are indirect spin-offs of defence spending which have a positive effect on growth. Military training, the provision of work to an underemployed labour force, road and other construction activities, disaster relief and so forth could have a growth-inducing impact. In addition the military is claimed to be a 'modern' institution and the values of modernization and nation building have positive externalities for the other more traditional institutions of society. In countries with large arms production activities there may be aggregate demand creation as well as inter-industry linkages which boost the output of other intermediate products.

On balance, however, the economic benefits of the military are far less than the opportunity costs of resources lost from productive investment.

Deger (1986; 1990; 1993) shows that most econometric studies seem to reveal that military spending has a negative impact on growth rates across a large cross-section of developing countries. The major (and possibly only) true economic benefit of the defence sector is that society derives utility from military security and indirectly productivity rises with greater security. No country can prosper or develop until and unless it has security from external threats. Only within the environment of secure inter-state relations can the rewards of development be found, since in the absence of such an environment long-term investment is simply not possible. In addition, countries with internal security problems, such as a civil war, will find it impossible to grow rapidly.

Does military expenditure, which reduces growth through resource misallocation, help to create a secure environment, which must be the minimum necessary condition for development? It is possible that at relatively 'low' levels of defence spending, additional amounts allocated to the military improve economic growth since the positive security effects counterbalance the negative resource effects. However, as defence spending rises, the relative effects are reversed. The marginal returns from security through higher military spending tend to fall as defence expenditure rises. At the same time, the marginal costs tend to increase with higher defence allocations. Figure 15.1 shows the nature of these two functions; security gains and resource costs (both measured in terms of economic growth) are made a function of the share of defence in GDP or central government expenditure (CGE) (m – often called the military burden. The curves also help to determine analytically what is 'excessive' defence spending. This concept can be defined at either the level m_1 or the level m_2. The former shows the case where marginal costs and benefits are equalized and the net returns are maximized. The latter level depicts the case where the net benefits are negative and defence expenditure causes a decline in growth rates.

These concepts can be generalized to more than one country (Deger and Sen, 1984; Sen, 1992a). Security may be a public good with positive externalities within a country. However, in a regional arms race, it has negative externalities for other countries in the neighbourhood. Increases in defence allocation by one country then create an action–reaction mechanism and both countries raise their military burden more than would have been warranted in the absence of the negative externality. This produces a prisoners' dilemma game which it is difficult to improve towards a cooperative game framework. When the negative externality is taken into account, the levels m_1 and m_2 will shift downwards and excessive military expenditure levels will be attained faster.

An analysis of military expenditure and arms imports can help in understanding the links between military and economic security (Deger and Sen,

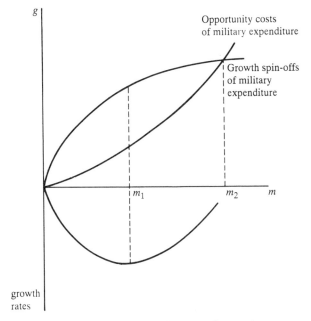

Figure 15.1   Military expenditure and growth

1990). There are a number of reasons for this. First, the link between military and economic security focuses attention on the wider notions of security, since defence spending could enhance military capability and yet have a
trade-off in terms of lower economic growth and a reduction of economic
security. Second, it is a measure which can be used analytically to explain
the many dimensions of security – military, political and economic. Third, it
is a tool for linking analyses of domestic developments to foreign policy
concerns, a linkage becoming increasingly important as the result of
globalization. Fourth, it is an aggregate measure of defence input. Under
well specified input–output relationships, it can also serve as an aggregate
indicator of military capability. Fifth, it is a measure that can be easily
understood and can also be used as a means of comparison, thus being useful
for political persuasion. Sixth, its growth or decline indicates the preferences
and perceptions of policy makers. Seventh, its expansion, within a dyadic
framework, is an indicator of an arms race with implications for war and
peace which have serious implications for development. Eighth, it measures
short-term economic costs for a weak economy and shows how vulnerable a
country can be to non-military threats to security. Ninth, its long-term effects
(as opposed to short-term costs), when adverse, affect the spending country's economic growth, industrial competitiveness and overall security. Tenth,

it is often used as a measure for calculating fair shares within an alliance as well as those of 'free-riders'. Eleventh, its reduction releases resources for domestic development and allows a country to reap the peace dividend. Twelfth, within a North–South framework, the reduction of world military expenditures could be a potential long-term source of international transfers from the rich countries (which are also the largest military spenders) to the poor countries.

Another problem is that the dividing line between internal and external security, threats and conflicts, is often thin in developing countries. Of the 32 conflicts identified by the Stockholm International Peace Research Institute (SIPRI, 1992) as major, and the over one hundred classified as less serious, many spring from internal upheavals – civil wars or foreign interventions directly related to internal instability. These are obviously the cases where poverty and developmental failures create the conditions for persistent conflict. The case for strengthening non-military security is strongest for such countries. Economic aid could be the most productive way to alleviate developmental problems, but the obstacles to providing effective economic assistance at a time of strife can be formidable. Multilateral aid agencies often abandon the country in which there is significant civil disorder. However, as the recent examples of Somalia and Bosnia show, aid can be channelled if there is sufficient political will.

An important aspect of the interrelationships between military and economic security is that governments are often asked to provide services that are required for the sustenance of both types of security. From the point of view of development, military expenditure is strictly unproductive. Another type of unproductive expenditure (in terms of forgone investment in physical and human capital) is that on debt servicing – often a product of past profligacy or of unpredictable external shocks such as the rise in world real interest rates. Countries could be excessively burdened with such expenditures, leaving little for the truly productive aspects of government spending, such as that on health and education. Table 15.1 gives data for military expenditure and external public debt service for a number of countries, as shares of current government revenue. The use of revenue share is appropriate for burden and opportunity cost calculations since aggregate expenditure can be artificially increased by running budget deficits which require further borrowing. The table shows that these two forms of so-called 'unproductive expenditures' could eat up a substantial part of government revenues, leaving very little for other items with far higher productivity.

A somewhat different, although related, way of looking at the linkages between the two forms of security, specifically focused on North–South relations, is to consider the levels of arms imports as well as net transfers on long-term debt as examples of unproductive external expenditures. Table

Table 15.1   *Military expenditure and external debt service payments as shares of current government revenues, 1988 (all data as percentages)*

Country	External debt service payments	Military expenditure	External debt servicing plus military expenditure
Argentina	22.3	15.2	37.5
Colombia	54.3	16.7	71.0
Chile	19.6	24.6	44.2
Egypt	10.8	18.1	28.9
Indonesia	51.6	12.0	63.6
Jordan	67.1	51.4	118.5
Morocco	26.2	20.5	46.7
Pakistan	20.6	41.8	62.4
Philippines	49.0	9.1	58.1
Sri Lanka	24.7	16.8	41.5
Zimbabwe	22.8	18.1	40.9

Source: Deger and Sen (1992a).

Table 15.2   *ODA, arms imports and net transfers of developing countries (billions of US dollars)*

Item	1985	1987	1989
Official development assistance	29.4	41.6	46.7
Arms imports	32.5	43.8	39.3
Net transfers on long-term debt	−19.7	−32.2	−42.9

Source: Deger and Sen (1992a).

15.2 gives data on arms importation by developing countries, which, incidentally, was predominantly exported by the industrialized countries. In addition, net transfers were negative, showing massive resource flows from the South to the North. By 1989, these two outward flows exceeded US$80 billion, dwarfing the level of ODA that was flowing in. By 1989, the level of net transfers on external debt and arms buying was almost twice that of ODA provided by the DAC members of the OECD and over one and half times the level of ODA from all sources.

III   The international public good aspect of foreign aid

The foregoing discussion alerts us to the fact that one way to enhance economic security is through the optimum use of increased foreign aid (from the donors' point of view) while at the same time attempting to reduce unproductive expenditures (from the recipients' point of view). There has been a major structural change in the resource flows to the countries of the South during the 1980s, as Table 15.3 shows. Total net resource flow in 1991 was 31 per cent less in real terms than the 1980 figure. The share of official development finance (which includes aid or ODA) rose from less than 30 per cent to over 55 per cent of the total net resource flow. Bank lending collapsed and private (non-official) flows were halved. Direct investment increased somewhat but still remained a modest proportion (around 20 per cent) of the total. Interest payments and dividends paid by developing countries, which represent the reverse transfer from the South to the North, remained stable at around US$100 billion (in constant 1990 prices and exchange rates) during the decade of the 1980s. It is instructive to note that such payments from the South represented 40 per cent of aggregate resource flows in 1975. By 1990, at the end of the 'lost decade', the ratio was approaching 75 per cent. Such data show that ODA is not only important but occasionally vital for the continuing economic security and prosperity of the South. Yet, as aid dependency rises, there are continuing worries that aid volume will not rise sufficiently to meet these needs, or even fall in some cases, while tougher conditionality will mean that the cost of receiving aid will rise, leading to a decline in 'consumers' surplus'.

Table 15.3   Resource flows to developing countries (at 1990 prices and exchange rates, $ bn)

	1980	*1990*	*1991*
Official Development Finance (ODF)	54.2	69.9	70.4
of which: ODA	43.1	52.7	54.0
Export credits	27.2	4.7	3.0
Private flows	103.5	52.7	53.6
of which: direct investment	17.7	26.9	27.5
bank lending	77.4	18.5	6.8
Total net resource flow	184.8	127.3	127.2
Memorandum: interest & dividends paid by LDCs	100.3	93.3	92.9

Source: *Development Cooperation: 1992 Report*, OECD, Paris, 1992.

The principles that guide the allocation of foreign aid by the donors from the OECD (which constitute the overwhelming proportion of the total) have changed significantly over time. The initial emphasis on projects changed later to programme aid, which looked at the broader framework within which each individual project would be implemented. This itself evolved towards the emphasis on macroeconomic structural adjustment programmes which looked at the overall economic climate before committing the donor to providing greater aid. Recent emphasis is on domestic policies such as good governance and internationally acceptable good conduct, such as the protection of human rights.

The use of defence conditionality (see Deger and Sen, 1992a; Sen, 1992a; Sen, 1993), whereby ODA is used as an incentive or sanction (for countries having appropriately defined 'excessive' military expenditures) so that un-productive government spending is reduced, has now become part of the policy dialogue of individual donors such as Germany and Japan. In addi-tion, multilateral institutions also tend increasingly to discuss this issue with recipients. Military expenditure reduction is considered to be a part both of macroeconomic management (cuts in budget or trade deficits) and of the move towards a better governed society. However, before such a scheme is to be successful, foreign aid itself has to be utilized to produce an interna-tional public good – economic development and security for the South (Tinbergen, 1990).

It is important to emphasize that the transformation in the objectives of foreign aid, from project to programme to policy to politics, is only feasible if foreign aid, and consequently economic development for the South, are considered to be international public goods. Thus the rewards of develop-ment must be both non-excludable and non-rivalled in benefits. One simple measure of the public good aspect of foreign aid can be understood from the data in Table 15.4, which gives information for the early 1970s and the early 1990s. In addition to the volume of net ODA, the table also shows the share of ODA as a proportion of the total for major OECD donors as well as the share of ODA in GNP. These are alternative burden-sharing measures. For a public good it is expected that the smaller donors (members of the group who will enjoy the benefits of *international* development) will tend to 'free-ride' by having disproportionately smaller shares or alternatively by spend-ing less on ODA relative to national output (Sandler, 1992). The data show that this has not happened. The smaller Scandinavian countries, for example, have increased their burden (in terms of either of the two measures) consid-erably over the 20 years while the USA, France and the UK have reduced their burden-sharing indicators. There are still considerable 'private' ben-efits to be gleaned from aid disbursement.

Table 15.4   The volume and distribution of economic aid

Country	Volume of net ODA ($ bn at 1990 prices)		Share of OECD total (%)		ODA as % of GNP	
	1970–71	1990–91	1970–71	1990–91	1970–71	1990–91
USA	8.98	11.13	31.8	20.0	0.3	0.20
EC	13.21	25.91	46.8	46.6	0.42	0.43
of which:						
France	4.56	7.36	16.1	13.2	0.68	0.61
Germany	3.14	6.55	11.1	11.8	0.33	0.41
UK	2.73	2.85	9.7	5.1	0.42	0.30
Italy	0.86	3.31	3.0	6.0	0.16	0.30
Netherlands	1.01	2.52	3.6	4.5	0.60	0.90
Japan	2.79	9.53	9.9	17.1	0.22	0.32
Canada	1.20	2.48	4.2	4.5	0.41	0.45
Sweden	0.58	2.01	2.1	3.6	0.40	0.91
Norway	0.18	1.20	0.6	2.2	0.33	1.15
Total	28.24	53.85	100	99.9	0.34	0.33

Source: *Development Cooperation: 1992 Report*, OECD, Paris 1992.

Policy coherence is possible, and collective action is optimal, when there exist public goods or private goods with significant externalities. If donors in aggregate are serious about the progress that the South makes towards economic development, political pluralism and achievement of economic as well as military security, then they must consider foreign aid as a good which cannot be excluded from recipients at will and whose benefits will not be reduced as the numbers of recipients increase (as is happening now with the entry of the East into the market for aid). In the 'new world order' it is fashionable to consider international security a public good for the world as a whole. The military engagements in Iraq, occupied Kuwait, Somalia and Bosnia provide clear examples of this trend. In the last two cases, a clear relationship has been established between military and economic security. However such a trend cannot be maintained if military security is considered an international public good while economic security is not. The use of ODA to foster economic security is vital. In the short run foreign aid is an input into economic security and in the long term it fosters development which should be regarded as a public good by the international community.

IV   The peace dividend

As mentioned earlier, one source of resources in a cash-starved recessionary world could come from military spending. The key to obtaining the disarmament dividend is reductions in worldwide military expenditures, which in 1990 stood at around US$950 billion. Industrial countries, including those in Eastern Europe, spent about 84 per cent of the total, while the remaining 16 per cent came from Third World countries. The distribution of aggregate spending was approximately US$800 and 150 billion, respectively. The former Soviet Union and the USA, the two largest spenders, accounted for almost 60 per cent of the world total. The European Community countries together expended almost 18 per cent of the total – about US$168 billion.

These shares had changed significantly during the decade of the 1980s (Deger and Sen, 1992b). In particular, the military expenditure of the former USSR and the United States increased rapidly with the arms race of the early 1980s. In contrast, Third World military expenditure either remained stable or fell. In the period 1980–88, on average, developing countries' total spending had been almost 20 per cent of world military expenditure, but by 1990 this share had fallen to around 16 per cent.

On the other hand, the economic burden for developing countries was quite high. The ratio of defence spending to GDP, termed the military burden, measures the opportunity cost of security. For all developing countries taken together, the military burden has hovered between 5 and 6 per cent throughout the two decades 1970–89. In comparison, the developed OECD countries had a military burden of less than 4 per cent in the same period. Only by the late 1980s and in the early 1990s has the Third World burden fallen, to around 4.5 per cent. This is a sizable economic cost. Other indicators, from alternative sources, point to a grimmer picture. It has been claimed (Sivard, 1989) that less developed countries' defence spending increased four fold in real terms since 1960 and by the late 1980s had achieved a level almost equal to their aggregate health and education expenditures.

Economic constraints, and technological oversophistication of weapons systems leading to ever increasing costs, had begun to put a structural brake on international defence spending by the late 1980s. World military expenditure began to fall around 1987–8. The aggregate is strongly influenced by the behaviour of the two (then) superpowers who both found that further increases were unsustainable. US national defence outlay in 1988 was 54 per cent higher than in 1980. Soviet military outlays also rose after the slowdown of the late 1970s, in the process far exceeding the growth of national income. In the 1985–90 plan, which Gorbachev radically altered, military spending was set to rise by 45 per cent, compared to a projected national income growth of only 22 per cent in the five-year period. Clearly it was impossible for such increases to be maintained for such long periods of time.

Economic and technological factors contributed substantially to the reduction in defence expenditure in the late 1980s. Elsewhere we have described this process (see Deger and Sen, 1990) as Technological and Structural Disarmament (TESD). As budget deficits began to bite, and recession slowed down the economy, resource constraints forced defence cuts. Defence procurement demanded new-generation weapons whose unit costs rose substantially to incorporate ultra-sophisticated technologies initiated by military research establishments. 'Invention became the mother of necessity', rather than the other way around. However huge sunk costs and fixed equipment expenditures were difficult to recoup unless procurement demand was large enough. As budgets shrank because of economic problems so also did the number of systems purchased. This raised unit costs and created a vicious cycle.

Political changes in Europe have somewhat hastened the underlying process of military expenditure reductions and concomitant demilitarization. However, outside the socialist countries and the USA, the cuts have not been dramatic. The forces of TESD are still predominant in producing a steady but rather slow decline. There are major plans for restructuring and changing procurement patterns, but as yet there are few tangible signs. The withdrawal of Germany from production of the European fighter aircraft, and the plans for reducing tactical and medium-range nuclear weapons by Britain and France are the few fundamental changes that have occurred in European NATO. These countries' military spending remained stable in the late 1980s, falling very marginally in 1991. Only the USA has gone for a bigger overhaul. However it should be noted that the level from which US defence spending is declining is very high indeed. It is now estimated that only by 1997–8 will real defence spending arrive at the level seen in 1980. In other words, US military expenditure will have passed through a long cycle of almost 20 years – not dissimilar to the Vietnam era.

Weapons procurement expenditures show a somewhat faster restructuring, but again nothing dramatic. In spite of cutbacks, equipment spending in the USA in 1990 was still higher than what it was in 1984, at over $75 billion. In 1990, European NATO's equipment expenditures exceeded the level seen ten years before, even though it had been falling steadily since 1987. World procurement spending on weapons systems was about $257 billion in 1989, falling to around 250 billion by 1991 – a significant but hardly dramatic fall. The message is similar. Political changes on the European continent and the dissolution of the Soviet empire acted as a modest catalyst but did not produce a fundamental transformation.

Another aspect of the military sector deserving attention is that of defence-related research and development (R&D). By the late 1980s, government-financed military R&D expenditure amounted to around US$95–100 billion, accounting for 9–10 per cent of world defence spending. At least 600 000 scientific personnel (scientists and engineers, full-time equivalent) were engaged in military research, with the overwhelming majority in the former USSR and the USA. In the sphere of military R&D, the greatest concentration continues in the USA, France, UK and Germany. (The Russian position is uncertain.) In all these countries, except arguably in Germany, the share of R&D in the military budget is stable. Therefore there are reductions but not of a very high magnitude.

These changes show that the peace dividend is yet to appear in the developed world. Rather, current emphasis is on the costs of disarmament as well as the costs of converting military capacity to civilian use. At the time of writing (1992), the world military sector – particularly among the developed countries (the West including Japan) – contains very large financial and physical resources, built up during the period of the Cold War to counteract specific threats and to fight world wars. Neither the threat, nor the possibility of such wars, exists any more. Unlike Ceasar's wife, military expenditure should not be beyond question and, albeit in the long run, these resources are usable for social and economic purposes. This is the rationale of the peace dividend.

The case is significantly different in the socialist countries, where rapid spending cuts have taken place since 1988. In particular the former USSR has pursued demilitarization actively since the Gorbachev reforms (Sen, 1992b). Between 1988 and 1991 the former USSR cut its defence budget by at least 25 per cent. Even though comparisons are difficult, because of the break-up of the Union, Russian military expenditure will probably be at least 25 per cent lower in real terms in 1992 compared to the level of 1991 (estimated contribution of Russia in the Union budget). However major structural problems have impeded the successor states, particularly Russia, in their attempts to capture the economic rewards of peace. The problems of economic transition and the transformation from socialism to market reforms have made conversion a costly problem. This is predominantly because of wrong policies; once again the peace dividend has been elusive.

V   Concluding remarks

The end of the Cold War and the realignment of international relations allows a unique opportunity for the North and the South to move towards a more equitable level of development, with greater security overall (Sen, 1993). Within accepted and plausible security guarantees from the major military powers, who are all in the North, the South could be freed from the perennial problems of conflicts and threats. This would help in the reduction of military expenditures and the attainment of the internal peace dividend.

However, as aid conditionally increases, interventionism rises and asymmetric development continues, true security encompassing economic and political emancipation from poverty and dependence will not be achieved. The role of ODA is vital for the future growth of the poorer countries of the

South and short-term economic recession should not be allowed to create long-term aid fatigue in the North. The use of the peace dividend in the long run is a rational and credible way to increase aid allocations. International development is a public good which will benefit all countries of the North. In a world of increasing globalization it is simply not possible to ignore localized deprivations. Thus, in spite of significant costs of transition to the demilitarized world economy, ultimately the rewards of disarmament must be gathered and distributed equitably.

References

Benoit, E. (1978), 'Growth and defence in developing countries', *Economic Development and Cultural Change*, **26**, January.

Deger, S. (1986), *Military Expenditure in Third World Countries: The Economic Effects*, London: Routledge.

Deger, S. (1990), 'Military expenditure and economic growth', paper prepared for the *World Bank Symposium on Military Expenditure and Development*, Washington, December.

Deger, S. (1993), 'Military expenditure and development', paper prepared for the *OECD Workshop on Military Expenditure in Developing Countries*, Paris, February.

Deger, S. and S. Sen (1984), 'Optimal control and differential game models of military expenditure in less developed countries', *Journal of Economic Dynamics and Control*, **7**.

Deger, S. and S. Sen (1990), *Military Expenditure: The Political Economy of International Security*, Oxford: Oxford University Press.

Deger, S. and S. Sen (1992a), 'Military expenditure, aid and economic development', *Proceedings of the World Bank Annual Conference on Development Economics 1991*, Washington DC: World Bank.

Deger, S. and S. Sen (1992b), 'World military expenditure', in *SIPRI Yearbook 1992 World Armaments and Disarmament*, Oxford: Oxford University Press.

Sandler, T. (1992), *Collective Action Theory and Applications*, London: Harvester Wheatsheaf.

Sandler, T. and J.F. Forbes (1980), 'Burden sharing, strategy and the design of NATO', *Economic Inquiry*, **18**, July.

Sen, S. (1992a), 'Economic aid and defence conditionality', paper prepared for the *United Nations University Conference on Military Expenditure and Economic Development in the Post Cold War Era*, Tokyo, November.

Sen, S. (1992b), 'The economics of conversion: Transforming swords to ploughshares', in G. Bird (ed.), *Economic Reform in Eastern Europe*, Aldershot: Edward Elgar.

Sen, S. (1993), 'Policy coherence and coordination in the interrelationships between economic and security issues', paper prepared for the *OECD Workshop on Military Expenditure in Developing Countries*, Paris, February.

SIPRI (1992), *SIPRI Yearbook 1992 World Armaments and Disarmament*, Oxford: Oxford University Press.

Sivard, R.L. (1989), *World Military and Social Expenditures*, Washington DC: World Priorities.

Tinbergen, J. (1990), *World Security and Equity*, Aldershot: Edward Elgar.

Index